MW00609687

2 Para's Battle for Darwin Hill and Goose Green

by
David J. Kenney

2005

Author's Copyright Note

All the text contained herein is the sole ownership of David J. Kenney. The content and format of the text are the original work and intellectual property of the author, unless otherwise accredited. All material is copyrighted and all copyrights are reserved. Material found herein may neither be republished or redistributed in any way without permission of the copyright owner, David J. Kenney.

Published in the United States of America in 2006 by
Oak Square Press
Upperville, Virginia

Printed by Berryville Graphics, Berryville, Virginia.

© 2006 by Oak Square Press. All rights reserved

Library of Congress Cataloging-in-Publication Data
Kenney, David J.
   2 Para's battle for Darwin Hill and Goose Green / edited by Guadalupe Paz
      p.   cm.
   Includes bibliographical references and index.
   ISBN 0-9660717-1-9 (alk. paper)
   1. The beginning of the story 2. The run-up to the Falklands war: Failed intelligence and desultory negotiations 3. The Falklands war and its political players: A myopic Thatcher versus an autistic Galtieri 4. Goose Green 5. Myth and truth 6. Conclusion: Cui bono?

Printed and bound in the United States of America.
Cover photo provided by Nigel Hawks, © Photographs by Nigel Hawks OBE.

∞ The paper used in this publication meets the requirements
  of the American National Standard for Permanence of
  Paper for Printed Library Materials Z39.48-1992.

5   4   3   2   1

This book is dedicated to

John Petersen Elder

and to

Herbert John Spiro

of

Lowell House, Harvard College

Contents

Acknowledgements

This book should not need to have been written. Had Thatcher's government and its intelligence services showed even ordinary competence, the blood would not have flowed. Many of those listed below went beyond the bounds of my questions to provide me with information that I had not known to exist. All but two of the senior participants in this conflict have declined, when asked by letter, to answer questions on the war or to comment on it. Not a few of those who agreed to provide information said the right word at the right moment to prod me out of a temporary slough of despond. Trolling around three continents has proven once again that people devoted to the honest written word continue to exist. I have tried not to dishonor them.

Special acknowledgment goes to the following:

Boston Athenaeum's intrepid searchers
Jorge Rafael Bóveda, without whom this book would be different
Carlos Braghini
Britain's Small Wars' far flung staff
Joan Carroll, AP/Wide World Photos
Eleanor Driscoll at the Imperial War Museum
Vincent Ferraro of Mt. Holyoke College
Max Goepp
Nigel Hawks
Dr. Rick Jolly
Chris Keeble
Greg Lang of the Haverill Library
John Lehman
Jim Love
Massachusetts Historical Society's staff
Museo Storico Navale, Venice
National Maritime Museum's very patient diggers
Chris Plant
Raúl Alfredo Pürzel
Guy Sheridan

Cheryl Steinberg at the NJ Historical Society
Oscar Teves
Julian Thompson
U.S. Naval Library
Sarah Walker
Sylvia Weedman, Bostonian Society
Caspar Weinberger
Jorge Gustavo Zanela
The many senior and junior NCOs who won their awful engagements one by bloody one
Sir Percy Craddock's, Sir Nicholas Henderson's and Sir John Wilsey's books have proved extremely valuable
Nick Vaux granted me the favor of writing so good a book on his 42 Commando's attack on Mt. Harriet that I avoided use of that singular operation. Nothing more need be said on this near perfect infantry attack.

Finally, I could not have completed this book without the patient assistance of Guadalupe Paz who, as many in Washington's foreign affairs community claim, can do anything.

Foreword

Argentina's invasion of the Falklands surprised me because I considered Thatcher too smart to have let such a disaster occur on her watch, and because I had high regard for the British Intelligence Services. As a reserve and junior naval officer, I had worked briefly but happily and productively with my British service counterparts. How could a ramshackle fleet with no combat experience drive up to British islands unopposed and take the capital? I wondered how the Argentine leadership, about whom I knew very little, could think to defeat those whom I considered very competent soldiers and sailors. I started to collect newspaper clippings, bought a map of the Falklands, and spoke with as many people on both sides as I could. The faces on television told the tale. From Argentina, young Apollos appeared wearing white scarves and laughing in front of their airplanes, while from the South of England, tough little unsmiling men climbed aboard the sort of ship I once knew well. It was clear who would win.

This book, or something like it, was conceived many years before the war in the Falklands. My former wife had germinated the idea of a book on Dame Rebecca West, and I went along to South Kensington to listen to that splendid person, and, as it turned out, to finish off the last drops of her late husband's cellar. Not a few had preceded me in this effort. Henry had been especially partial to one shipper of decent Burgundy, as was—and am—I. A good, if testing, friendship with Rebecca ensued. Dinners were exchanged and we became guests at one of her two birthday suppers held each year at about Christmas time. We went along to the more liberal and less America-bashing session. The wine and conversation merited the trip. Toward the meal's end, two themes invariably emerged. Looking down the table, Rebecca would declare that there was great hope for the human race, such a splendid gathering were we. This after saying that: "Mosley [an old chum] wasn't so bad." Then she announced in a now Scottish accent: "That woman from Somerville [Oxford] is going to be the first woman Prime Minister." Divination of the woman's identity demanded the author's consumption of yet more of the said Burgundy. Finally, the name Thatcher emerged. Later, I was one breath and half a glass away from getting Anthony Blunt's name as the Fourth Man, but that is another story. Rebecca knew that side of London's life too. Mrs. Thatcher did not attend the birthday parties at which I was present.

From the western side of the Atlantic I followed Margaret Thatcher's career in a cursory way, and found myself delighted that Rebecca had been correct and that an energetic and handsome woman sat in front of the dispatch box. No old goat from The Drones' Club or its St. James' brethren was she. I knew and know little about British domestic politics. In truth, I fancied her because I entertained a mild dislike for some of those who went for her throat. That said, I have no axe to grind in Albion, and my frequent visits thither over the past 45 years have always been made as though to the "next parish over." I remain a closet royalist and I read Kipling, who once lived just up the road from where I stayed in Vermont. Still, I was of two minds—each opposed to the other. Should I spend evenings, weekends, and holidays rusticating with my animals and visiting delightful places or should I pore over the printed page in the hope of finding something new to say? It seemed that everyone, except the stokers, had written about the Falklands War. Vanity won out. Serious research began, only to be interrupted by embarkation on a new career and a trying illness.

This book was much on my mind as a witless naval surgeon looked down at me before doing God knows what to my intestines and asked: "Are your documents in order?'" In such circumstances I do the anesthetists' count backwards in Russian. It annoys them, and I have potentially the last laugh. Rude good health followed, Rebecca had died, and I restarted the book. I met some who fought and a few who bled at Goose Green. Many, nameless, have declined to speak with me. An American interested in H. Jones VC and Goose Green! What can he possibly want? Well, certainly not a job or money or notoriety at my advanced age. One distinguished officer, whose evidence and views I very much respect, passes me in silence, cuff link to cuff link, in a London Club that we both frequent. The youngsters tend to speak about Goose Green only among themselves. That is a sacred privilege and I respect it. In the end, many have helped me, a few in tears, and to them I owe much. I can repay only by telling the truth as best as I can dredge it up.

To stay healthy, societies should tell the truth about themselves. Britain maintains an Official Secrets Act of which much could be changed without damage to The Realm. There are, however, no tales out of school here. Neither have the facts been trimmed to fit the niceties. Those respondents who cherish their anonymity have been respected. After a great event such as a war, the British Government appoints an Official Historian—and the Falklands' historian is a very good one—who has access to papers that few others may see. In America, we have Congressional Committees and sometimes awful journalists who get to the bottom of almost anything very quickly. It hurts sometimes, but that is the better way. Then, too, in the interest of objectivity, at least one foreigner not related to its participants should recount any major event. When British write about British, especially if most involved have emerged from the military womb, the Philby syndrome comes into play: "He's Widmerpool's nephew and went to Pryn's. He's a good fellow, did well at Bisley, lunches at The Mop, married old Scrumble's daughter. You'll like him." Or the reverse happens: Colonel Bearskin savages General Cumberbatch for some barely remembered, and perhaps imagined, incident during the 3rd Muckinese campaign. Not so fast! Besides, God knows American politics and wars have provided nice livings for many strangely accented scribblers. Turn about is fair play.

Why write a history of the battle for Goose Green? Few brief military encounters yield as much fodder for argument, discussion and gossip. Staff Colleges and Schools of Infantry have their meat for the next few decades. One skillful Commanding Officer faced an opponent who knew nothing of war, yet the battle's conduct was one of bloody intensity that was almost lost to the less competent side. Goose Green was a manageable episode of violence, small in comparison to the struggles on the Normandy beaches, but its loss would have brought down a government and shriveled the world's view of Great Britain. There can be no question but that Lt. Col. H. Jones VC knew of his involvement in something far larger than a brutal infantry fight. The very roots of the battle return to the Elizabethan age with all its scoundrels, looters, and pirates disporting themselves 8,000 miles from home. None of the Falklands' discoverers knew that their British patrimony would be secured by a stray American frigate in 1831 and retrieved in 1982 by a half-American at the head of roughnecks from Nottingham, Liverpool and Manchester. And few of them knew that less than half of any crew dropping anchor in the 18th century at Stanley or Port Louis would live to see home. If ever history had a bizarre continuum, it is this bloody stretch of affairs.

Fascination for views contrary to the accepted canon about the war intruded. Samuel Butler comes to mind: "I never write on any subject unless I believe the opinion of those who have the ear of the public to be mistaken." The gutters of history should be flushed from time to time.

Was the Falklands War a surprise? Not if you could read. Was Thatcher a warrior Prime Minister? Hardly. Were British forces, superb at what they do, adequately prepared? No, and not their fault. Was Jones VC a hero? Yes, but not as the government's blather would have it. It is a much richer yarn than that, and why should some have poisoned a hero's story with the politics of envy and whine? Was the Franks Report an honest reappraisal of the run up to the war? Now, there's a Brooklyn Bridge for sale.

Any history, especially one like that of Goose Green, should be written for perusal and perhaps study by the young who will govern the society that they enter. No matter what the pundits and analysts of stock markets blurt, the future is always terra incognita. History does not tell the reader what to do, but it does recount what torments can afflict persons and societies who claim ignorance or prescience. Classical literature polishes the mind, but it rarely describes or celebrates a corporal's leap over a trench to rescue a wounded mate. As for rank or social class, almost no one who takes part in a great event lacks interest. Anyway, competence and honesty are all that matter.

War is terrible, but wit and humor emerge from it everywhere; indeed, they may provide the richest fuel for victory. The sergeant who answered, "No, you haven't, mate. It's right over there," after his soldier shouted, "I think I lost my leg," existed in direct line of descent from those East Enders upon whom I eavesdropped 50 years ago from behind a gun mount on the deck of a British destroyer. Admiral Nelson would not have been surprised. What follows is the story of islands discovered by chance, settled by outcasts, and run by absentee toffs. Narration, not enchantment, is the goal here. This is a story of war begun from malign ignorance, of a battle fought out of the cheapest political necessity and of deaths and mutilation that should never have occurred. It is the tale of a failed bureaucracy redeemed by singular human valor. The English Language is a wonderful thing and this tale is not the best example of it. But the account is tallied as best as can be just now.

1

The Beginning of the Story

Why did Lt. Col. H. Jones VC and so many of his soldiers die at Goose Green? The story began long ago. Captain John Davis from Devon cleared Plymouth on August 20, 1591, in the ship *Desire*, 90 feet long and 136 tons burthen.[1] The ship sailed as part of an expedition formed by Sir Thomas Cavendish to discover a passage to the Orient and to the Spice Islands.[2] His expedition's purpose was not precisely stipulated, at least in print, but Cavendish was known more for pillage than for his scrutiny in exploration. A thirst for glory was there, too. If Cavendish was avaricious—he had squandered his substantial inheritance—his adroitness among the toffs at court did not translate into the hard won skills of the era's celebrated pilots and navigators. Nor did his lust for plunder match the demands of leading men and ships through danger and back to safety through rough seas. However fierce the resolve of this adventurer, his predatory instincts could be satisfied only with the help of a skilled captain or two in durable, well-manned bottoms. Captain Davis had held royal patents in 1585 and owned a reputation for astute and safe navigation.[3] He had searched for the Northwest Passage in 1586, 1587 and 1588, and returned. His crews did not mutiny. He was available. He fit the bill.

Davis' employment by Cavendish was a necessary feather in his cap, for this courtier-dandy-merchant-sailor-adventurer was a shady if singular player on his era's stage. Cavendish had restored his squandered fortune by a successful voyage of plunder and destruction up the west coast of South America that ended with the capture of a Spanish treasure ship containing 122,000 pesos in gold.[4] His fame and fortunes recouped, Cavendish made Plymouth on September 9, 1588, two years and two months after his departure. On that voyage he had titled himself Admiral of his quirky fleet, though he did not hold the Queen's commission for such rank. It is clear that whatever skills he lacked afloat, he drew fully from the knowledge of his sailing master, Thomas Fuller of Ipswich. Feted for his circumnavigation of the known world and for the treasure he paraded at home, Cavendish' reputation rivaled Drake's. By 1592 he was fresh for new adventure and prepared to finance it himself.

The age's sheer exuberance prodded the many as never before. Marlow's Tamburlaine said it well:

Nature
Doth teach us all to have enquiring minds;
Our souls, whose faculties can comprehend
The wondrous architecture of the world
And measure every wandering planet's course,
Still climbing after knowledge infinite,
And always moving as the restless spheres
Will us to wear ourselves and never rest.

Surely, Lt. Col. H. Jones VC brought the same set of mind to his assignment as commanding officer (CO) of 2 Para and to the job at hand on Darwin Hill. Most in his circle thought Cavendish exceeded himself. Blood-bought loot, velveted by navigational discoveries, fueled his swagger and sway at court. He soon gained approval for his next expedition, even though it originated from a woolly conclusion that a southwest passage to the Orient could be found in southern latitudes through which British ships might freely trade with the Spice Islands. His record for such speculation did not inspire confidence. He had explored the frozen coasts of Northern Canada for such a passage at great cost and without success. A colony that Cavendish planted in Virginia fizzled and had to be brought home in 1586 by Sir Francis Drake.

Still, the search for an easy way to the Pacific continued, in part because Dutch competition for the same routes excited British merchant seafarers. Elizabeth enthused over her gallant courtiers' distant adventures, especially if her treasury did not pay. Cavendish, gilded by Spanish treasure and by favor at court, had the resources to set out once again. It is not beyond probability that Elizabeth and her circle—Burghley, Walsingham and especially Drake—wanted to be shut of Cavendish. Even Elizabeth's splendid court could tolerate just so much of Cavendish' naked flamboyance. In order to form a judgment of the man, no further evidence is needed than what he wrote of himself: "I navigated along the coast of Chile, Peru and New Spain, where I made great spoils. I burnt and sank nineteen sails of ships small and great. All the towns and villages ever I landed at I burned and spoiled. . . . A great ship of the king's, which I took at California; which ship came from the Philippines, being one of the richest of merchandise that ever passed those seas."[5]

Cavendish put to sea on August 26, 1591, with three tall ships and two barks. Then, as now, failure, accident and lack of human resolve dogged the Falklands. From the outset, mutinous sailors, poor seamanship and cruel mismanagement plagued this outlandish admiral and his expedition of five sail. He put sick crew members ashore on the freezing Patagonian mainland where they had scant hope of survival, and enjoyed cordial relations with few of his officers. Deep in the South Atlantic, concern for his own safety prompted a transfer between his own ship, the *Leicester*, to Davis' *Desire*. Like many before and after him, Cavendish was stymied by the Straits of Magellan and its storied weather: "We have been almost four months between the coast of Brazil and the Straits, being in distance not above 600 leagues; which is commonly run in twenty or thirty days."[6] Despite his earlier success in passing the Straits, this time Cavendish fled the Straits' turbulence once again aboard his flagship, the *Leicester*. Shortly afterwards, he abandoned his fleet under circumstances yet to be fully explained and sailed off northwards alone. With his heart set upon the spice trade and plunder and his eyes fixed upon the best route to increase it, Cavendish may be forgiven for his inattention to any lands that promised no trophies for court or trees to repair his damaged spars. Cavendish never saw the Falklands.

Davis, in contrast to his absent leader, stayed on through that summer's awful storms but failed twice to beat through the Straits' devilish waters. After the first failed attempt, Davis headed *Desire* northward, sure of his latitude but without accurate measures of longitude. The prevailing winds at that time of year made sailing due north almost impossible. Worse, the current, a branch of the South Pacific Westwind drift, pushes through the Le Maire Straits often at six knots and flows northeast until it reaches the Falklands Stream.[7] Davis' crew, exhausted after hundreds of tackings in the Straits, could not have manned his ship as smartly as on the way south. No wonder then that Davis' battered and broken sparred ship failed to hug the Patagonian coast and was thrust northeast out into the Atlantic. By chance, Davis made landfall on the Falklands probably on August 18, 1592, but did not go ashore.[8] Another attempt to pass the Straits got Davis barely into the Pacific on October 2, 1592, but winds and current forced him back through Le Maire's perilous narrows into the Atlantic and he retired; his Admiral and the other four ships of the fleet still nowhere to be found.

Captain Davis had named his earlier discoveries after wealthy patrons or investors in his voyages. That he conferred the pedestrian name of "Southern Islands" on this discovery suggests that then, as now, the Falklands promised scant gain and drew little attention from London's nabobs.[9] Elizabeth's great captains, like Frobisher and Gilbert, had other fish to fry. Besides, the court had a few pesky problems at home. Elizabeth I dallied for the last time with a possible husband, the Duc d'Alencon; the Scots' fidelity to her had weakened alarmingly and signs of a resurgent Catholic presence poked up everywhere. Enough intrigue bubbled along the Thames' banks for several queens without bothering about audacious but profitless trips to the South Atlantic.

Davis put in to Brazil in late 1592 for spars, cordage, food and water. He had failed in his principal goal, but survived Cavendish' recklessness and mismanagement to make discoveries not included in his remit. On the trip home, 11 of Davis' men died. Of the 16 who survived from the original crew of 70, only 5 were fit to work when *Desire* put in to an Irish port. Meanwhile, Cavendish, still looking for trouble at sea, accused Davis of abandoning him and of attempts to supplant him as "Admiral." How this accusation could be proven, after Cavendish had absented himself from his own ships and from Davis' second attempt to try the Straits, is difficult to understand. As he skulked around the South Atlantic, Cavendish seems to have spewed venom over most of the officers who sailed with him. Scant evidence for his charges exists, and much supports Davis' valor, determination and judgment. No one else seems to have taken Cavendish' calumnies to heart, for Davis was hired by other venturers for five more lengthy voyages. This extraordinary man, wrongly unsponsored in history, was chief navigator for the first East India Company's voyage to the East in 1601–1603.[10]

Cavendish never saw England or Davis again. His crew on the *Leicester* refused to sail south, and he mounted a failed attack on Portuguese ships that left half the assault party dead or wounded. His escorting ship, the *Roebuck*, refused to answer his orders and sailed alone for England.

Cavendish died in late 1592 or early 1593 at sea under mutinous circumstances as his ship stood off St. Helena. He left a malign legacy. The penumbra of confusion, hardship, malevolence and misfortune had fallen over the Falklands on his watch.

The South Atlantic was not a bell jar. A few known and many unrecorded captains found their way to the South Atlantic by intent or accident. Skulking southward was a proven way to avoid troubles with the law. In any case, most ships made for the Spice Islands, and only one sure route existed to them. Sir Richard Hawkins, holding the Queen's commission, sighted the Falklands on June 12, 1594, and named them, not surprisingly, Hawkins' Land. He described the sighted land as, "not mountainous but much of the description of England."[11] Scotland in the dead of winter would have been more like it, but an easy metaphor brought his rediscovery more notice at home.

While the English Channel and the North Sea were the cockpits of European contention at the 17th century's outset, the maritime search for commercial triumphs in the East shunted considerable traffic past the Falklands. Winds and currents rendered it a fair possibility that, if lost or damaged below 51 degrees south, a ship might make one of the Falklands. Then, too, the prevailing Elizabethan scheme of values enhanced the effect of chance and bravery at sea. The Elizabethan world sought to know and to tame the complete order of the universe as God had created it. Using technology, as it then was mated to courage, intrepid seamen reckoned it necessary that all terrestrial matters be found, described and tucked away into the political scheme of the day. The sea was a natural venue for such undertakings because, in short order, it could take adventurers from the known into the unknown, from the commonplace to the exotic, from the secure to the perilous. Theology helped too. If man's spiritual struggle involved rising above his baser nature, it was a small step to rise above courtiers and clerks mired in their Thames side intrigues. If God's will could be fulfilled, if the universe were explored and catalogued in its fullness, if obstructive quill drivers at court could be left in the shadows and a few pounds gained on the side, how better could a decent man spend his life?

British seamen were not alone in beating through the South Atlantic's harsh waters. A Dutch expedition led by Jacob Mahu left Rotterdam on June 27, 1598, and headed for the Far East through Magellan's Straits. The explicit goal here was riches won by legitimate, if rough-edged, commerce in spices and valuable oddments gleaned from the still exotic Indies. In a successful passage through the straits, one of Mahu's ships, the *Geloof* under Captain Sebald de Weert, sustained sufficient damage to prevent its sailing on to the Spice Islands. While limping home, De Weert sighted three of the Falkland Islands on January 24, 1600. The Falklands' bays invite beleaguered mariners to this day, and Captain de Weert almost certainly put in for food, water and rest. He had no one to spare from his demoralized crew after the beating the *Geloof* had absorbed in the Straits, and did not plant a colony. Here begins the confusion over the Falklands that has dogged the islands ever since. Upon De Weert's return home, Dutch cartographers named the islands the Sebaldines.[12] Nicholas Visscher, the most famous and creditable mapmaker of his day, has De Weert finding the islands in 1599: "Ainsi nommées par celui qui les decouvrit l'an 1599."[13]

It takes little imagination to understand that, of the frequent traffic around the Horn into the Pacific, many unrecorded ships of all nationalities sighted or landed on the Falklands. The seas were too rough and the mishaps too frequent for those quiet bays not to serve as safe havens for distressed ships on legitimate errands and the many embarked-on less licit quests. But the Falklands were not 21st century New York or Southampton. The absence ashore of spars, cordage and merry maids serving tankards of ale to thirsty sailors heightened the undesirability of the islands for all but the most vexed by other difficulties.

In August 1683, Captain John Cook, aboard the *Bachelor's Delight*— a decent vessel recently pirated from Dutch seamen off Sierra Leone— departed Accomac on Maryland's eastern shore and headed south in search of a "rich wreck."[14] Captain Cook and his associates, who included William Dampier, the celebrated navigator, and a Mr. Ambrose Cowley, scribe, advisor and resolute thief at sea, were, beyond doubt, seasoned pirates. They had already captured two ships, sold their cargoes, dealt harshly with the crews and burned one of the ships to destroy the evidence of their successful endeavors. These scallywags might well have rested on their laurels ashore but for the fact they would have been arrested in most of the ports available to their ship.

On January 8, 1684, John Cook sighted a tree-covered island and named it Pepys Island. Ambrose Cowley, the onboard scribe, noted the latitude as 47° 40' S, far distant from the Falklands. This discovery was duly printed on charts of the area, such as the later edition of Visscher's that was reprinted with his widow's permission.[15] Confusion over this error lasted for 100 years, for no other navigators found land at this latitude. Almost certainly, Cook had rediscovered Southern Isles, the Falkland Islands, also known as Sebald's Islands.[16]

The squabble in law over nations' ownership of the Falklands cannot be said to have begun until January 27, 1690, when Captain John Strong went ashore from his 270 ton ship *Welfare* and named the waters where he had anchored Falkland Sound after Anthony, Viscount Falkland, a commissioner of the Admiralty. Strong had sighted the Falklands five days earlier on January 22, 1690, but British claims date from his physical presence on the island. Even so, this claim is weak because sovereignty demands occupancy and Strong neither stayed nor planted a colony. In fact, Strong's sailing orders, like many of that time, bade him search for a "rich wreck."[17] Planting colonies lay outside his brief.

Indeed, an unassailable claim to sovereignty demands not only permanent occupation, but also the paraphernalia of governance: judges, deed keepers, police, harbor masters, surveyors, property and birth records, customs officials and a bureaucracy, however small. Strong left none of these. Sadly, too, Strong's trip turned no profit and, on a cheerless run up the west coast of South America, he lost eleven crewmen, sent ashore to get water, as prisoners to Chilean authorities.

No evidence suggests that Strong or his mentors at home yearned for the Falklands themselves. Centuries later, Margaret Thatcher's government showed about the same disinterest. Possession of those wet, stone-riven islands never did promise gain from trade in tea, spice, rum or slaves. Almost certainly, the motive for Strong's landing lay in England's desire to supersede Spanish and Dutch influence wherever found. After the Spanish Armada's defeat in 1588, that country's sway waned, and Papal decrees that granted Spain virtual ownership of the New World ossified. Soon thereafter, political acts, devised principally in Europe but backed by blatant military and commercial realities, formed the new order for the division of new found land, exotic cargoes and quickly subdued peoples. The diplomatic machinations of those times are well explicated in other sources, but it can safely be said that maritime exploration in distant and intrinsically useless territories grounded many of the era's economic and political realities in Europe. Among all the European powers, Britain intended in the late 16th century to maintain preeminence in these often heartbreaking and bloody endeavors, just as it did in the spring of 1982.

French mariners from St. Malo and La Rochelle sought fire where they knew their British competitors had seen smoke, and darted about the South Atlantic with as much success as Captain Strong had enjoyed. An

Italian map maker, P. Coronelli, put the islands of "Sybald de Werde" very close to their true location in his *Planisfero del Mondo Nuovo, descrito dal P. Coronelli Cosmografico Pubblico* that was published in 1592. This large map, almost one square meter, showed the two largest islands and was, interestingly, published in French as well as in Italian.[18] A French expedition of six warships under Jean-Baptiste de Gennes left Brittany's ports in 1695, ostensibly to find and destroy Spanish shipping. A little exploration and commercial do-gooding lay further down the list. The Straits had other ideas, however, and, after a failed passage, De Gennes hauled his battered ships close aboard the Falklands for rest and repairs. If anyone went ashore, it was on French leave. Those few who deserted and stayed had insufficient numbers to form a colony or even a small settlement, and no French claim was made for sovereignty. Finally, in April 1697, his crews diminished by injury and sickness and, with his voyage a military and commercial failure, De Gennes dropped anchor in La Rochelle.[19] Louis Antoine de Bougainville, in his travels to the East Indies, planted the first permanent colony in 1764—buildings, primitive government structure, garrison and all. This entrepot, named Port Louis, existed in ignorance of other settlements on the island, so complete was the struggle for survival and the yearning for secrecy. The colony fell into disuse and was removed when France decided to yield all such petty holdings to Spain. Either from fear, ignorance or lethargy, a few settlers remained.

During the 17th and 18th centuries, almost everyone of note in the exploration and plunder business, and a few who were not, dropped in or passed by the Falklands. Captain Woodes Rogers of Bristol saw the Falklands on December 23, 1708, but disdained landing there. Rogers' finely developed commercial nose told him that there were better fish to fry elsewhere. Brawn, sometimes cruelly used in his piratical wonderings, and brain—his navigator was William Dampier, the best of his day—brought him such enormous success that he acquired, by Crown lease, the island of Jamaica. Fortified by an injunct to stamp out piracy wherever found, he ruled his demesne as Governor off and on until his death in 1732.

The Falkland Islands were first considered a strategic outpost, at least in Great Britain, by Admiral Lord Anson who, after seeing them on his round-the-world voyage, viewed that scruffy outpost as useful for controlling commerce around the Horn. He recommended in 1744 that they be settled, and Captain John Byron was deputed in 1765 to take possession for the "Crown of Great Britain, his heirs and successors." Byron planted a vegetable patch, named his discovery Port Egmont and left.[20] De Bougainville's colony reached two hundred persons, but they and Byron existed in ignorance of each other until 1771 when the French handed over to the British. However, on July 14, 1771, the British departed, encouraged by a vastly superior Spanish force of 5 ships and 1,400 men. The colonists' next home remains unknown to us, but they did leave, perhaps against the faint hope of their return, a bronze plaque attesting to British sovereignty. The vegetable garden failed to survive. The name Port Egmont lives on.

British efforts to harass and diminish the Don dotted the 19th century. By then, it was clear to the most greedy adventurer that the risks involved in rounding Tierra del Fuego for the Asian trade outweighed probable gain. The British Foreign Office and London's maritime establishment decided upon another tack. In order to secure the sea routes to Asia around the African Cape, Great Britain dispatched substantial ground and naval force to Capetown and seized it from the Dutch in 1806. In command was Commodore Sir Home Popham, by virtue of his scientific works a member of the Royal Society. An attractive presence in London society, he gained favor from wealthy merchants for his views on enlarging British trade at Spain's expense. Restless in Capetown, and ambitious too, Popham convinced the local army commander to add a regiment of foot to Popham's own expeditionary force of sailors, marines and wharf rats that he intended for the River Platte—all this done on Popham's sole initiative without any sort of order or permission from London. Popham did not plan a reconnaissance in force or a raid, but in fact an expedition that was designed to snatch a country and a trading entrepot from a moribund Spanish empire.[21]

By June 8, 1806, Popham and the British Army commander, Brigadier-General William Carr Beresford, had landed 2,000 men under arms and menaced Buenos Aires. Quite unexpectedly, a Catalan, Captain Santiago de Liniers y Bremond, raised bands of irregulars to harass the British regulars from the rooftops and stone walls of Buenos Aires. Unable to adjust from frontal combat to guerilla warfare in city streets, the regular infantry suffered heavy casualties that broke theirs and their commander's will. On August 12, 1806, Beresford agreed to quit the country. Popham returned home to face a court-martial by his masters and to receive a jeweled sword from his supporters in the City of London. He had, with great fanfare, begotten an Argentine tradition whereby extra-legal governmental acts—De Liniers' bands of irregulars were in no sense an army of the

United Provinces—were thought immune from universal scrutiny, owing especially in the Falklands' case to their remoteness and perceived insignificance. A second expedition, this time authorized by London and intended to expunge Popham's and Beresford's shame, ended a few years later in similar defeat and humiliation. An embryonic political tradition was incubated here too. An Argentine military combine, however shabby, united cattlemen, city dwellers, artisans, merchants, clergy and society's dregs against an external foe. When this coalition disintegrates or turns against the government, radical instability looms. Still, an external foe, preferably English-speaking, got worked into the myth of Argentine history.

Napoleon's defeat of Spain banged the last few nails into the Spanish empire's coffin. By 1810, Ferdinand owned little sway in Europe and none in the South Atlantic. Britain expelled Spanish interests from the Falklands without demure, and the islands existed without garrison or governance from 1811 until 1820. The Spanish went away, never came back, and thus proved they had yielded rights to Great Britain.[22] Even if this agreement were not recognized by the United Provinces, the islands de facto became *res communis*, open to all and ruled by none. It is this lacuna in ownership and physical possession that invalidates Argentine claims to have inherited Spanish dominion in the South Atlantic. From 1811 onwards, Spain simply had no interest in the Falklands, having ceded to Great Britain possession of the Islands. Spain could not, from that date, pass on to the United Provinces or any other party rights that it did not possess. The abject Spanish departure only mirrored the mainland's reality, because on May 25, 1810, a committee of Creoles in Buenos Aires formally removed the Spanish Vice-Roy from office and arrogated to themselves such thin functions of government as could be said to exist. On January 8, 1811, the new government or junta decreed the end to its own and others' colonizing of the Falklands and proposed to withdraw all settlers.[23] The arrogance of this proposal amuses, because the Creoles had no navy and no citizens on the Falklands.

It was only six years later, on July 9, 1816, that the United Provinces' rulers thought to publish a formal Declaration of Independence. Legitimacy before the world had taken second place to the awkward business of cobbling rancorous factions into the semblance of a sovereign state. Nothing of serious military or political import happened on or to the Falklands until 1823, when a certain Don Pablo Aregusti got himself appointed governor of the islands at the same time as commercial concessions were granted to Louis Vernet and Don Jorge Pacheco.[24]

Vernet's commercial adroitness and the United Provinces' desire to succeed to Spanish interests in the South Atlantic, however bogus, soon convinced authorities in Buenos Aires that Vernet, a German from Hamburg, would make a useful governor of the islands. On August 30, 1829, Vernet, as the islands' new governor who took umbrage at foreigners carving up his fishing domains, ordered the fishermen out. It is well to remember at this point that sealers, commercial fishers, skippers in search of fish, fowl and water were often storm thrust from Brazilian waters and sought the Falklands' safe harbors as a matter of course. Then as now, sailors are as rough as the seas over which they sail. Vernet's curbs on his free-wheeling Falklands visitors met with scorn and rejection. Still, sound governance demanded that examples be made of the more egregious malefactors. In the end, its skipper's failure to recognize Vernet's authority got the American schooner *Harriet* seized on July 30, 1831, and sent with its captain to Buenos Aires for trial. Vernet chose an American ship out of well-grounded suspicion that its presence suggested American authority in the region. If Great Britain and the United States saw little value in the South Atlantic, they wanted no one else to dominate it.

British Foreign Secretary George Canning's Overture in 1823 for a Joint Declaration with the United States on the Spanish Colonies in America demonstrated Vernet's point:

My Dear Sir:

Before leaving Town, I am desirous of bringing before you in a more distinct, but still in an unofficial and confidential, shape, the question that we shortly discussed the last time that I had the pleasure of seeing you.

Is not the moment come when our Governments might understand each other as to the Spanish American Colonies? And if we can arrive at such an understanding, would it not be expedient for ourselves, and beneficial for all the world, that the principles of it should be clearly settled and plainly avowed?

For ourselves we have no disguise.

1. We conceive the recovery of the Colonies by Spain to be hopeless.

2. We conceive the question of the recognition of them, as Independent States, to be one of time and circumstances.

3. We are, however, by no means disposed to throw any impediment in the way of an arrangement between them, and the mother country by amicable negotiation.

4. We aim not at the possession of any portion of them ourselves.

11

5. We could not see any portion of them transferred to any other Power, with indifference.

If these opinions and feelings are, as I firmly believe them to be, common to your Government with ours, why should we hesitate mutually to confide them to each other; and to declare them in the face of the world?

If there be any European Power which cherishes other projects, which looks to a forcible enterprise for reducing the Colonies to subjugation, on the behalf or in the name of Spain; or which meditates the acquisition of any part of them to itself, by cession or by conquest; such a declaration on the part of your government and ours would be at once the most effectual and the least offensive mode of intimating our joint disapprobation of such projects.

It would at the same time put an end to all the jealousies of Spain with respect to her remaining Colonies—and to the agitation which prevails in those Colonies, an agitation which it would be but humane to allay; being determined (as we are) not to profit by encouraging it.

Do you conceive that under the power, which you have recently received, you are authorized to enter into negotiation, and to sign any Convention upon this subject? Do you conceive, if that be not within your competence, you could exchange with me ministerial notes upon it?

Nothing could be more gratifying to me than to join with you in such a work, and, I am persuaded, there has seldom, in the history of the world, occurred an opportunity when so small an effort, of two friendly Governments, might produce so unequivocal a good and prevent such extensive calamities. I shall be absent from London but three weeks at the utmost: but never so far distant but that I can receive and reply to any communication, within three or four days.[25]

Canning entertained a nettlesome anxiety that the victor in the War of 1812 might show more than a benign interest in the South Atlantic's affairs, but that is another story. John Quincy Adams' reply to Canning's letter is instructive in many ways. The key sentence: "The president was averse to any course which should have the appearance of taking a position subordinate to that of Great Britain."[26] In other words, we were to be partners as regards the South Atlantic; the United States was not a client state of Great Britain.[27] The second sentence: "We should at least keep ourselves free to act as emergencies may arise, and not tie ourselves down to any principle which might immediately afterwards be brought to bear against ourselves."[28] Here read that America may annex Texas and Cuba and does not want British interference. The sense of the cabinet's discussion suggested that America was open to a request for assistance from Great Britain, that America would not assume a position or hold interests subordinate to Great Britain in the South Atlantic and that matters would be decided on a case-by-case basis. Thus America put its official toe in the waters of the South Atlantic. No mean diplomat himself, Adams also sent to Baron Tuyl, the Russian Minister, a note after the meeting on November 7, 1832, that was certain to reach the Spanish. The note emphasized that Adams considered Spanish interests in the South Atlantic dormant, and that he expected they would remain so. In his inaugural address, delivered on March 4, 1829, President Andrew Jackson, a ground soldier, had preened himself on the growing U.S. Navy and its dockyards, all for the benefit of his foreign audience. Surely, Adams took due notice of this ebullience.

American desire to prevent anything like "foreign" control of the South Atlantic can be traced to the first voyage to Vancouver of the ship *Columbia* and her tender, the *Lady Washington*, under Captain John Kendrick of Wareham. The first American ships to transit the Straits took 11 months from January 1788 to reach Vancouver. By this voyage, Kendrick opened the New England states to Canton and to the China trade by way of Vancouver; it is unlikely that he made this expensive and perilous trip in the face of opposition from the new American government. *Columbia*'s trip to Vancouver was intended to acquire furs there for sale in Canton, lest the British establish a monopoly in that lucrative commerce and set astronomical prices for China goods sold to America. Of course, the founding fathers did not object to commercial brashness that confirmed their own political independence. Captain Kendrick's enterprise was the first such, but not the last. All through the early 19th century, New England's ships followed in Kendrick's wake and plowed the waters from Massachusetts around the horn to the sealing grounds in the North Pacific, thence to Canton. Rarely was Port Stanley without an American visitor. In the best mercantile tradition, nails, cloth and bits of copper got in return salmon, otter and seal skins. These were exchanged in Canton for tea, silks and chinaware that found their way to the kitchens, dining rooms and ladies' closets of the prosperous Atlantic states. The odd side trip to the Cochin coast on the way home did no harm to profits either. All this business was done by ships not much longer than 100 feet. By January 1789, voyages to the East were part of Massachusetts' maritime life, and berths for them were advertised in Boston's newspapers. Profits and the exoticisms of the East outweighed storms and pirates any day, and young men of substantial families signed up in numbers for these lengthy hard riding voyages. Ashore, the merchants of Boston and Salem, their bankers, their relations in London and proud Andy Jackson were not about to allow the hint of an obstruction to this hazardous but lucrative trade.[29]

Against this background, a series of events occurred that stamped the Falklands as British ever since, and drew the United States into an arrangement that culminated 150 years later in America's moral and materiel assistance for the British in combat against Argentina. In 1820, the new regime that called itself more in hope than in fact the United Provinces sent the frigate *Heroína* to the Falklands with orders to assert sovereignty over the islands. The United Provinces had just slipped ties with Spain and claimed that right as the proper heir to Spanish interests.[30] The *Heroína*, probably not a frigate as defined by European navies, was commanded by Colonel Daniel Jewitt, an adventurous Englishman in Buenos Aires' pay who ordered all other ships in port to cease hunting ashore and to abstain from fishing around the islands.[31] As many as 50 foreign ships were in port at Stanley or at Port Louis or scattered about the islands; Jewitt could not have fought them all, the hooligans there would probably have strung him up in short order, and he contented himself before his departure with planting the United Provinces' flag. He also posted notice that skippers of offending ships would be sent to Buenos Aires for trial. The impossibility of his one ramshackle ship patrolling all the harbors, bays and inlets of the Falklands seems not to have compromised Jewitt's satisfaction with his impractical decree. It was later reported by the one-eyed jacks charged with enforcement of the United Provinces' decree that foreign vessels had respected their agents' orders. From this distance, history's skeptical eye cannot gauge the truth of that claim. No record exists of harbor fees collected or births and deaths recorded from that time. Still, a certain brashness at sea might lend symmetry to Buenos Aires' strenuous efforts to order its dissident provinces. By 1823, a governor sent from Buenos Aires was in place at Port Stanley. He had little power beyond that of self-protection, and the United Provinces' attempt at planting a self-sustaining and viable colony on East Falkland failed.[32]

True, the United Provinces had the slimmest reason—the right of propinquity—to confirm their nascent sovereignty over these distant islands; yet their petty legalisms challenged the interests and subjects of those foreign nations that offered this loosely sewn country the most benefit and took the most risks in doing so. The English colony in Buenos Aires had long been substantial and influential; by 1825 it exceeded 1,000 people. The British bank, founded in 1822, became Buenos Aires' center of foreign trade and opened up commercial relations with English-speaking North America. Britain was the first European country to recognize the United Provinces in 1824 and to grant it most favored nation status. Simultaneously, Barings Bank of London granted the new nation a loan ostensibly for port and harbor development, but in fact, to shore up the United Provinces' fledgling administration. The British pound was the accepted medium of commerce and Barings Bank itself a distant ministry of treasury. A Treaty of Friendship with Great Britain guaranteed safety of each nation's citizens and belongings. In casting off Spanish shackles, the United Provinces had become as near as made no difference, the client state of Great Britain.

That this shaky newborn conglomeration of dissident provinces should assay the Falklands as a maritime province—hundreds of miles from Buenos Aires—while it lacked a navy, even a fishing fleet, a taut hold on its home ground, a viable colony of citizens, a self-sustaining economy and a garrison to enforce its laws contrasts almost comically with its declaration of sovereignty. The United Provinces did not claim or even know the extent of the lands that constituted what turned out to be Patagonia. The weather there was awful, the land mostly uninhabited and the soil infertile. More noticeably, the United Provinces' proposed expulsion of foreign ships from Falklands fishing grounds flew in the face of the open seas policy that the Dutch, French and British had encouraged and defended over the years.

The American government's first official engagement with the Falkland Islands came under unfavorable auspices for the newly formed United Provinces of Argentina. The year was 1833. Andrew Jackson, no one to mock, was the ebullient and self-confident president. The Monroe Doctrine was in full flower, and tinkering with the political status quo in either hemisphere caused more than raised eyebrows. Not by chance, the scantiness of American naval resources left it to the Royal Navy to establish a virtual *mare clausum* in waters where U.S. ships could not adequately patrol.

The Monroe Doctrine, promulgated on December 2, 1823, stipulated that European interference in the Western Hemisphere's affairs would not be countenanced—that was a thumb in the eye of the French and Spanish—and that the United States reserved the right to normalize the behavior of those countries who could not manage their own affairs. That put the makeshift countries of Latin America on notice that they could not interfere with American ships, their navigation and their commerce. The Doctrine also meant that American economic and military influence would set matters aright at sea and on the South American littoral. This cheeky dogma could not, of course, have been enforced by America's tiny navy alone. The real muscle behind the Monroe Doctrine and Andrew Jackson's brashness was the Royal Navy. The slow accretion of British imperial power grew as much from the travails of dogged seamen as from the finely wrought decisions of the Foreign Office. Captain Jones and bosun Smith were as necessary as Palmerston, Canning and the Foreign Office.

Woodbine Parrish, the British consul-general in Buenos Aires, and George W. Slacom, the American consul there in 1831, were clearly of one mind about imperial growth, the New World's stability and ownership of the Falklands. In the brazen world of the Southern Coast, the unfortunately named Slacom saw the prospects for easy profits; he developed friendships especially along the Brazilian coast that led to a prosperity not usually found among minor consular officers. His was an easy interpretation of the regulations governing his position as consul and of the commerce that flowered under his gaze. Whatever Slacom did with his free time, he found it entirely natural that two English speakers, both representing English-speaking nations in a Creole world, would share similar views on many subjects, and it is clear they knew each other well. The Brazilian coast and the South Atlantic in general were crowded with ships of every flag on all sorts of business, some legal, much questionable and not a few both. Chicanery and worse was the order of the day and notice of the River Platte's rambunctious commercial life soon reached Washington. Levi Woodbury, the American Secretary of the Navy, bade Commodore Duncan USN: "make sail and shape your course for the coast of Brazil. . . . It will be your duty to protect the commerce and citizens of the United States and maintain the National character by all lawful and honorable means."[33]

On April 28, 1828, Louis Vernet, the cultivated English and French-speaking native of Hamburg, received the exclusive right to fish around the islands. By extension, all others were forbidden this practice. Vernet went further and got himself named governor of the islands, and, on August 30, 1829, ordered the departure of all fishing ships that did not fly the United Provinces flag. The order was greeted with derision. On July

30, 1831, Vernet seized three American ships: *Harriet, Superior* and *Breakwater*. The latter soon escaped. With Vernet aboard, *Harriet* arrived in Buenos Aires for trial on November 19, 1831. *Harriet*'s seizure was soon known in Buenos Aires, and Slacom protested the outrage fiercely to Anchorena, the United Provinces' foreign minister who sent a condescending reply that supported Vernet's actions in seizing the *Harriet*. Duncan of the *Lexington* took it upon himself to demand of Anchorena that Vernet be tried and punished under the laws of Buenos Aires.[34] His cheeky note received an equally impudent negative response from Anchorena.

After the death of John Forbes, the American minister, George Slacom had become the American government's senior representative in Buenos Aires, but lacked the powers of chargé d'affaires. Vernet's breach of laissez-faire and his gratuitous insult to the United States (as many as 50 ships from many nations loitered about the Falklands under various pretexts; why pick the *Harriet*?) sent George Slacom into action despite his very junior consular rank. The American frigate *Lexington* stormed back to the Falklands on a mission of retribution, doubtless orchestrated by Woodbine Parrish, the British consul-general, Slacom and Silas Duncan. *Lexington*'s skipper did a complete job. After finding good evidence that four American fishing vessels had been taken and fitted out as United Provinces' warships, he recaptured them. He freed Vernet's prisoners, spiked his guns, rendered his tiny garrison impotent, proclaimed the islands free and sailed off with six prisoners of Duncan's own clapped in irons.

Skipper Duncan then removed the colony consisting mainly of Germans from Buenos Aires and returned them to the mainland. All this with no orders from Washington to liberate the Falklands and no record in his log that any such events had occurred. Slacom knew his president and Duncan took his orders and his Secretary of the Navy seriously. The Americans wrapped up in this affair were a free-spirited lot who knew that it would have required more bravery to thwart Jackson's brashness than to practice it. Many a commanding officer, before and since, has prayed for similar opportunities. HMS *Rattlesnake* joined in the spirit and in the event had stood off *Lexington*'s quarter while Duncan set matters to right. Commodore George Rogers of the American Brazil Squadron arrived in May 1832, and by way of soothing ruffled feelings, returned Duncan's prisoners to the authorities in Buenos Aires. He reported to Navy Secretary Levi Woodbury: "The people here, whilst desirous of friendly intercourse with us, still hold out the idea of recolonizing the Falkland Islands."[35]

The Falklands had lacked, since December 1823, a government by any definition and even any form of political organization. The islands were, quite simply, one of those storied safe havens for ships and people who hid from other ships and other persons. There, no questions were asked and no explanations were offered. Ashore, wandering plunderers who had nothing, stole from the few who had little. No financial gain was ever promised by dropping anchor in one of its seductive coves. In the end, common sense told that Vernet, neither a military representative nor even a citizen of the United Provinces, lacked the right to seize American fishing boats and to imprison U.S. citizens. Slacom was correct in protecting U.S. persons and interests against one who was in every respect a private citizen.[36]

On January 1, 1833, Commander John James Onslow, CO of the 18-gun frigate *Clio*, detached from Sir Thomas Baker's South Atlantic squadron, made Port Egmont and surveyed the coast where he found Spanish-speaking survivors of the United Provinces' regime. These he ejected peacefully and sent to Buenos Aires. The true nature of the United Provinces' intent became apparent with Onslow's discovery of the prison hulk *Sarandi*, a leaky, barely seaworthy assemblage of planks and spars that was home to many of Buenos Aires' undesirables.[37] This, too, was returned to the mainland at Onslow's insistence, though not before several of its inmates had escaped into the wilds of East Falkland. Onslow returned *Sarandi*'s United Provinces' flag and crew of 25 to Captain José María Pinedo in a civil gesture that had lethal consequences. Later in 1833, Matthew Brisbane and William Dickson, agents of the crown charged with surveying the interior, were murdered by outlaws who had escaped from the *Sarandi* before its enforced departure for the mainland.[38]

During their brief occupation of the Falklands, the United Provinces never fulfilled the criterion for the achievement and maintenance of sovereignty. In fact, questions can be raised about the status of the United Provinces as a nation (it had no defined borders) when it claimed in 1833 to own the Falklands. In any case, the United Provinces could not assure the Falklanders' safety there or abroad, collect taxes, keep property, birth and death records, provide for defense or negotiate with foreign powers. No ship or person could be forced to leave or to stay in port, nor were customs fees collected, nor borders patrolled. In fact, the Falkland Islands were a junkyard for the refuse, both human and materiel, of the South Atlantic. One certainty remained: America and Great Britain had determined that it was to be their junkyard.

The South Atlantic was a high crime area even after the Falklands were handed over to what slender British hegemony existed in that day. In searching out a West African port, Commander Henry Dundas Trotter in HMS *Curlew* recognized the schooner *Panda* as a pirate vessel. In fact, piracy was carried on those days more by small ships such as *Panda* than by the many-gunned behemoths of the cinema. Trotter followed *Panda* westward to the coast, where it blew up because of careless handling of powder—or so it was reported. *Panda* survived long enough to deliver to an American captain, Loney of the USS *Savage,* four of *Panda's* seamen and their master Pedro Gilbert. After due process and trial, these five were executed on June 11, 1835, in Boston.[39]

Civil administration began straightaway and British occupation has continued since 1833. Once ownership was settled, British authority grew apace. In 1840, the British government decided formally to colonize the Falklands, although they did not acquire colonial status until 1892. Lieutenant Robert Lowcay RN in the ketch *Sparrow*, having styled himself "Officer In Charge of The Falklands," established a military presence against a threat from the United Provinces that never materialized. Port Stanley was designated the capital, a town was laid out and its port was named a free port with "Good Water at 2/6 per Ton," this to be supplied by the Falkland Islands Company at Stanley. By 1847, the known population had risen to 270, almost all English-speaking, with the exception of a Mr. Lafone of Montevideo who farmed large tracts and formed a rump faction that kept to itself in the wilderness. Horses and sheep were introduced from Patagonia, and, by the middle of the 19th century, 1,000 ships per year visited Stanley. Few tarried. Imports and exports—lime, hides, fish, iron, tallow and sundries—were recorded to the last shilling by a small government that in mid-century consisted of at least a governor, two clerks, a surveyor, surgeon, harbor master, a magistrate and a chaplain. Parliament voted the equivalent of US$24,000 in pounds during 1851–1852 to support its distant and clearly impecunious holding.[40] Over time, the islands became in practice the property of the Falkland Islands Company that secured its London base with a small but vocal lobby.

On February 6, 1856, John Washington, the Royal Hydrographer, gave notice by way of a permanent sign written in English, French and German that a fixed light mounted on a 60-foot iron tower had been erected at Cape Pembroke. After all, the government's chief purpose in maintaining the Falklands was to keep an eye on traffic passing Cape

Horn, and what better way to do that than to invite them safely into a snug harbor for water and repairs. It was cheaper than keeping a squadron of ships at sea there, and no bad thing either for the Colonial Office's drones who saw opportunity for a small, if harmless, expansion of their fiefdom and its dreary paperwork. For those interested in landing for food, water and repairs, information was made handy at No. 59 Gracechurch St., London. Much of this activity could not have been tried, let alone accomplished, but for a detailed survey of the islands and their shores by Capt. Bartholomew Sullivan RN, who from 1834–1839 traveled the land, took soundings and made sure that good solid British names identified the prominent features.[41] His work allowed the Colonial government to stipulate, for example, that the 200 islands consisted of about 6,300 square miles. Port Louis remained Port Louis, but good British names like Kidney Cove, Wickham Heights and Port Harriet got familiar for the cartographers who followed Visscher.[42]

A few fish were caught, a few ships repaired and thousands of sheep got sheared. The Kelpers, as the islands' inhabitants came to be called, occasionally sent children to school in England and employed Chileans to help the farming. Life was dull, predictable and, while dips in the price of raw wool caused grumbling and some hardship, no one who worked starved. Dignity and survival came from sweaty or freezing outdoor toil. Except for a growing myth on the Argentine mainland that Britain had filched what belonged rightfully to Argentina, the world left the Falklands alone and vice versa. Rogues of every sort found their way to the islands and some, not all, got their comeuppance too. Hear Rear-Admiral Grey RN, from HMS *Cleopatra*, in his diary January 1, 1837, entry at Fanning's Harbor: ". . . we came upon a small schooner, entirely dismantled and secured to the shore, her masts were standing but everything else had been carried away. I had heard before of this vessel as being owned by an American of bad character who went about the island ostensibly only to kill seals but who also destroyed great numbers of wild cattle. The vessel was not worth much, but manned by runaway seamen and without any regular papers, I had determined to seize her wherever I might find her and therefore sent a party to break her up next day as we were in want of firewood she answered our purpose well."[43] This incident was neither the first nor the last of its kind. Jones and his 2 Para were still trying to restore order a century-and-a-half later.

This remoteness got shattered in December 1914 when the German Admiralty, perhaps aware of Admiral Lord Anson's advice that Cape Horn and the Falklands held supreme importance for a naval power bent on European domination, sent out a cruiser fleet 10,000 miles distant from its normal operating area. Steaming near the Chilean coast under Admiral Graf von Spee, the Germans defeated Admiral Craddock's very surprised squadron and sank HMS *Good Hope* and HMS *Monmouth*. In hasty retribution, the Royal Navy sent Admiral Sir Doveton Sturdee to avenge the unexpected disgrace.[44] On December 7, 1914, Sturdee put paid to this bizarre German excursion by sinking four of its five ships, including *Scharnhorst* and *Gneisnau*. The German Admiral von Spee and his two sons were killed in the action, and the South Atlantic reverted to its normal pacific, not to say inert, state of affairs.

Notes

1. Some have placed Davis' date of departure at August 26, 1591, and his ship's tonnage at 120. The differences are slight and at this remove insignificant.

2. A few skeptics have, in 19th century writings, questioned the authenticity of Cavendish's knighthood. In writings on him he was called Mr. and Captain-General. Not above any mischief, Thomas probably did get Elizabeth's sword on his shoulder.

3. John Davis (1550–1605) invented Davis' Quadrant, a piece of navigational gear well ahead of its time. Its use prevented blindness incurred by those sighting the sun with earlier instruments. Davis completed two books on navigation, which still stand. He wrote *The World's Hydrographical Description* and *Seaman's Secrets*. The latter, first published in 1594, was a compendium, the best of his era, of all that he had learned in his many voyages of exploration, principally in the Northern Atlantic. Davis lent his knowledge to mapmakers who produced noteworthy, if less than precise, charts of the newly discovered lands and seas. Long before H. Jones VC landed on the Falklands, England celebrated a champion who trolled distant possessions when Shakespeare wrote in *The 12th Night*: "He doth smile his face into more lines than are in the new map with the augmentation of the Indies." William Shakespeare, *12th Night* (Roslyn: Black's, 1937), pp. iii, 1, 89. Davis was killed by Javanese pirates near Sumatra in 1605.

4. See Christian Isobel Johnstone, *Lives and Voyages of Drake, Cavendish and Dampier* (New York: Harper Bros., 1840).

5. Ibid, pp. 148–149.

6. Ibid, p. 132.

7. See Julius Goebel, *Struggle For The Falklands* (New Haven, CT: Yale University Press, 1927), for a troublingly exhaustive description of some early navigational efforts in these waters.

8. Albert Hastings Markham, editor, *The Voyages and Works of John Davis the Navigator* (London: Hakluyt Society, 1880).

9. Goebel, *Struggle For The Falklands*. Professor Goebel, in prose even more tortured than his logic, advances the cases of Vespucci and Camargo as earlier

discoverers of the Falklands. The most charitable comment about his assertions is the Scottish verdict: "Not Proven."

10. For a good and overdue description of Captain Davis and his accomplishments see, Samuel Eliot Morison, *The European Discovery of America* (Oxford, UK: Oxford University Press, 1971), p. 583 et seq.

11. C.R. Drinkwater Bethune, editor, *The Observations of Sir Richard Hawkins, Knt., in his Voyage into the South Sea in the Year 1593* (London: Hakluyt Society, no. 1, 1847 [reprinted from the edition of 1622]).

12. See the chart by Nicholas Visscher, *D8537*, in the National Maritime Museum, Greenwich, England.

13. Ibid.

14. Charles R. Low, *Maritime Discovery* (London: Newman, 1881), vol. 11, p. 110.

15. The widow Visscher was rumored to have earned modest profits from sales of her late husband's labor, which delighted herself then and gossipy historians later.

16. Johnstone, *Lives and Voyages*, p. 250. While the error in calculating latitude is large, it may be forgiven. As Thatcher's soldiers and marines discovered, everything about the Falklands is wet or at least damp. A 17th century navigator, probably undernourished and certainly dead tired, who took sun or star sightings from a pitching quarterdeck and then entered them into a soggy notebook, deserves only sympathy.

17. Low, *Maritime Discovery*.

18. On exhibition, Museo Storico Navale, Venice, 2004.

19. Low, *Maritime Discovery*, pp. 115–116.

20. John Percival Egmont, the 2nd Earl, engineered land booms, far from his native Somersetshire, in Florida and in Nova Scotia during the 1760s. In Nova Scotia, he sold off parcels of 20,000 acres that later included the author's family farm. There remains an Egmont Harbor in Nova Scotia. See Sir Lewis Bernstein Namier and John Brooke, *House of Commons 1754–1790* (London: Oxford University Press, 1964), pp. 266–268.

21. See Henry Stanley Ferns, *Britain and Argentina in the Nineteenth Century* (Oxford: Clarendon Press, 1960), pp. 46–47, for the story and its background. Popham had seized the Cape of Good Hope from the Dutch in 1806, had his own ship seized from him by the East India Company, and was court marshaled, but proven innocent, for fiddling with ships' repair monies. He wrote the signal book used by Admiral Nelson to order his warships at Trafalgar. See Peter Kemp, editor, *The Oxford Companion to Ships and the Sea* (London: Oxford University Press, 1976), p. 660.

22. The Spanish renounced all rights here. Thus the Argentine claim to have inherited Spanish ownership of the Falklands is invalid because one cannot inherit what does not exist.

23. Goebel, *Struggle For The Falklands*, p. 433.

24. Little is known of Pacheco. It may be assumed, however, that Vernet entertained substantial ambitions for his new role in the Falklands because he ordered his piano sent from Buenos Aires to Port Louis. Nothing is recorded of

Vernet's repertoire or skill, but his musical instrument was almost certainly the first such on the islands.

25. The author is indebted to Professor Vincent Ferraro of Mt. Holyoke College for this letter sent to Minister Rush.

26. John Quincy Adams, "Account of the Cabinet Meeting of November 7, 1832," documents relating to American Foreign Policy before 1898. Mt. Holyoke College, courtesy of Prof. Vincent Ferraro.

27. This notion came into play again during April and May of 1982.

28. Adams, "Account of the Cabinet Meeting."

29. See Samuel Eliot Morison, *The Maritime History of Massachusetts, 1783–1860* (Boston: Houghton Mifflin Company, 1921), p. 46, et seq., for a rousing description of this social and maritime escapade. It was also clear that Canning did not wish an American presence in South Atlantic waters so forthright that it might compromise presumed British hegemony there.

30. British Foreign and State Papers, vol. 20, p. 422.

31. The ship in a later incarnation was deemed a pirate ship and so dealt with by the courts. U.S. State Department Papers, Argentine Dispatches, September 26, 1832.

32. British Foreign and State Papers, p. 369.

33. American Secretary of the Navy Levi Woodbury, letter to Duncan dated June 10, 1831. U.S. National Archives, Washington, D.C.

34. Duncan was no stranger to trouble. He had fought against the British in the naval encounter on Lake Champlain and against the Algerian pirates in the Mediterranean. He appears a punctilious naval administrator, too. He demoted the *Lexington*'s chief master at arms for calling another sailor: "A Damn Yankee Son of a Bitch."

35. Rogers' letter to SecNav, 1832. Navy and Old Army Branch National Archives, Washington, D.C. Courtesy of Rebecca Livingston.

36. From 1829 to 1832, the senior Governor among the United Provinces was Juan Manuel Ortiz de Rosas, the Governor of Buenos Aires. He conducted foreign affairs for the United Provinces. While the absent Ortiz de Rosas cleared Indians from his porous borders, his wife, Doña Encarnación, ran a spy network that kept both aware of possible intrusions into their hegemony. Dissenters from their rule were sent to the Falklands, possibly without due process.

37. William Laird Clowes, the best maritime historian of this era, calls *Sarandi* a "War Schooner." Pity those who went to war in it.

38. Peter Calvert, *The Falklands Crisis: The Rights and the Wrongs* (London: Continuum International Publishers' Group, 1982), p. 71.

39. William Laird Clowes *The Royal Navy: A History from the Earliest Times to the Present* (London: Chatham, 1901,vol. 6), pp. 272–273.

40. National Maritime Museum, Greenwich, D8544.

41. Sullivan must have been a close and reliable observer of scientific bent, for Darwin uses his evidence to build some complex conclusions. Darwin quotes Sullivan several times in C. Darwin, Esg., F.R.S., F.G.S, "On the Geology of the Falkland Islands," in *The Quarterly Journal of The Geological Society of London* (pt. 1, 2, 1846): 267–274.

42. National Maritime Museum, Greenwich, D8539.

43. Ewen Southby-Tailyour, *Falkland Islands Shores* (London: Conway Maritime, 1985), p. 84.

44. Sturdee's squadron consisted of: battle cruisers *Invincible* and *Inflexible* and cruisers *Cornwall*, *Kent* and *Glasgow*. Von Spee's squadron had five ships: armored cruisers *Gneisnau* and *Scharnhorst* and light cruisers *Dresden*, *Leipsig* and *Nurnberg*. The British carried 8×12 inch guns, while the Germans fired 8×8.2 inch guns. Von Spee knew the odds and tried for home. He lost the encounter with *Dresden* alone, escaping only to scuttle three months later upon being discovered by two British cruisers. British losses were small; the Germans lost 2,000 men.

2

The Run-Up to the Falklands War:
Failed Intelligence and Desultory Negotiations

Desultory negotiations between the two countries in London, Buenos Aires and New York had failed to reach arrangements satisfactory to the British, the Argentineans and the Falklands' inhabitants. The Foreign and Commonwealth Office (FCO) made several attempts, racing from the impalable to the disastrous, to ease the Kelpers from their obduracy into arrangements that might placate whatever Argentine government was in power that day. For example, Nicholas Ridley, a senior politician and junior minister in Thatcher's government, visited the islands in 1980 and came away with the notion that a transfer of sovereignty to Argentina and a lease back to the Crown would satisfy all parties concerned. His explication of the arrangement in parliament got him savaged as few before and none after. His plan encompassed, in the end, the Kelpers' union with Argentina and that notion was unacceptable to the Falklands lobby, the islanders and many on both sides of the isle. Ridley's misjudgment of the whole affair did nothing to assist him into No. 10 Downing Street.

The Argentine decree of April 30, 1970, that made any child born in the Falklands an Argentine citizen, failed to bring a flood of applicants for Argentine passports. The vacuous effect of that nonsensical legislation caused no surprise. Both sides' diplomats resembled no one so much as the English convict Harvey Crippen, who dismembered his wife's body and carried its severed head in a bag through London's streets with a view to throwing it into the English Channel. After all, few, if any, would sniff felony in an ordinary man walking soberly through London's streets. By malevolent chance, Crippen and the head were caught and he was executed. By winter of 1982, the FCO implicitly concluded that it had successfully temporized and that the head of Argentine demands remained hidden in the bag. The junta, marching to its own drumbeat, concluded that it had been mocked and humiliated by British stubbornness. The duration and turgidity of the negotiations, and their absence of thermonuclear content, sapped the final negotiations in winter of 1982 of any immediacy. The stacks of memos, the hundreds of meetings and the sheer unimportance of the islands had created near terminal ennui in both foreign offices. Except for a few prescient souls, the belief abided that words, not blood, would continue to flow.

Then, too, the slender skein of reason that snaked through the British negotiations lacked the intellectual and political punch to gain their alleged purpose. Boredom, confusion over method, perhaps a touch of condescension towards a nation known best for bloody political repression and fast polo ponies, all made for dilatory behavior. After all, there was no great evil about the Falklands—and not much virtue either. They were distant, cold and bereft of involvement by the North Atlantic Treaty Organization (NATO). Decent men could skirt the problem without besmirching their consciences. In negotiation there was no valor, no cowardice and no fame—only tedium punctuated by good lunches in New York's best hotels. Both sides favored The Pierre. Those involved in the Falklands' discussions—honest men—knew that they wrote footnotes, not chapters, to British diplomatic practice. In fact, no one predicted an end to British ownership of the islands because few, if any, knew of its origins.

For its part, British obduracy fuddled a mushy-minded Argentine foreign office that stumbled deeper into failure, enjoined as it was to bail its masters out of domestic breakdown by pressing the jejune notion that the Falklands belonged to the heirs of Perón. A none too perceptive observer of the moment, and never a historian, the junta's leader, Leopoldo Galtieri, resorted to the only course sure to destroy him: war against an undervalued enemy. On December 15, 1981, the just-elected Argentine junta of Galtieri, Jorge Anaya and Basilio Lami Dozo ordered Vice Admiral J. J. Lombardo to prepare for an invasion and occupation of the Falklands.[1] Lombardo set up a five-person cell and commented after the war that he expressed no views on the matter at hand to his seniors, but as a serving officer simply obeyed their orders. Lombardo said he knew of no reason to believe or to deny that Thatcher would permit Argentine seizure of the islands and that Nicanor Costa-Méndez, the Argentine

Foreign Minister, would be the better person to ask. No date was set for the landing, although those around the junta who knew of the plan concluded that Anaya, the junta's de facto leader, would wait until two new destroyers, store bought from the UK, became operational, until the small carrier HMS *Hermes* had been delivered to the Australians and until HMS *Endeavor* had ended her assignment as guard ship in the Falklands and South Georgia's waters. That meant September or October 1982. Poor old Gloucester said it best: "Tis the time's plague when madmen lead the blind."[2]

Anaya was thought by many to have convinced Galtieri to support the invasion from a conviction that the British would not fight, and the two dragged in a less than enthusiastic Lami Dozo, head of the air force. Galtieri was born of immigrant Calabrian and Genoese stock into the seedy provincial life of the barracks where his father was a senior NCO. The salons of Buenos Aires that accompanied political success came to his family much later. Alike in the sly energy they brought to their life's work, the son was of a different stamp from his father. Galtieri attended U.S. military schools, lived lengthily in America, visited there often and made few mistakes as he climbed his army's greasy pole. Never a combat soldier, he was an engineer of no little crude charm who mastered the minefield between his country's military and civilian politics. He garlanded his anti-Communist credentials with graduation from the American "School of the Americas." With either foresight or disgust, it is difficult to choose which, he stood idly by while others of his own profession perpetrated atrocities on their own countrymen. The army and the dirty war that it had instigated were in his bones.

The myth that the Falklands constituted a legitimate part of Argentina lay embedded in the interstices of the country's political and social traditions. Maps, stamps and children's schoolbooks all included the islands as part of the national entity. Every politician made that notion a given in his political platform and no office seeker could survive without slanging the unlawful British occupiers. The paradox was bizarre: British banks, polo games, clubs and tailoring comprised an essential part of good living for sophisticated Argentineans, while Her Majesty's government remained a sworn enemy. Argentina banked in London, where it maintained huge debit balances and bought, on credit, quantities of military oddments from a very willing Ministry of Defense. From their election in December 1981, Galtieri and his junta entertained a false security in drawing on that insistant and schizophrenic animosity towards Great Britain.

The notion of an Argentine invasion of the Falklands had been bruted by the Argentine military and political establishment since 1977, when it was formulated under the title of Plan Goa. The Argentine plan for an actual invasion of the Falkland Islands, a refinement of Goa, equated roughly to what in NATO language is termed an "Op Plan," that is, an outline of military goals to be met and the subordinate tasks that had to be completed in order to accomplish those tangible goals. That plan was finished on February 23, 1982, just as 2 Para began to prepare its deployment from England to Belize, British Honduras. Despite Argentine military preparations, muffled hope still lurked about the Casa Rosada—the Argentine White House—and in the Argentine Ministry of Foreign Affairs that the Falklands might be won through negotiations. For his part, Galtieri repeatedly asked his planning officer, Lombardo, at what point the operation could be cancelled. This tentative behavior was unusual for a general officer who had studied for a year at the U.S. Army's Engineering School at Fort Belvoir, VA, because there he would have learned that any Op Plan, or the Op Order that puts it into play, can be terminated at any time until the troops step onto the beach. Galtieri's diffidence was a normal reaction, however, for a leader undecided about whether his enemy would fight or accept a fait accompli. As it happened, the Argentine order to invade was given on March 26, 1982, but the troops did not secure Port Stanley until April 2nd, ample time to call off the invasion.

But first a digression and a lesson must intrude! One absolute truth applies here. Countries cannot go to war without very obvious preparations like clearing rail heads, moving troops, issuing live ammunition, erecting barriers with ships, closing ports, canceling scheduled maintenance, recalling critical officers from schools and leave, closing roads and airfields, shutting down overseas telephone calls, increasing radio traffic or going silent, increasing reconnaissance, performing increased training exercises, stockpiling fuel and supplies, etc. Certain places of low entertainment see their patronage greatly diminished. In the case of an invasion, ships and planes foregather. None by itself means much, but, taken together, they usually spell trouble.

Indications and Warning

The business of predicting countries' hostile moves is called: "Indications and Warning" (I&W).[3] It means that Country A's intelligence service writ large tries to predict moves by Country B or by anyone else that could

28

harm its (Country A's) interests. A few caveats! Watchers over potential enemies must not concern themselves with their own country's policies or lack thereof. They are irrelevant to the I&W crowd's concerns. Worrying about the success or failure of U.S. initiatives dulls the acuity needed to focus on the enemy's hostile moves, if any. Tolerance or liking for the status quo must not breed watchers' indifference to distasteful change.[4] Equally, graduate watchers or keeners must not entertain too much respect for their seniors' leanings or for current policies. Mimicking past judgments can be fatal; matters change often overnight. Cartesian clarity is useful, but rough-edged weight of evidence is the totem here. Mental powers are not enough, for keeners must have the guts to say and to write against the grain and perhaps to risk temporary unpopularity. Not to worry, good keeners gain immediate respect and are a joy to the government and to the administration that they serve.[5] Their prosperous employment is almost guaranteed. The situation under study may bore, but the watcher/keener may not ever be bored. Anything can happen and often does. Only one question exists: How, when and where can Country X or Group Y hurt us?[6]

America and other great nations spend billions of dollars on satellites, human intelligence, signals intelligence and what have you, to gather fodder for their analysts to masticate.[7] What is regurgitated is mostly a dog's breakfast and that is good because it means that nothing is happening. Occasionally, brilliance surfaces and that means trouble because one of the keeners has discovered that Country X is about to be "naughty."

Who are the keeners? First, one must be a simple and interested watcher. Anyone can join—historians, physicists, economists or someone who fancies a country well. The nastier prejudices about religion, ethnicity, etc., disqualify immediately, not just because they are intrinsically bad, but because they cloud the mind. Not all bright people are good at this craft and not all dull normals fail.[8] The trick is to notice change. Let us say that Vizerian fighter pilots fly thirty hours per month year in and year out. Suddenly, and for no apparent reason, they fly forty then fifty then sixty hours per month. They reach a very high level of military competence. Simultaneously, your chum who watches tanks observes that two battalions of every tank regiment are on exercise, a departure from the norm of one battalion.[9] A third, bright, young person notes that more fuel trucks (bowsers) are being left forward with their communications gear after a week's exercise than has been normal. He or she probably possesses *fingerspritzengefuhl,* that sine qua non of the successful intelligence officer.[10]

29

Now a keener will note that Vizerian intentions seem to exceed their capabilities, always dangerous for the region's tranquility. At this point, somebody senior tells somebody else up the administrative chain that the Vizerians menace the Nampitian border. More reconnaissance is ordered and a chain reaction proceeds up and down the foreign policy establishment.[11] Formulators of policy toward Nampitia and Vizeria are roused from their torpor. Often, academics from universities are called in to evaluate potential crises and to share the blame if matters go badly awry. After all, you are as good as your last war. In most cases the I&W gang preens and, after a decent interval, goes back to work looking for more trouble. It is a very Manichean business.[12]

After Galtieri solidified his control of the Argentine government, it was apparent to all that one of Argentina's recurring periods of political and economic turmoil was about to begin. By autumn 1981, the country was nearly broke. Inflation ran at 600 percent per year, factory output declined 23 percent, and real wages—how much bread and meat can one buy—declined 20 percent in the past year.[13] That the state practiced an especially abhorrent form of terrorism against its own people did not exclude it from the comity of civilized nations, but it came close. Any reader of the serious Argentine press knew that the Falklands were a vital interest to whatever Argentine government held power, and that this condition, almost a national psychosis, stood little chance of changing. The story of the Malvinas and the terrible British was part of children's curriculum in grade school. In June 1955 the Argentine legislature passed laws making the Falklands and its dependencies a province of Argentina.[14] All the factors that suggest or deny a run-up to war must be read against this background. In winter 1982 the ground swell of hostility towards Great Britain became a roar, and most informed persons in Buenos Aires knew that the government must fall or the Falklands returned to Argentine ownership. Most wars have a large dollop of failed intelligence in their causative structure, wherein proper information was not gathered and given to the policymakers or, alternatively, it was given to them who then failed to take appropriate action. Falklands is the star example. Might Jones and his men not have died at Goose Green if their masters in Whitehall had been as scrupulous in their watch over Falklands as they were assiduous in pursuing Soviet intentions?

What follows is a collection of indicators, taken from British and Argentine open sources, that separately mean little but together have the unmistakable smell of Argentine preparations for war over the Falkland

Islands. It is best to start with the establishment of Plan Goa that formalized, during 1977, the Argentine national myth about repossession of the Falklands. That written plan, the first known of its kind, laid down certain stipulations about the Argentine recovery of the Falklands by military means. It had the virtue, from the Argentine point of view, of asserting what Argentine leaders had murmured in secret for generations.

Indicators of War: Preparations

- **Autumn 1976.** The Argentine military seized and retained, despite British protests, South Thule, an island possession of Great Britain about 1000 miles southeast of the Falklands.
- **November 15, 1977.** The British Joint Intelligence Committee's report to Overseas Defense Policy Committee says Falklands could be taken without a shot being fired.[15] [Could not an Argentine staff study have concluded similarly?]
- **December 1977.** Argentina cut off fuel supplies to the Falklands.
- January 27, 1982. The Argentine foreign office sent to British Ambassador Williams in Buenos Aires a demand that a permanent negotiating commission be established to settle the Falklands matter once and for all.[16]
- **From 1980.** Argentine pilots, when arriving bi-weekly at Stanley's airport, refused to speak English when contacting the tower. Instead, they used Spanish. Aviation's international language is English. Years prior to the hostilities, members of the Argentine Air Force and their families lived in Stanley in order to run the local offices of the Argentine state airline, LADE. No reciprocation was sought or given.
- **December 1981.** A Spanish and English speaking KGB officer, a Russian Intelligence Service officer, arrived at the Soviet Antarctic base.[17]
- **December 20, 1981.** An Argentine ship, *Almirante Irizir*, entered Stromness Bay and Leith Harbor. Kept radio silence and moved furtively. Constantine Davidoff, a scrap merchant, was aboard and with others inspected the whaling station. Argentine Commodore Trompetta stopped sending out weather reports to all and sundry as he had done for years whenever he was at sea. [This incident occurred five days after Galtieri told Lombardo to write a plan for invading the Falklands.]
- **January 1982.** An Argentine officer asked for and received an architect's plan of the Government House.

- **January 21, 1982.** HMS *Endurance*'s cocktail party at Ushuaia not attended by invited Argentine Navy guests. Soccer game cancelled and Captain Nick Barker and his crew on HMS *Endurance* denied the use of the field. Such an incident had never happened before.
- **January 22, 1982.** Argentine Navy Captain Russo told Captain Nick Barker of HMS *Endurance* that Argentina would war against Great Britain. Russo told Barker that he was in the "Falklands War Zone." [Russo would not have had his job without Anaya's approval. Russo spoke from the horse's mouth.]
- **February 1982.** Roberto Gamin, an Argentine C-130 pilot, arrived as LADE (Argentine civilian airline) officer in Port Stanley. He replaced Air-Commodore Héctor Gilobert.
- **February 2, 1982.** Carlos Busser, the head of the Argentine marines, established a planning cell for the Argentine marines' part of the seizure.
- **February 9, 1982.** The Buenos Aires Herald, an English language paper, discussed the pros and cons of military action against the Falklands.[18]
- **February 13, 1982.** Veal and Scrimgeour of the British Joint Services Expedition found yachts *Isatis, Kim* and *Caiman* looting Leith harbor in South Georgia.[19] The crews and passengers called themselves filmmakers.
- **February 16, 1982.** *Caiman* is taken to King Edward Point, South Georgia. *Kim* left for Rio and *Isatis* regularized.
- **March 2, 1982.** Foreign Minister Costa-Méndez announces that further negotiations would be fruitless and cancels talks. Colonel Stephen Love, the British Defense Attaché in Buenos Aires, sent to the Governor of the Falklands, to Robin Fearn at the FCO and to Defense Intelligence in London his appreciation that Argentina could invade the Falklands in the event negotiations lacked progress or if Galtieri needs a diversion from his failed domestic policies. Love had many contacts in the Argentine military. His report was not circulated within the Ministry of Defense (MOD).
- **March 8, 1982.** *Caiman* left for Argentina carrying loot from Leith.
- **March 14, 1982.** Yacht *Cinq Gars Pour* arrived at King Edward Point (KEP), South Georgia from Buenos Aires and began begging for food and medical supplies. A .22 Rifle with a silencer was confiscated. Upon inspection, the yacht was found not to have been damaged so as to need harboring and to possess ordinary amounts of provisions.

- **March 18, 1982.** *Bahía Buen Suceso* arrived AM at Leith, South Georgia under radio silence.[20] Captain Gastón Briatore claimed permission from the Commonwealth and Foreign Office (CFO) and would deliver fresh food.
- **March 19, 1982.** Full-scale Argentine landing exercise by Argentine marines on the Argentine coast. Constantine Davidoff, the salvor, landed men salted with military personnel on South Georgia. They remained as Davidoff left.
- **March 20, 1982.** Protest given Briatore. The Argentine flag at Leith was hauled down. Both Argentine Foreign Minister Costa-Méndez and Enrique Ros refused to see British Ambassador Williams.
- **March 22, 1982.** *Buen Suceso* departed at 0400, leaving 39 Argentineans on South Georgia.
- **March 23–24, 1982.** Royal Marines were invited aboard a Russian tug and got very drunk. The Russian tug was far from its normal South Atlantic operating area near Elephant Island.
- **March 25, 1982.** *Bahía Paraíso* arrived at Leith before dawn and unloaded cargo and Special Forces.[21]
- **March 26, 1982.** *Bahía Paraíso* left Leith and loitered offshore.
- **March 26, 1982.** The Argentine frigate *Guerrico*, undergoing overhaul, was taken from the yards and put into operational status. The Argentine fleet sailed for an exercise with Uruguay. [There was no exercise.] All Argentine submarines at Mar del Plata were put to sea.[22] Costa-Méndez stated that the Argentineans on South Georgia would be given full protection.
- **March 26–27, 1982.** Twenty AMTRACS (amphibious vehicles that carry troops from ship to shore), which are broad, noisy and bellow smoke, loaded from Puerto Belgrano along with their Argentine marine crews from the 2nd Marine Infantry Battalion.
- **March 30, 1982.** Captain Nick Barker on HMS *Endurance* intercepted and passed on to Government Communications Headquarters (GCHQ) signals of war.[23] An acquaintance of the author watched from his balcony in Buenos Aires as trucks laden with troops drove to the port.
- **March 31, 1982.** Air-Commodore Héctor Gilobert, the Argentine Air Force officer deputed to LADE, returned to Stanley to complete an audit. This was a new event.
- **April 2, 1982.** *Bahía Paraíso* sailed into Cumberland Bay and left shortly. It messaged that an important announcement would follow.[24]

However incompetent the Argentine foreign office was in sensing American reaction to the invasion after it had occurred, it had, earlier in 1981, gotten two matters right. First, withdrawal of the *Endurance* did signal a lowered British interest in defending the Falklands and a reluctance to defend them with blood and treasure. British Minister of Defense Nott's decision to remove HMS *Endurance*, purportedly for lack of money, gave the junta its needed thrust toward war because it convinced the fence sitters that the British would react with words not bullets.[25] Second, the parliamentary vote for the British Nationalities Act, that removed Commonwealth citizenship from 3rd and 4th generation Falklanders unless they could prove British birth within the United Kingdom, deprived about half the islands' population of the normal protection afforded to British subjects. Even more rankling to the Kelpers, this provision did not apply to Gibraltans. All could see that the Falklands held vastly diminished interest for the British government and specifically for the Ministry of Defense under John Nott and the Foreign and Commonwealth Office of Peter Carrington.[26] The Argentine military staff concluded, as it monitored Port Stanley's fall, that the American Intelligence Service and its satellites had caught the invasion force and that the subsequent ease with which it took the Falklands indicated a tacit consent to the whole affair. The storm around Thatcher came as a complete surprise to the junta and its planners.[27] The battle and casualties of Goose Green had their roots in these events.

The Joint Intelligence Committee (JIC) was a British interdepartmental committee that works for the Prime Minister's office and sends intelligence appreciations to the cabinet and to the Prime Minister. It sits on top of the British intelligence community's pyramid of assessment. If Barker, Hunt and Love could hear the dogs of war begin to bay, Whitehall's minions, those who wrote memos and papers for the JIC, then headed by Sir Antony Acland, turned a deaf ear. Colonel Love was later horrified to hear that his appreciation on the possibility or indeed probability of war (contained in Appendix A) had been frozen at a very low level of the bureaucracy and had not been circulated among those who might have forewarned their masters. Captain Nick Barker's cogent and crystal-clear forebodings, written from his perch as CO of *Endurance* and sent to London from the man nearest the point of troubles, were taken as a crude attempt to shore up the Royal Navy's budget and not as indications of imminent hostilities. The JIC had not treated the Falklands matter since January 1982, nor had Foreign Secretary Carrington or Nott made the Falklands an issue for serious discussion in the Cabinet until March; in fact, the Falklands were not put on the Cabinet's agenda until war broke. The reasons why provide material for a treatise on bureaucratic bumbling whose malign effects ended in war.[28]

It is useful to digress here to recall that all the good intelligence in the world, properly formatted for politicians' consumption, has little value if the recipient politicians are predisposed to mute inactivity. In fact, no paper on the Falklands problem was tabled for the Cabinet meeting of March 16, 1982. Of course, one clever but ultimately self-defeating administrative practice entailed FCO members sitting as chairmen on the various JIC subcommittees, thus the FCO judged the success of its own policies.[29] Even more stultifying, a Foreign Office member headed the final national assessment committee and controlled whatever counsel, memos or recommendations wended their way to Thatcher and her colleagues. In the end, Foreign Secretary Carrington controlled the group that measured his own policies' success—or in the Falklands' case, failure. It would have required a supremely courageous act by a civil servant to propose that the policies of one's masters had failed. Even in retrospect, it is not pleasant to revisit a cabinet composed, by and large, of intelligent men and women who simply waited for events to occur to which they might respond, instead of taking up the reins themselves.[30]

British Politics and Diplomacy at Work

Thatcher's comment that the war was a bolt from the blue is metaphysically impossible, but it drew sympathy from a middle class whose soldier ancestors had punished recalcitrant foes in the back of beyond dozens of years ago. Thatcher, tottery mistress of city and shire that 1982 winter of her discontent, knew that political foes of the day fade and that failed policies get forgotten. Alert to shifting political winds at home, she had failed to understand that nations' intentions, benign or malevolent, remain roughly constant over time, whatever gloss successive political regimes use to disguise them.[31] All said, when her winter of trials passed, the British public revived its patriotism and landed it on Margaret Thatcher that tumultuous Falklands weekend in early April 1982.

After Sir John Kerr prepared the Government's side for Thatcher's appearance in the Commons on April 2nd, his and Sir Geoffrey Howe's car was nearly overturned on its way from No. 10 Downing Street to Parliament by a mob that shouted its anger that the islands had been taken and proclaimed its support for Margaret Thatcher. Just as quickly, Kerr cherished U.S. assistance from the highest levels of government and recalled that Secretary of Defense Caspar Weinberger had penciled on a memo "Give them what they want and arrange payment after the war."[32] Quietly but forcefully, Weinberger overrode objections from dark cornered Pentagon baronies whose petty concerns seemed fruitless, fuzzy and unnecessary then and now. Three days after the Argentine invasion, Thatcher had captured the ingredients for success in the war: tangible encouragement from her once alienated electorate and open doors into America's warehouses. All this should have been unnecessary.

Galtieri's seizure of the Falklands in April 1982 could not have been more poorly timed for Margaret Thatcher. Race riots in English cities, two million unemployed and back-bench grumbling had eroded her dominance over the Conservative Party and the House of Commons. A national poll published at the time in the Daily Mail contended that 80 percent of the electorate blamed the British government (and not the Argentine government) for the invasion, and 36 percent held Thatcher herself responsible. A few days later, The London Times' poll found her to be the worst Prime Minister in British history.

By the morning of April 3, 1982, when it was clear to all that Port Stanley had surrendered to the Argentine invading forces, it is safe to say that Thatcher's cabinet was not with her. As a courtesy to her opponents, she fired her Foreign Secretary. Although that move was useful and necessary under the circumstances, Thatcher had to accept as a replacement Francis Pym, whose hawkishness towards the Argentineans and loyalty towards Thatcher herself remained in doubt until and after the war's end.[33] Despite the daggers thrust in the bowels of his own government, Pym continued to speak and to act in the dovish mode both privately and in his utterances to the House of Commons, so much so, that Thatcher's characterization of "Wets" was always thought to put Pym at the top of the list. Thatcher and Pym shared a mutual dislike and mistrust on professional grounds too. Her Foreign Office, now headed by Pym, had committed that gravest of bureaucratic blunders—it had gestated a minor perplexity into a major crisis. She could not repose confidence in her intelligence community after its failure to assess accurately Argentina's overt preparations for war.[34] A new political party, the Social Democrats, had risen to a 40 percent approval rating in nation-wide polls and threatened a major victory over the Conservatives at looming local elections. Unlike Churchill, Hume or Macmillan, Margaret Thatcher had never participated in a war, let alone led her country in an armed conflict. Thatcher's weakness in this respect prevented her from dismissing her government's intelligence chiefs, as Churchill did during World War II, and from sacking a third of the cabinet as Macmillan once did.

Early in her reign, Thatcher reportedly stated, "Must I do all this international stuff?" and the obvious response was, "You can't avoid it."[35] No crisis management team swung into action during those first days because, like most congealed bureaucracies facing crises, the initial reaction of Thatcher's cabinet was denial that a crisis existed. At midday on April 2nd, Humphrey Atkins MP, the government's spokesman on foreign policy in the Commons, stated that no invasion had occurred and that Downing St. had heard from the Falklands not two hours earlier. This statement was untrue, because on that day at 5:15AM Falkland's time, Rex Hunt, the Falklands Governor, had advised London that the invasion had begun. Hunt surrendered the islands and their garrison five hours later at 10:30AM. Through the night of April 2nd and the following morning, the unmistakable scent of a government's imminent fall wafted through Whitehall and the Houses of Parliament. At an emergency session of parliament on Saturday, April 3, Thatcher offered the curious alibi that no government could have stationed deterrent forces on the Falklands, so prohibitive would have been its cost. A few months, 255 lives and several billions of pounds later, this excuse seemed fairly lame. During that rancorous Saturday session on April 3rd, Parliament contented itself with mauling some ministers, a few of whom resigned, but Thatcher carried the Commons and stayed.[36] Her party's qualms about their leader weighed less than their loathing for Galtieri and a probable loss of the next election.

As soon as Thatcher made clear to the House of Commons and to the outside world that she intended to retake the Falklands, major fleet units homebound from spring exercises near Gibraltar reversed course, loaded war stores and sailed southwards. Other Royal Navy ships were put on four hours notice to move. The navy's tiny amphibious staff, moribund after cuts in its budget, cobbled together ships, men and plans for an opposed landing over unknown beaches. The Royal Marines' 3 Commando Brigade, Britain's sole amphibious force, was put on 72 hours notice to move and to have all its officers and men recalled from leave, schools and even a marriage. With all of that, many weeks would pass before troops could assault Port Stanley.

"Mrs. Thatcher respected intelligence and had a keen appetite for it. She was aware from personal experience that we lived in a dangerous world."[37] Few would have agreed with the quote's first sentence during that first chaotic weekend of April 1982. All would have shouted "yea" at the second. In the meantime, Thatcher needed a dramatic event to keep her cabinet with her, to put Galtieri on the defensive, to still her domestic opponents, to preserve U.S. support, to rally the free world to her side and to convince the captive Kelpers that they might get their freedom back. The cur dogs already nipped at her heels.[38] James Callaghan, Labor's spokesman on defense, accused Thatcher of a "gross blunder" in letting the Falklands fall.[39] From Thatcher's own party, the Falkland Islands lobby shouted "I told you so" so stridently, that a Foreign Office spokesman was moved to retort that: "Air Commodore Frow [the lobby's spokesman] has no official standing whatever. The crisis is entirely a matter for the British government."[40] "To this day I remember vividly the Chairman of the Select Committee on Defense [Timothy Kitson] hanging about the Tea Room Corridor, telling anyone he could waylay that *Hermes* had propeller shaft trouble; that *Invincible* had sailed without her electronics, etc."[41] There was the Argentine angle, too. If, despite his self-adulatory bluster, Galtieri could be persuaded that Thatcher meant business, he might heed the provisions of UN Resolution 502 and quit the islands after a dramatic British diplomatic or military move.

By April 3, 1982, Anthony Parsons, Britain's delegate to the UN, had shepherded through the UN's Security Council Resolution 502, which called for Argentina's immediate removal of its armed forces from the Falklands as a condition precedent to negotiation about the Falklands' future sovereignty. Parsons' brilliant diplomacy at the UN, a bare few hours after Argentina's invasion, put the Falklands center stage among the world's vexing affairs and convinced a heterogeneous assortment of Third World, industrialized and non–English speaking states to oppose in public the junta's military adventurism. Parsons' diplomatic triumph qualified the Argentine invasion as a universally accepted act of military aggression for all the world to see. That gave Secretary of State Haig the cover to attempt a diplomatic solution and, most important of all, gave the United States justification to supply its principal partner with the vast amount of military and intangible aid that headed south. British Ambassador Henderson's elegant work got the headlines, but Parsons had done the heavy lifting that set in motion the diplomatic and military steps that Thatcher needed for a quick and fairly bloodless victory. Absent Argentina's removal of its military forces, Britain could now take military steps to retake the Falklands.

The Soviet Union failed to veto the British resolution, and non-aligned states mutely resisted the Argentine ambassador's pleas for their help. Much to the surprise of Argentina's foreign office, settlement of border disputes by armed force was not a precedent modern nation states could stomach. The reasons were clear. Even passive approval of Argentina's invasion and the lack of solid British victories on the Falklands would leave open the possibilities of military initiatives almost anywhere else along the Brazilian and Argentine border and at the Amur River, for example, where China and the Soviet Union contested in a not always cold war.[42] More was at stake than even ambitious battalion commanders like 2 Para's Jones knew. Major Sheridan's bold initiative had retrieved South Georgia for the crown but, in the absurd calculus of Galtieri's junta, this Argentine defeat did not count for much. Absent Pym's fanciful expectations of a truce and Brigadier De la Billiere's coup de main by the SAS that would win the war on every front, the problems lurking behind a single battalion's actions weighed more heavily than the squadies could imagine. From very early April, Jones lobbied for his 2 Para to be included in the ground force that would be needed to retake the islands. He put himself in the cross hairs of history and it would take much to believe that Jones did not know this in his bones.

The pre-invasion dinner that UN Ambassador Jeane Kirkpatrick enjoyed with Esteban Takacs, the Argentine ambassador to the United States, gave rise, with no factual support, to the notion that the event signaled a closeness with South American dictators that would trump the Special Relationship. Hear Nott: "Apart from Weinberger and the Pentagon, the Americans were very, very far from being on our side."[43] That view is equally far from reality, as evidenced by President Reagan's letter to Margaret Thatcher dated April 1, 1982 (see Figure 2.1).

Kirkpatrick claims, on her part, that President Reagan ordered her to attend the Takacs dinner even though both knew the invasion was on and that, as a result, she felt exploited.[44] Few of senior rank inside the government or the foreign policy establishment sided with or acted in behalf of Argentina during the war. The Senate, led by Sen. Charles Percy (R), voted in Senate Resolution 382 of April 29, 1982, to support Great Britain, to condemn Argentina's actions and to call for the withdrawal of Argentine forces from the islands as a condition precedent to negotiations about sovereignty. The vote was 79 to 1. The resolution was supported by Senators Moynihan and Biden, both Democrats, and by Senator Malcolm Wallop, Republican of Wyoming, who stated: "We do have a policy and it

---

Figure 2.1: Text of Letter from President Reagan to Margaret Thatcher, April 1, 1982

Dear Margaret:

I have just talked at length with General Galtieri about the situation in the Falklands. I conveyed to him my personal concern about the possibility of an Argentinian invasion. I told him that initiating military operations against the Falklands Islands would seriously compromise relations between the US and Argentina, and I urged him to refrain from offensive action. I offered our good offices and my readiness to send a personal representative to assist in resolving the issue between Argentina and the UK.

The General heard my message, but gave me no commitment that he would comply with it. Indeed, he spoke in terms of ultimatums and left me with the clear impression that he has embarked on a course of armed conflict. We will continue to cooperate with your government in the effort to resolve the dispute, both in attempting to avert hostilities and to stop them if they should break out. While we have a policy of neutrality on the sovereignty issue, we will not be neutral on the issue involving Argentine use of military force.

Source: Reagan letter to Thatcher (Galtieri intends to use force) [NSC draft], April 1, 1982, Margaret Thatcher Foundation, www.margaretthatcher.org.

---

is on the side of our traditional ally, Britain."[45] Percy did not stop after his formal Senate resolution had passed: "I think she [Kirkpatrick] does tremendous disservice . . . and I think she misled the Argentines by buttering them up."[46] Percy went on to say that Kirkpatrick may have misled the Argentine junta into misreading American resolve in backing Britain.[47]

The barons of the U.S. Senate had stated a policy in line with the president's letter to Thatcher that was to hold; it created an umbrella under which government departments—Treasury, Defense and Commerce—could assist Great Britain virtually on their own. At every level of government, the spigot opened a flow of overt and covert aid to the British, whatever the misperceptions of some abroad.[48] One can hardly escape the conclusion that this near unanimous vote, which was taken a month before Goose Green and remained in force for the war, was greater at least in percentage terms than the support that Thatcher had conjured up from her own government. The Anglo-American lobby inside the State Department, so contemptuously scolded by Kirkpatrick, stayed alive and well and pro Thatcher from the outset of the conflict. Those who spent their lives thwarting the Soviet Bloc in Europe determined that jejune pride in one hemisphere should not trump principles held dear in the other hemisphere. War is the way that most nations go from point A to point B in their national lives. More than a few in Great Britain and many in Buenos Aires failed to understand that Britain's American allies— Lawrence Eagleburger, Alexander Haig, John Lehman, Caspar Weinberger, etal.—wanted point B set on the correct side of the chasm that fenced off zealous democracies from barren despotisms. However cheeseparing the British Foreign Office and MOD had acted regarding 2,000 Kelpers, Al Haig and Cap Weinberger were the last persons to put nearly indecipherable texts from moldy documents ahead of common sense.[49]

Much gauzy meaning has been drawn from Ambassador Jeane Kirkpatrick's support for Argentina. Her actions at the UN, where she was the U.S. ambassador, and her discourse on Meet The Press on June 6, 1982, have given rise to the notion that American support for Thatcher was a close-run thing. That is barely understandable, but erroneous. British writers and politicians have seldom understood how American policy gets made. A heterogeneous nation's discussion that includes political bluster, grandstanding, and simple ignorance of the problem at hand confuses onlookers who have not lived within the interstices of Washington's political society. The White House, Congress, its important committees, the Think Tanks, the Pentagon, the State Department, the CIA and the Boston-Washington axis rarely center on the same problems at the same time with a singular voice and never with similar conclusions. No government whip snags everybody into line. The tenor is existential; anticipation is little practiced. Problems are solved when they arrive. For example, the problem of the Falklands was not included in the very detailed Carter to Reagan transition papers that catalogued in excruciating detail issues that President Reagan might be forced to handle immediately upon entering office.[50] Nor was the Falklands an issue between the United States and Great Britain or the United States and Argentina. British and Argentine striving after the islands appeared on no one's radar screen.[51]

What counts in Washington is the interface between the problem, in this case war between Great Britain and Argentina, and the department or departments assigned to handle the problem. Even then, senior bureaucrats can run "fast desks" or "slow desks" to hasten or to delay any action. Mrs. Kirkpatrick never had any executive authority over what actions the United States took or failed to take to assist Great Britain. Her misunderstanding on this point is barely comprehensible. Certainly her post at the UN apparently failed to fulfill grander ambitions. "I'd rather be in

Philadelphia." Ambassador Kirkpatrick characterized herself at the UN as an "intellectual among bureaucrats."[52] Alan Clark, one of Thatcher's junior ministers, thought otherwise, and after lunch with Mrs. Kirkpatrick characterized her as: "Odious, totally Stalinist, humorless."[53] However scanty Kirkpatrick's true power as Ambassador, she called the job quite realistically: "Death in Toronto." She might bray as she wished; true power to act in favor of the UK or against its interests lay in the Pentagon and the White House. Yet her failure to help Britain's Anthony Parsons push through UN Resolution 502 that gave Thatcher the moral and diplomatic high ground, provided fodder for sappy London gossip meant to denigrate the extent of America's help and to weaken Thatcher's resolve. It is true that Kirkpatrick told Sir Anthony Parsons that she would try to block Parson's submission of 502 to the Security Council.[54] It is equally true that her boss, Al Haig, did not order her to so act. Quite the opposite! Like Nott and Admiral Lewin, Kirkpatrick either failed to know where true power resided in the administration that she served or, realizing it, chafed under the reality. Kirkpatrick's utterances resembled balloons at a country fair. Colorful and large, they floated over the hoi poloi and finally fell because they contained only air.

When the president and the leaders of the U.S. Senate, the Pentagon and the Defense Department take broad agreement on a political or military initiative, as they did in April 1982, said initiative becomes a matter for action by the subordinate bureaucracies. Whining over the purported absence of immediate support for Britain, Nott's statement in the Daily Telegraph on March 20, 2002, that, "If replacing Washington had been in the hands of the East Coast Wasps things might have been different" is as invidious as it is incorrect.[55] Washington's foreign policy establishment has for the last 75 years been very liberally salted, and often led by persons of German, Irish, Jewish, Polish and African-American extraction, whose attractive accents contrasted happily with Boston twangs normally found in Harvard's classrooms (e.g., Secretaries Al Haig, Henry Kissinger, Colin Powell, Cap Weinberger and National Security Advisors Zbignew Brzezinski and Condoleezza Rice).[56] Nott's statement that he "sometimes wondered if [Reagan] even knew or cared where Europe was" stands as perhaps the most mindless judgment ever publicly made about the president whose policies and actions later led to the destruction of the Berlin Wall and to the fall of the Soviet Empire.

Nott's retention as Minister of Defense was understandable in the context of British cabinet politics, but lamentable for those whose professional lives depended on his views. He had been assigned to cut the defense budget across the board, if necessary, to pay for Britain's nuclear deterrent.[57] The Royal Navy was hardest hit, as became woefully clear during the all-too-successful Argentine air raids on the British ships in San Carlos Bay. But despite Nott's failures, politics demanded that he remain Minister of Defense. Thatcher doubtless wanted the man who had gotten her into the disaster to get her out of it, and, in the event that she lost the war, Nott could swing for at least part of the disaster. Nott knew the ways of Whitehall, but the decisions that he had made there—the withdrawal of HMS *Endurance* from the Falklands and the navy's emasculation—had been disastrous, and ultimately threatened both Thatcher's primacy and Britain's eminence as America's principal NATO ally.[58]

Sir Nicholas Henderson was the British Ambassador to Washington and, as many believed—perhaps even he—self-appointed don to the city's foreign policy elite. While he jogged, all collar points askew, from Washington's TV studios to New York's TV studios back to Capitol Hill in his quest for American support, the reality of American planes landing on Ascension Island with the oddments of war that Nott's ministry either could not or would not provide, told the tale.[59] Henderson's efforts, clever, theatrical, unnecessary and powdered with a light coating of mock disillusionment over the workings of a duplicitous world, gladdened the media and amused some of their audience (see Figure 2.2 for his fair summation of the affair). Here was a British Robert Frost preaching the old verities. He need not have done so, for as one American politician remarked: "Argentina is a dictatorship. . . . And one of our best friends and allies of all time has been the United Kingdom. To say that we stand neutral was a mistake."[60] It was clear to many that Henderson's numerous appearances on TV ended too soon for him. Energized rectitude was wanted and Henderson offered that by the liter. In a curious way, Henderson and the FCO missed out on American judgments just as they had ignored the junta's preparations for war.

As Sir Nicholas velveted his way through what he saw as the corridors of power, tangible American assistance—fuel, bullets, medical supplies, air-to-air missiles, etc.—had been flowing towards the South Atlantic since before the Argentine landing. It is not difficult to sense that, while Henderson's interlocutors at the U.S. State Department were sighing in sympathy with their artfully rumpled colleague, they knew full well what their own juniors were perpetrating far from the Potomac's banks. Henderson's picture taken for the New York Times in the office of Senator

---

Figure 2.2: Text of Letter by Sir Nicholas Henderson, March 30, 2002

By **Sir Nicholas Henderson**, who was British ambassador in Washington

During the evening of March 31, 1982, I went to see Alexander Haig, the US Secretary of State. When I said we thought Argentina intended to invade the Falklands, he said he didn't believe it. Tom Enders, the assistant secretary for inter-American affairs, said the US ambassador in Buenos Aires had been assured that they would not invade. I then showed them our intelligence. Haig jumped out of his chair. "Why wasn't I told this," he exclaimed.

After a while, he asked: "What do you want us to do?" I had to consult London. Lord Carrington had just returned from a trip and I was put through to Margaret Thatcher. It was 4am in London and the Prime Minister was asleep. She had to be woken up. She just said: "I'll leave it to you."

President Reagan offered to send George Bush (then vice-president) to Buenos Aires, but Galtieri would not see him. The President also spoke to Galtieri for 50 minutes by phone, but could not prevent the invasion.

I spoke to Haig every day afterwards. We needed American support: intelligence, diplomatic and political. But the problem was that, for America, it was difficult to come out openly on our side at first, because of its interests in Central and South America. There was also considerable doubt in Washington whether we could pull it off militarily.

Mrs Thatcher thought that the idea of a negotiated settlement would cheat us and would be bound to fail. She saw it simply as a sign of weakness. In retrospect, I think the Prime Minister underestimated the difficulty America faced.

Jean Kirkpatrick, the US ambassador at the UN, drew a distinction between an authoritarian and totalitarian regime in Buenos Aires. She regarded the junta as authoritarian an not totalitarian, which was a false view. It was also her view that Argentina had helped America in combating communism in Latin America. So it was never a foregone conclusion that Washington would come down on our side. I also

---

John Tower (R-Texas) with that very influential Washington insider was a coup no Argentine diplomat could match. The image of a wise and weary servant of the Queen confiding his needs to a powerful and receptive American senator awaited only the brush of a master portraitist to enshrine the pair into the pantheon of British diplomatic triumphs.[61]

The Argentine side lost the battle of public relations straightaway, but it remains a matter of conjecture as to whether the citizens of, say, Butte Montana knew or cared more about the Falklands after Sir Nicholas' discourse than they knew or cared earlier. A senior British officer still remembers from Ascension what he calls "the chain of American planes that landed on that tiny island." That was what mattered. In fact, the logistical efforts of

appeared on American television almost every day. It was vitally important to get public opinion behind us.

Haig took part in exhaustive shuttle diplomacy, the failure of which was later to cost him his job. It must be said that Mrs Thatcher was always suspicious of Haig, but he made it absolutely clear to me that, "We are not going to do to you what we did at Suez". Reagan, himself, was also pretty distant.

There were a number of quite acrimonious exchanges with the Prime Minister. When we landed on the islands, Haig was terrified there would be a terrible slaughter. He kept on saying that we must be magnanimous. It made the Prime Minister mad. They also wanted a ceasefire before we had finished them off, but it was not something Mrs Thatcher was prepared to consider.

It must be said, however, that, when it was absolutely clear that the Argentines would not agree to a negotiated settlement before the fighting started, the Americans came out publicly on our side.

Before that Caspar Weinberger, the US Defence Secretary, had undertaken to give us anything we wanted militarily. I'm sure Haig did not know of that at the time, because it would have compromised his position as an honest broker. I'm not sure whether Reagan knew either.

At the end of May, Weinberger even offered us an aircraft carrier. It was during a garden party at the British Embassy. He took me aside and said: "If you want me to provide an aircraft carrier, I can do it." The Royal Navy was astonished. They didn't know whether to take him seriously or not. But he was very serious. As it was, we didn't need one.

But the Americans provided us with equipment and intelligence facilities from their satellites. I think even the Prime Minister has conceded that, without the new Sidewinder missiles that the Americans provided, we would not have won the war. We have a lot to be grateful to the Americans for, even if there were difficulties along the way.

Source: Letter to the *Daily Telegraph*, March 30, 2002, p. 65.

both countries and the line of Royal Navy ships heading south, all stridently bannered in the world's press, assured almost all that support for Argentina, aside from the diplomatic niceties, would be fruitless and perhaps in the end embarrassing. As some in Washington remarked, "As soon as we saw the fleet going south we knew Thatcher couldn't afford to lose."[62] Whatever doubts members of the British government might entertain about ejecting Argentina from the Falklands, Washington determined that Britain would prevail. While London was not so confident about the war's outcome, most of Latin America's chanceries saw the beginnings of a major Argentine embarrassment. It was possibly a good thing that Brigadier Thompson RM and Lt. Col. Jones of 2 Para were not aware of this ironical divergence as they prepared for their first battle. To Ronald Reagan, the president who more than any other brought down the Berlin Wall, helping the British and, even more, defeating an aggressive dictatorship, was a certain choice.

Al Haig was Secretary of State when the war began. He knew nothing of the run-up to it and became a peacemaker as only an old combat veteran can be.[63] He neither needed nor wanted adulation for his daily efforts. In retrospect, it is clear that his actions on behalf of Great Britain during April of 1982 diminished his tenure in office. When the war began, Haig was busily engaged on other fronts. True, his deputy, Thomas Enders, had visited Buenos Aires on March 8, 1982, with a message to Galtieri not to stir up trouble. Enders had received a delegation of the mothers of the "disappeared" and noted their agony both privately and officially. Remember, though, in 1982 the preeminent duties of the State Department and the Washington foreign policy community were containment of the Soviet Union, its allies and the client states that were signatory to the Warsaw Pact. All else was secondary, even the diaphanous threat posed by the strangely Marxist countries in Central America. Cuba made the most noise. It maintained an army of 15,000 troops in Africa and had established a seedy intelligence net to cover the Caribbean basin. After the Cuban missile crisis, Soviet troops remained in Cuba, but all said the United States suffered no military menace from any part of Central or South America. Careers were not made there.

On March 28, 1982, Sir Nicholas Henderson brought U.S. Secretary of State Haig a letter stating that Argentine forces had landed on South Georgia. No bells rang. Haig and possibly others at State considered the Falklands "an amusing anachronism."[64] Haig remarked that the Argentine chief of military intelligence landed in Washington the same day. That worthy did not see Haig. Neither Henderson, if he knew, nor Takacs, the Argentine ambassador to the United States, had seen fit to inform Haig that a storm was brewing in the South Atlantic. Apparently, Haig was not briefed that Carrington had told his Argentine opposite number by way of a note dated March 23, 1982, to remove from South Georgia the Argentine landing party, which was clearly composed of military persons dressed in civilian clothes. After Henderson's visit, Haig did the gentlemanly thing and offered to mediate the incipient dispute. In consequence of this tender, Galtieri "refused American good offices and a Bush visit."[65]

By April 8, 1982, Haig was in London, at the start of an exhaustive shuttle among Buenos Aires, Washington and London. U.S. policy at that moment aimed at getting both parties to step back from war and to reach a settlement that allowed for future negotiations on the Falklands' fate. Haig had few cards to play. Whatever either side might say or hint or posture, a few fundamental truths dictated the non-negotiable positions of all involved. The Kelpers' self determination could be hinted at but never became a position to be compromised. Galtieri had vainly mouthed anti-Communist platitudes to disguise the Argentine junta's brutal repression of even the most timid opposition to his regime. However glib his spoken banalities, the international community well understood that the underlying truths of Galtieri's rule were terror and economic reliance on the Soviet Union, which bought 80 percent of Argentina's grain crop.[66] Far from the Northern Hemisphere's wealth and military power, Galtieri's Argentina was in no sense an American client state, or a Russian one for that matter. The junta simply existed, solitary and without direction. Whatever Haig did or said, a tactical reality intruded on the junta's speculation. One Argentine editor put it succinctly that after Argentina's invasion of South Georgia: "Galtieri and the generals are cornered; they have nowhere to go but forward. If they go backward, they will be swept away."[67] The junta had to fight—they could not be seen as having negotiated away their conquest—and the war was on. It mattered little that Goose Green was the first site for the resolution of this unnecessary folly and that Lt. Col. H. Jones was its protagonist.

The apparent graciousness of Haig's meetings in London with Thatcher and her cabinet disappeared once the American Secretary of State had departed Downing Street. In the course of the smarmy dithering that characterized much of the cabinet's and Northwood's discussions on the war, Thatcher introduced a new expression into diplomacy's vocabulary. It was "Haigism," she complained, that prevented full American support for her position. It was "Haigism" that kept the diplomatic ball bouncing unpredictably so that Britain lacked global support, and "Haigism" that may have infected those FCO members of her coterie who, as closet wets, seemed less than firm in their support for Thatcher's obduracy.[68] None of the PM's pouting held the least scintilla of truth. A novice in global affairs, she was only being shown how the outside world works and, possibly for the first time, examples of American Realism and Idealism, the twin roots of U.S. foreign policy since Ben Franklin labored at the court of Versailles. In fact, it was her own FCO that had never shown any spine in defining the Falklands as a vital interest at risk to which military attention might, one day, need be paid. In truth, Haig's negotiations were conducted in a way that garnered, quietly but force-fully, the international community's support for Thatcher and gave her time to get a coherent military force in Falklands' waters ready to invade the islands if the junta did not remove its troops.[69] Underlying Haig's efforts was the fact that he had seen the rows of body bags in Vietnam and he wanted no more of such awful scenes from anyone.

The sticking point for Galtieri came now at the confluence of two per-sistent realities: The Special Relationship between the United States and Britain and the foundations of American domestic and foreign policy.[70] The datum from which all U.S. foreign policy has sprung since WWII is self-determination and diversity. These principles, sometimes tortured or misapplied, remained during 1982 valid and in place. Haig, for himself, would not side with a time and blood-worn dictator or be seen as the front-page ally of the junta that made the disappeared disappear. Even more potent, the Vietnam syndrome perdured: the United States was not to be seen in the company of criminals, if it could be at all helped, no mat-ter Kirkpatrick's lame distinction between good dictators and bad dicta-tors. In the back of many minds were the facts that Argentina had remained neutral during World War I, only joined the allies very late in World War II and, after the war, harbored many Germans thought to be war criminals. Le Tout Argentina had always considered itself a European outpost rooted in a Latin tradition, and a 19th century one at that. Fifty-five percent of its people were of Italian extraction, but Spanish was the language of conversation and English the language of banking; a lightly veiled animosity towards the Anglo-Saxon North had always alloyed Argentina's view of the world. Those who, despite the hollowness of their remarks, grabbed the TV cameras at every possible opportunity to spout anti-British and anti-American twaddle, expressed a petty national feeling but, in the end, did their country no good. The special relationship remained firm. Costa-Méndez apparently forgot who had attacked whom first when he stated, "Britain violated the principles of international law while negotiations are on between two countries."[71]

Oddly, Haig found himself "plus royaliste que le roi" in the face of temerity from the very British leaders whose cause he defended. For example, Denis Healey, the shadow Defense Minister, called for the UN's Pérez de Cuéllar to appoint an interim administrator for the Falklands until a long-term solution could be found.[72] That move would, of course, have nullified British sovereignty over the islands, cast aside the wishes of the Falklanders themselves and rendered superfluous the fleet and troops that approached the islands. Healey's proposal would also have rendered useless the vast American aid that even that first April weekend poured into Ascension.

Failed Negotiations

The story of these jello negotiations between Great Britain and Argentina is banal. No substantive point ever got nailed down. At bottom, the paramount issue of sovereignty was not negotiable.[73] "Sovereignty is not under consideration because it is Argentine," said Roberto Baltiérrez, a spokesman for Galtieri.[74] The Argentine junta reneged on one set of proposals that might have averted war, just as Haig sat in his plane waiting to take off from Buenos Aires. Haig later lamented: "The shuttle ultimately failed because politics within Buenos Aires made it impossible for the junta to negotiate in good faith."[75] It was as much the daily mechanics of negotiation as its substance that bedeviled Haig, because no one person had authority on the Argentine side to give him a firm offer or counter offer for transmittal to Thatcher. Almost comically, the Argentine foreign minister Costa-Méndez carried a different message to Haig each day. No one on the Argentine side strained to get the king's ear because there was no king.

On the British side, Thatcher could not lose the military war that was soon to begin or be thought to have lost a political battle against a third rate power. By going to war, Thatcher admitted her government's error in diplomacy, in the early warning of war and in the composition of her defense budgets. Of course, politicians' singular gaffes are usually rectified by blood, and this conflict was no exception. Even so, she floated the notion that she was willing to yield Galtieri a small administrative role in the islands' administration by way of giving him a ladder from which to climb down. That offer was never taken up. Goose Green and the subsequent battles loomed almost inevitable. Jones and 2 Para got the first job.

Each day of the war up to Port Stanley's fall, Thatcher had constantly to look over her shoulder at her own party, at Julian Amery, whom she had narrowly defeated for the Prime Ministership, at Pym and his small but niggling coterie of assorted "wets," at Parkinson, a member of the war cabinet who awaited a blunder by Thatcher to receive a summons from the Queen, and at Nott, who believed reconquest would fail. Still, however sharp the waiting knives of her party's nabobs, she had mastered the British middle class and the immediate spate of American aid would continue. More to the point, bluff Al Haig, Henry Kissinger's prize pupil, had

49

no truck with desk-bound Argentine Generals and their late middle-aged adventurism. From the beginning, Nott, Thatcher and others kibitzing from the cheap seats failed to grasp the premise of Haig's work as he explicated it: "To see in what way we can, as allies and friends, assist in the realization of UN Resolution 502 which calls for the withdrawal of Argentine forces from the islands and a diplomatic solution to the problem."[76] In other words, the junta's troops must leave the Falklands before any substantive talks may begin. Haig wrapped up his sleep-depriving efforts at finding peace in one trenchant phrase: "An exercise in bad faith that is unique in my experience as a negotiator."[77]

After Haig discontinued his own efforts at a negotiated settlement, he dispatched General Vernon Walters, a trusted friend, who contacted the junta, several of their army corps commanders, and others in South American countries who might form a coalition of anti-war cabals. Haig sent Walters to Paris to discuss a cessation of hostilities with Federico Schames, an old friend of Walters and the Argentine ambassador to Paris. These, the thinking went, might shame Galtieri into compromise. Walters also brought with him the counsel that Thatcher would fight, with America as ally, and would win. Walters' pleas fell on deaf ears.[78]

Thatcher's litany that "the wishes of the islanders are paramount" peppered her statements throughout the conflict, though it is doubtful that she would have stopped the seizure of the islands by military force under any circumstances. Along with Jones' 2 Para and their like, the task force sailing south carried her entire political capital. But the bane of British parliamentary politics—that those committing indecent acts inside her tent could bring her down, while those caught in the same act outside the tent could only bray in the wilderness—remained her most vexing encumbrance throughout the war. The wets slinked menacingly inside the cabinet's tent until the war was well won. They seemed blinded to the sense of all the American discussions that followed the Argentine invasion and to President Reagan's prescient exhortation in a 50-minute call to President Galtieri on April 1st.

With much of the Argentine task force still at sea and all the Argentine troops still not landed, Reagan asked Galtieri to stop the invasion and warned that, if it continued, the British would take military action and that America would support Great Britain.[79] Here go back to the junta's intentions as they were stipulated both publicly and privately after the war. Some confidence may be lent these assertions because it is clear that the junta and its staff, with very few muffled exceptions, did not believe that Thatcher would fight. After the Argentine landing, it was planned, the assault force would be withdrawn and a small occupying force would remain while final negotiations to transfer sovereignty would occur. Plan Goa and subsequent determinations explicitly envisaged such moves. Indeed, much of the Argentine marine force was removed shortly after it had landed, but when the British task force sailed, thousands of army troops from the just exited class of conscripts were rounded up, put on trucks and flown or shipped to Port Stanley. So dramatic was the roundup that mothers in at least one northern Argentine village hid their children from the press gangs.[80] As the British fleet sailed south, Thatcher and Galtieri both upped the ante. The Argentine Exocets were prepped and a flood of American supplies almost submerged Ascension Island. On the other hand, many of the Argentine troops arrived on the Falklands without cold weather clothes, weapons or tactical organization. Clearly, Britain was set to win this war, absent a disaster like *Canberra*'s sinking or a major military blunder. It was against this backdrop that Thatcher sought a military victory that could be publicized widely and understood thoroughly by the middle classes whose sons were being killed. A thumb in the eyes of those timid souls who doubted her would not hurt her either.

Notes

1. Lombardo's written answer to author's questions, February 24, 2000.

2. William Shakespeare, *King Lear* (New York: Penguin, 1972).

3. The literature here is enormous. Try first, James Bamford, *Body of Secrets* (New York: Anchor, 2002); and David T. Lundgren, *Trust But Verify* (Annapolis: Naval Institute Press, 2000).

4. In the case of the run-up to this war, British watchers and their seniors failed to notice or disregarded change. Their underlying axiom was: "Nothing has happened so far, therefore, nothing will."

5. The opposite is true. Bad or lazy watchers cause no end of trouble. They are soon gone. They have missed opportunities to aid their government and to have great fun by not attaining the status of true keeners. Thatcher needed Goose Green and the other bloody victories to compensate for mistakes that her watchers or their clients should never have made.

6. The first question the author asked of himself when assuming a watch was: "What can happen in the next 24 hours to harm the United States, its people or its interests?" When he strayed, several inquiring and energetic colleagues set him straight forthwith.

7. All countries can inflict some damage to some person, entity or country somewhere. The trick is to discover when the peckish diplomatic adversary is about to challenge a vital interest. Definition of vital interests is set not by the intelligence

community, but by its political masters. Neither the British government of the moment nor the Commonwealth and Foreign Office (CFO) had defined and publicized the Falklands as a vital interest. That Margaret Thatcher defined possession of the Falklands *in pectore* as a vital interest, and that she failed to communicate this fact to her own Foreign Office, her Defense Establishment and to the Argentine junta was the single biggest step on the road to war and, in terms of lives lost, the biggest blunder of her career. Two British sergeants, one from Goose Green, remarked to the author: "We never knew the Falklands was important."

8. The vote here goes to those with educations in the classics. After years of declensions and conjugations, one notes asymmetries very quickly. The I&W crowd also gets into Intentions and Capabilities. This is the mystical theology of the intelligence profession and discussion of it must be avoided here.

9. Watching tanks is said to be fun, rather like train spotting or bird watching.

10. Keeners notice what does not happen but should. This particular skill takes time to develop. Partners in a lengthy marriage understand this.

11. In such cases, the communications among those concerned are far less formal and scheduled than Franks implies (the Franks Report, a summary of British action prior to the war, is treated extensively in the latter pages of this book). Most good intelligence is passed word of mouth to him or to her who needs the information. Lengthy papers are frowned upon if for no other reason than that the information may be out of date before it reaches the customer. The word "assessment" is a portentous word in Franks. Any intelligence watch officer or area analyst worth his or her salt keeps a running assessment in his or her head at all times, often at the expense of a good night's sleep. A pretty good and very timely "assessment" is available on an hour's notice from any competent watcher or keener. Committees are not needed here. In fact, they should be shunned.

12. While involved in such efforts, the author had in his group a young enlisted man (NCO), a carpenter from West Virginia, very bright and uneducated. He spoke no foreign language and had no degree. He did register the subtlest change. When he said: "Sir, did you notice?" the day or night or both would be long. He was not simply a watcher, he was a true keener. He was marvelous and much more productive at a quarter the pay than the humorless Ph.D.s who ooze into the business.

13. See International Monetary Fund (IMF), *Blue Books 1981–1982* (Washington, D.C.: IMF, 1981–1982) to understand in what fiscal and monetary straits the junta found itself.

14. Bank of London and South America Fortnightly Review, June 11, 1955. The Argentine bill erred. The Falklands had no dependencies.

15. Tony Benn, *The Benn Diaries* (London: Arrow, 1996), p. 434.

16. Nick Barker, *Beyond Endurance* (London: Cooper, 1997), p. 123.

17. Barker, *Beyond Endurance*, p. 111.

18. Barker, *Beyond Endurance*, p. 124.

19. British scientists. Falklands' flora and fauna delighted the hardier investigator.

20. The Argentine Navy used this ship to transport supplies and troops.

21. Barker, *Beyond Endurance*, p. 142. Allegedly a civilian ship under contract to the Argentine Navy.

22. Barker, *Beyond Endurance*, p. 144.

23. Barker, *Beyond Endurance*, p. 235.

24. From March 26 to April 2, 1982, the British intercept service picked up electronic signals that made war certain. See Nigel West's recounting of these incidents in *The Secret War for the Falklands* (New York: Little-Brown, 1997).

25. Conversations with and correspondence from Argentine military and civilian officials.

26. The Joint Intelligence Committee that watched over such matters for Thatcher's government did not see fit to deal with this and other overwhelming evidence that predicted hostilities as well as anyone could want. A study of Great Britain's catastrophic lacuna in this regard would hold high interest for those practitioners or academics in search of the way not to do things. That study must await a better day.

27. See Dr. Juan Carlos Murguizur, a teacher at the Argentine Army Staff College, "The South Atlantic Conflict: An Argentinian Point of View," *International Defense Review* 2 (1983): 136.

28. For starters, see Simon Jenkins' essay in *The Times*, April 2, 2002.

29. It is safe to say that for its own assessments the American Intelligence Community did not rely on the JIC's findings.

30. A few have asked how better the U.S. government would have handled the matter. Answer: a committee or subcommittee of the House or Senate that dealt with foreign policy would have carefully monitored the Falklands affair and howled to the White House and to the Press when the indications of war became more frequent and blatant. Parliament had no such corrective or admonitory instruments. Here Bagehot's comment on the "Bovine Stupidity" of MPs becomes apposite. See Walter Bagehot, "The Bovine Stupidity of the Average MP," in Richard Crossman, *Godkin Lectures at Harvard 1970* (Cambridge: Harvard University Press, 1972).

31. "No one in London could ever understand the degree of almost religious fervor that the Argentines had for the islands . . . one cause that could unite all the Argentines." Derek Ashe, *The Guardian*, June 19, 1982.

32. Author's conversation with Sir John Kerr, May 1997. Weinberger remarked later that he had eliminated "fifteen in-boxes." At the time, Howe was the British equivalent of the American Treasury Secretary.

33. On April 18, 1982, Francis Pym told the House of Commons that force would not be used as long as negotiations continued. That policy would have prevented Operation Paraquat, by which Major Sheridan RM recovered South Georgia. Either Pym had not been told of the plans to retake South Georgia by force or he had decided to formulate his own policy on the war. The former is more likely. Pym was forced to return to the House later on the night of his misstatement and to withdraw his remarks. Margaret Thatcher, *Downing Street Years* (New York: Harper, 1993), p. 204.

34. After the war, Thatcher's sour experience with her Foreign and Commonwealth Office led her to appoint an Adviser on Foreign Affairs at No. 10 Downing Street: first, Ambassador Tony Parsons and, later, Sir Percy Craddock, who held the position from 1984 to 1992. The job description suggests a sorry history of Thatcher's grip on her country's foreign relationships: "[First, to] antic-

ipate crises and to see that the Prime Minister was briefed in advance of having to take quick decisions on Foreign Office recommendation; and, second, to interpret to the Foreign Office what was in the Prime Minister's mind in the field of international relations." Percy Craddock, *In Pursuit of British Interests* (London: John Murray, 1997), p. 10.

35. Margaret Thatcher to Sir Frank Cooper, Government Conference, 1977. Cooper was Permanent Under Secretary of Defense, 1976–1982. Quoted in Alan Clark, *Diaries* (London: Weidenfeld and Nicolson, 1993), pp. 218–219.

36. It is difficult to conclude that Thatcher's government was less well-off without the services of those who let the disaster occur.

37. Craddock, *In Pursuit of British Interests*, p. 44.

38. "The mob was always ready to wack MT if things went wrong, especially Timothy Kitson, Chairman of the Select Committee on Defense, a prey to blandishment from every quarter." Clark, *Diaries*, p. 64.

39. *New York Times*, April 8, 1982, p. A12.

40. *Washington Post*, April 11, 1982, p. A15.

41. Clark, *Diaries*, p. 64.

42. "The successful seizure of territory by force, in lieu of negotiations, could not be allowed to become the lesson derived nor the final conclusion drawn. With the history of western weakness in the recent past, it probably would have sent a very serious signal around the world, especially to the Soviet Union." Alexander Haig, quoted in Michael Charlton, *The Little Platoon* (London: Basil Blackwell, 1989), p. 15.

43. Thatcher's hold on British domestic politics remained just secure enough that she could afford a bumbler like John Nott who made erroneous decisions about almost every major military issue that he touched. He showed next to no awareness about the Special Relationship begotten during WWI and fostered throughout the rest of the century by such luminaries on the Senate's Foreign Relations Committee as Prescott Bush, the father of the vice president whom Galtieri refused to receive.

44. Michael Bilton and Peter Kominsky, *Speaking Out* (London: Andre Deutsch, 1997), p. 28.

45. *Washington Post*, April 29, 1982.

46 . United Press International, Domestic News, June 5, 1982.

47. Ibid.

48. Misperceptions about the power of the American Congress abound in the United Kingdom, where members of parliament are elected to gain a majority that forms a cabinet that does the real work and gets individual tasks done. See Bagehot, "The Bovine Stupidity of the Average MP." Under the American system, a near unanimous vote by a major Senate committee to accomplish something or to prevent something from being done is almost always taken by the departments of government to be a set of marching orders unless the president forbids such action. When the Senate voted as it did, whatever Jeane Kirkpatrick or others of her belief said or wrote, America had come down on the British side with all that it meant and implied.

49. For example, the Nootka Sound Convention of October 25, 1790, signed by Spain and Great Britain gave the United Kingdom the right to fish any-

where, to sail anywhere, to get to the fish and to land on any territory needed to support fishing rights, e.g. huts, etc. The Falklands could not be occupied as they were already occupied by Spain. Goebel, *Struggle For The Falklands* (New Haven, CT: Yale University Press, 1927), pp. 428–431.

50. Author's examination.

51. Washington's reaction to the Argentine invasion of the Falklands can be summed up in one senior official's comment: "My God, how could they have let this happen?" Anonymous.

52. See Linda Melvern, *The Ultimate Crime* (London: Allison & Busby, 1995), pp. 213–214.

53. Clark, *Diaries*, p. 71.

54. Sir Anthony Parsons quoted in Charlton, *The Little Platoon*, p. 200.

55. John Nott, *Here Today, Gone Tomorrow*, (London: Politico's, 1992).

56. One of the sergeants who organized the transfer of Stingers to Lt. Col. Rose's regiment may have had Saxon blood. Most of his colleagues believe that his principal ancestry was African. Neither Rose nor Nott refused the weapons.

57. Nott had studied economics at Cambridge University for one year and worked for an investment banking house for several years.

58. "Shortly before the reshuffle in January 1981, I was asked to visit the Prime Minister in her flat at No. 10. . . . I was delighted at the appointment (MOD). . . . I also asked Margaret whether she 'excluded a radical look at the Defense programme.' 'Oh no' she said unhesitatingly, realizing perhaps, at this early stage, what political discomfort a radical look at the Defense programme might involve." Nott, *Here Today, Gone Tomorrow*, pp. 200–201.

59. Tony Benn met Henderson in Paris when the latter was British ambassador to France: "A tall, grey-haired, scruffy man, almost a caricature of an English public school boy who got to the top of the Foreign Office. He was rather superior and swooped me up in his Rolls Royce." Benn, *The Benn Diaries*, p. 390.

60. Former vice president Walter Mondale, answering a questioner at a Press Conference at Yale University, New Haven, April 27, 1982.

61. "Crisis in the Falklands," *New York Times,* April 26, 1982.

62. Interviews and discussions with OAS diplomats and civil servants in Washington, D.C., 1996–1998.

63. Dewey Clarridge, a former senior member of CIA, stated publicly that it had no knowledge of major military action against the Falklands. Duane R. Clarridge, *A Spy For All Seasons* (New York: Scribner's, January 1997), p. 220.

64. Alexander Haig, *Caveat* (New York: McMillan, 1984), p. 261.

65. Haig, *Caveat*, p. 264.

66. Argentina's "agriculture first, industrialization second" policy was fathered by Emmanuel de Hoz, an Argentine graduate of Eton College some years before H. Jones of 2 Para.

67. Argentine Editor quoted in the *New York Times*, April 19, 1982.

68. Sir Nicholas Henderson, *Mandarin* (London: Weidenfeld and Nicolson, 1994), pp. 457–470. Henderson's picture of a distracted, sulky and almost panicky PM varies greatly from the official picture of a war leader in control.

69. Henderson was correct to point out in his memoirs that Thatcher's treatment of Haig, both in private and in her memoirs, was far less generous of him than the General ever was of her.

70. Henderson chronicled with great and probably intended delicacy Thatcher's lapse in judgment on Haig's efforts to secure peace under the Union Jack. Thatcher's petulance gave way, somewhat, after the war had been won and a sufficiency of olive wreathes was fetched up for transatlantic distribution. Thatcher's intellectual wanderlust, to the extent that it existed, never seems to have found a home in the U.S. Department of Defense where the Special Relationship was more revered than in her own FCO.

71. Costa-Méndez, *New York Times*, April 21, 1982.

72. *New York Times*, April 19, 1982.

73. Perón, in a moment of reverie during his reign, had remarked to a junior assistant that the Falklands issue should be let be, that Argentina had too many domestic problems to engage in strife with the UK and that Britain would win any confrontation. Author in conversation with a distinguished Argentine civil servant.

74. *New York Times*, April 19, 1982.

75. David Gompert, Haig's deputy, during negotiations, quoted in Michael Bilton and Peter Kominsky, *Speaking Out* (London: Andre Deutsch, 1989), p. 23.

76. Leonard Downie, Jr., "Haig Holds Talk," *Washington Post*, April 8, 1982, pp. 1, 14.

77. Haig, *Caveat*, p. 290.

78. Rear Admiral Woodward, the battle force commander, opined differently from his master: "General Haig was to me not much short of a disaster. . . . Every day he kept everyone chatting was another day's delay for us." Admiral Sandy Woodward, *One Hundred Days* (Annapolis: Naval Institute Press, 1992), p. 83. Aside from the disingenuousness of this statement, Woodward seemed not to realize that British unpreparedness was the cause for any delay. In fact, British forces were never hazarded by any American negotiation. Almost certainly, Haig's negotiation bought Woodward's force and other parts of the British military the time to organize for the invasion. In discussing the arrival to his battle force of HMS *Intrepid*, Woodward contradicts himself: "She would be the last ship to arrive, the last piece in the jigsaw, and so all the timings depended on her."

79. Five U.S. citizens and their nine dependents lived on the Falklands at the time of invasion. Bernard Gwertzman in the *New York Times*, April 2, 1982.

80. Argentine soldier's mother. Written note to author, September 2001.

3

The Falklands War and
Its Political Players:
A Myopic Thatcher versus an Autistic Galtieri

It is useful to speculate that what Thatcher and her advisors did not even guess at during early April 1982 would have changed the war. So loose was her Foreign Office's grip on the junta's tolerance for risk and the Argentine masses' limp acceptance of both the war and the junta, that no one in the United Kingdom thought to consider if shooting down the Boeing 707 that shadowed the British fleet, sinking one or more Argentine warships beside the cruiser *Belgrano* and/or sinking any Argentine flagged ship close to Buenos Aires would have stopped the war. Remember that Galtieri's truculence during winter of 1982 gave way to nearly constant doubt about the invasion's success as the landing date approached. Thatcher knew the language of domestic political strife in shire and slum sufficiently well to be crowned as the first woman prime minister, but she lacked the dialectic of war, and showed no evidence of wanting to learn it. That mixture of political and military argot, continuously exchanged between East and West, had let NATO and the Warsaw Pact countries snarl at each other across the Berlin Wall, but kept their tanks from rolling and their missiles snug in their tubes. Over the years, Haig had measured with great success the Kremlin's intent in the dark and hazardous craft of keeping the world intact.

No such deft touch existed in Thatcher's circle of advisors, who seemed blissfully unaware that the Argentine junta's will, the final mental effort, to invade the Falklands lacked adequate military preparation, and was innocent of the masses' buoying approval that the politicians need in order to save their own skins in case things go awry. Risk then piled on risk, for, absent the defined and articulated support of the electorate, the junta panicked and pushed up the date for the Falklands' invasion from autumn to April because the British threatened to take back South Georgia. Keep in mind that the Argentine forces were thought barely able to reach full mobilization by the earlier planned invasion date of September or October 1982.[1] The junta's staff officers opposed this hurriedly established April date principally because they wanted more time to plan and to train the Exocet pilots, each of whom had, by April 1, 1982, fewer than 100 hours familiarizing themselves with the missile's delivery system, and that flying time spent mostly in France rather than in their home areas of operation.[2] Galtieri went to war with the slightest of margins.

Keep in mind, too, that by the end of April 1982 most of the best Argentine troops were on the alert against Chile, that Lami-Dozo had not lengthened the strip at Stanley to take attack planes, that no South American country had delivered tangible assistance to the junta and that the OAS had backed out of the fray saying that it was a subsidiary organization of the UN and would hew to the provisions of UN Resolution 502. All during Haig's peregrinations the Argentineans had garrisoned the islands, but the junta had not strengthened their military position on the Falklands to the extent that they could win any possible fight there. True, C-130s flew night missions into Stanley, though much of the cargo space was taken up with creature comforts for Argentine officers. Untrained conscripts arrived in quantities and a single regiment of marines was sent over. As had been the case for dozens of years, the majority of Argentine front line troops and much of the best equipment remained poised against Chile. General Pita, possibly the best Argentine ground commander who had just returned from training in Great Britain, defended the Exocet base on the mainland. The Argentine submarine force, that had never established a barricade against the Royal Navy in what were claimed to be Argentine waters, remained neutered out of action.[3] By May 1, 1982, almost a month before the battle of Goose Green, Lami-Dozo's air force had been defeated, its best pilots killed, wounded, or otherwise out of action. The British naval task forces had not been defeated and the logistics chain to support all the ashore and afloat forces was safe.[4]

Oddly, the conflict continued despite Argentine staff officers' contention that the British, its task forces at sea, would win an air-sea-ground war. For his part, Galtieri contended that, in the end, the United States would come down on Argentina's side, no matter what.[5] He was immune, for reasons that American negotiators never understood, to Reagan's and to Haig's pleadings to stop the war. A member of Haig's party concluded that the Argentine junta were "a group of thugs . . . with no one in charge and each trying to outdo the other in toughness."[6] Running through the negotiations was a held Argentine belief that the United States would, in the end, pressure Thatcher to refrain from military action. The junta failed to understand that the Atlantic Alliance could not stomach another Suez nor tolerate the use of unprovoked military action against a sovereign ally. Unexpectedly, in a moment critical to the junta's declining optimism, fate intervened on the wrong side. HMS *Sheffield*'s sinking on May 4th, splashed on the world's front pages, gave spurious if temporary hope to Galtieri and Anaya. And their men prepared for the long haul.

The American Intervention

"Do you know what this means? It means war.
Do you know what war means? We have to try to avoid it by all
means."[7]

Haig wanted peace as only an old combat veteran can. Not enough on both sides of the Atlantic noticed how heroic, exhausting and reasonable were his efforts to stop the bloodshed and maintain relations with Latin America, while simultaneously preserving Great Britain as a puissant and reliable ally. By April 7, 1982, his attempts to stop the war were in full swing. Ultimately, three trips to Buenos Aires and the accompanying late night sessions produced little but frustration. At least one close observer has stated that America could have forced a peace if it wanted. This conclusion is faulty at bottom because Haig never could get the junta to agree on its fundamental demands and the methods and duration of their fulfillment. In fact, Haig found himself talking with so many generals and admirals that it became unclear who was negotiating what and who was really in charge. On one occasion, Costa-Méndez ran out to Haig's plane, as it was about to take off, to cancel a set of proposals that might have won acceptance from Margaret Thatcher and stopped the run up to war.

Haig's negotiations were doomed from the start, unless the Sea Harriers had shot down Argentine surveillance planes or nuclear submarines had sunk Argentine war ships or naval supply ships. Thatcher, who was never sufficiently sure or sufficiently powerful to disguise her uncertainty, lacked the political muscle to use military force before the landings. After the war, naval persons close to the junta have been unanimous in declaring that their greatest fear lay in Thatcher's unleashing her nuclear submarines on the Argentine Navy and on Argentine maritime commerce. In other words, sinking a few Argentine ships would have obviated the need for further British military action. Absent this kind of military response from Thatcher, Galtieri and his Foreign Minister Costa-Méndez were not interested in what the latter called a face-saving discussion. After all, both sides had spent years talking. What was the good of more words when years of talk had only gotten the parties to daggers drawn? Indeed, as Haig flew and talked and consulted, the Argentine position changed for the worse. Argentina would negotiate "on the understanding clearly stated from the beginning that Argentine sovereignty over the Malvinas Islands is nonnegotiable and that such a premise be unequivocally reflected in the results of the negotiations."[8]

It was not the junta's lack of intellect that did them in, but rather a failure to conquer their cupidity and fecklessness. After all, these were clever men who had taken over their country without tanks battering down the palace gates. By April 29th, after a last flurry of messages among Haig, Thatcher and the junta, both sides failed to yield and a Goose Green, by whatever name, was inevitable. After Haig folded his tent and stole away for a few nights sleep, bilateral negotiations went no further. Francis Pym, the reluctant dragon of Thatcher's War Cabinet and Foreign Secretary, remarked on May 18th that "there was no more than a 3 or 4 percent chance of success," for the negotiations in New York.[9] Each side had to see if the other would fight. On May 1st, the Royal Navy's Carrier Battle Group began the insertion onto the Falklands of the Royal Marines' Special Boat Service (SBS) and the British Army's Special Air (SAS) reconnaissance troops in order to gather intelligence for the inevitable landing. On May 2nd, the Argentine cruiser *Belgrano* was sunk by torpedoes fired from HMS *Conqueror*. The real war was on. The landing of Julian Thompson's 3 Commando Brigade could go forward.

Did Haig tilt towards his old NATO friends at cost to his standing in Washington? The answer is probably yes. Each squabble, no matter how victorious the chief emerges, chips away at the intangible capital needed to sustain power. The public slanging match with Kirkpatrick did neither any good, and the stock of Haig's enemies lurking in Washington's political thickets grew.[10] Certainly, his health had diminished. Haig was gone a few short weeks after the Falklands, his departure hastened imperceptibly but not caused by his brawl with Kirkpatrick. Thatcher's Minister of Defense, John Nott, wrote further that tilting too far and too visibly toward Great Britain would, the American State Department feared, lessen America's influence in Buenos Aires. Nott may have echoed a few American "Wets," but it can be safely assumed that American influence in Buenos Aires has never been of paramount interest to the State, Defense and Treasury Departments. Dependence went the other way. Argentina owed billions to New York banks and continued to borrow from the end of the war.[11] Neither American influence nor Argentine reliance upon the Northern Hemisphere diminished one iota during or after the war.

The lame Nott, following the blind Kirkpatrick, had erred again. A prey to misstatement and misjudgments before and during the war, Nott became the cabinet's chief grinner after the war. No complex machinery of state was needed to ease his departure from Thatcher's cabinet. After a barely decent interval, he left politics to seek his fortune in the City of London. Following the Argentine defeat, Raúl Alfonsín, friendly toward the United States and not so amicable with his own armed forces, succeeded to the presidency of Argentina. In the meantime, Argentina kept on borrowing from New York's and London's banks.

On the British left, Denis Healey spoke in support of Thatcher's intent to repossess the islands by any means necessary. It was a required and perfunctory statement. One or two levels down in the labor party, that generosity of spirit gave out. Dame Judith Hart and Tony Benn mewed on April 28th that military action should stop until further negotiations found a solution, and that "the question of sovereignty must be negotiable."[12] Seldom have so many erroneous statements been mottled by so many faulty judgments in so few words as in Tony Benn's views of the Falklands War: "Some 1,800 British settlers do not constitute a domestic population whose views can be taken seriously, or rather whose views can be allowed to lead us into war."[13] Benn did not stipulate the number needed for freedom and for self-determination. Nor did he correctly assess the situation when he stated that "the real issue there is the oil."[14] In fact, oil in the beds around the Falklands is among the most expensive oil to be found anywhere. The existence of large quantities of recoverable crude has yet to be proven and no profitable oil has been taken up from these fields as of 2004. He was further mistaken when commenting: "I don't think the Americans will support us."[15] Neither did he know of Reagan's letter to Thatcher promising support in the face of Argentine military aggression (see Figure 2.1). Nor did he foretell Haig's reiteration of that promise, when, as his fruitless negotiations ended, he summarized his travails and warned: "The President has also directed that the United States will respond positively to requests for material aid for British forces. There will, of course, be no direct U.S. military involvement."[16] American fuel oil for the Royal Navy was already on its way at the time of that writing—April 3, 1982. Benn, the politician, was not a historian.

The odd mixture of realism and idealism that has characterized American foreign policy since the days of Adams, Franklin and Jefferson came into full play those first days of April 1982. Benn once again misjudged the situation: "Galtieri . . . could be deposed. The Americans don't want that since the whole of Latin America would be set ablaze."[17] Neither Reagan, Weinberger, Haig, the Congress, the working military nor Navy Secretary Lehman supported Galtieri or his junta. As it turned out, Galtieri was deposed peacefully at war's end and Latin America did not find itself in an incendiary state. No one in Washington publicly regretted his departure. The countries of South America breathed a collective sigh of relief and very quickly resumed *status quo ante bellum.* Argentine borrowers, shoppers and students still flocked to Boston and New York. And the list of Benn's embarrassments goes on.

The real fault was Thatcher's. She never grasped that nations, especially those of the second tier, seldom change their long-term goals or methods. Tactics and timing yes, but the itching purposes of countries' international life remain frighteningly constant. Sir Percy Craddock, later Thatcher's resident advisor on Foreign Affairs, put it well:

> She had little sense of the forces moving the other side in international exchanges; of the history, the prejudices, the aspirations which drove her opposite numbers to adopt positions differing from her own but in their eyes equally valid; and of the overriding need to understand these forces, not as a prelude to a graceful surrender, but so as accurately to assess likely reactions to British moves and the strengths and weaknesses of opponents, or competitors, or partners. In other words, as a means for getting our way. She had a poor view of foreigners, other than Anglo-Saxons. . . . This lack of imagination about the other side was a real defect.[18]

All the blunders, negotiations, posturings and recriminations led to one fact. Lt. Col. H. Jones would plan and execute the perfect battle with the perfect battalion. Most commanding officers want only to win. Many, the Montgomerys and the Pattons, want theater too. Jones wanted none of that, but he did demand excellence and more from himself and his men. That is a vital distinction. That Jones was tepidly supported by his own civilian bosses and his military seniors, and moved against the correct judgments of his Brigade CO and his friend the CO of the 22 SAS Regiment Lt. Col. Michael Rose, did not matter. Jones believed himself the star in his own firmament, the very bright commanding officer of one of the best light infantry units. Of course, he had the Americans and the Toms on his side and that was all he needed.

Lehman, Weinberger and the Special Relationship

In the first days of May, just after the *Belgrano*, a British frigate and a Sea Harrier were destroyed, Nott and Caspar Weinberger, the American Secretary of Defense, met in Brussels to fix the extent and timing of American assistance.[19] American aid to British forces had been, prior to their meeting, immediate, broad and unequivocal from the very beginning of the war. U.S. Special Forces transferred Stinger AA missiles to their SAS colleagues, and fuel and the miscellaneous oddments of war were given the British without let or hindrance. A U.S. Carrier was put on standby for loan to the Royal Navy in case one of the two British carriers was sunk or disabled. Then Navy Secretary John Lehman said it best: "It is highly unlikely that even Jeane Kirkpatrick, the U.S. ambassador to the United Nations, or anyone at the State Department or the White House understood at first the extent of the assistance we were providing especially in communications and intelligence."[20]

Weinberger knew that a British defeat, actual or perceived, would diminish British worth as America's principal NATO and European partner and probably end Britain's role as a major entity in the world's politics. After all, the British side of this conflict was about to be fought entirely by professional soldiery. The British army could scarcely be expected to stave off the Slavic hordes on the North European plains, it was suggested, if it could not hold some distant islands that were British soil. Then too, there was a whiff of suggestion in the air that America might well compensate Great Britain in its moment of dire need for America's refusal to sanction the British invasion of Suez in 1956. The debt was all too real for being so ephemeral.

Caspar Weinberger, the second most powerful man in the American defense establishment whose actions constituted by themselves a foreign policy, wrote: "The normal course could not be followed if we were now to be of any assistance. Therefore I directed that all the British requests have immediate and first priority. . . . I also directed that each of those requests come straight to my desk. . . . Finally I directed that I be told, within twenty-four hours of our receipt of a British request whether it had been granted; and if not, why not and when it would be granted. The outward flow of materials of all kinds began immediately. . . ."[21] AIM-9L air-to-air missiles, fuel for ships and planes, an enlargement of the base at Ascension Island and a squadron of F-4 Phantom jets to keep the postwar peace were fruits of the "Give them what they need; they can pay later" policy.[22] The author stood beside a fuel trunk within the United States while a British frigate was refueled on its voyage to the Falklands. This was not the first event of its kind nor the last.

There was graciousness too. Weinberger stated: "Some said later that the British could not have succeeded if we had not helped. This is not so—I think the decisive factor was Mrs. Thatcher's firm and immediate decision to retake the islands, despite the impressive military and other advice to the effect that such an action could not succeed."[23] As Weinberger noted, U.S. national intelligence capabilities were, at great cost, put at Britain's disposal: "Shortly we were able to let the British see what we could see in that area."[24] By the end of April, Brigadier Julian Thompson, his 3 Commando Brigade and 2 Para were ready for war with the manifest support of the U.S. Government, but not entirely of their own.[25]

Passage of UN Resolution 502 that ordered Argentina to leave the islands gave Thatcher room and time to maneuver, but not much.[26] It gave American assistance to Great Britain some cover and legal validity. With one stroke, it recovered her from diplomatic isolation. She could sequester Argentina's holdings in London, stop trade between the two countries and lobby for other nations' support. Yet no cheap or easy answers to repossession of the islands presented themselves. She could not attack Argentine ships on the high seas because no war had been declared. She could not bomb the Argentine mainland because so disproportionate a response would turn new-found allies against her and she could not yet seize the Falklands because Britain's military was not in place.[27] As splendidly executed as it was, Parson's victory at the UN gave his Prime Minister a decaying asset that delay or a false step could quickly squander. Now that Thatcher had negotiating momentum, she had to follow up Parson's triumph with military accomplishment that could not await the month-long marshalling of Britain's invasion force. The British middle classes, whose wrath at Argentina's theft the Prime Minister had so deftly exploited, could not long exist on rhetoric; they needed blood. In 20 predominantly labor boroughs, 24 percent of potential Tory voters considered the Falklands crisis as the most important or an important factor in the upcoming elections.[28]

It was not altogether clear that Britain's professional military were of one mind about the repossession's chances of success. Nott declared that the islands could not be retaken.[29] Senior military men abroad issued mordant warnings about an operation for which British forces had neither the equipment nor the expertise to complete. Setting aside her allies' skepticism, her colleagues temporizing and her enemies' hostility, Thatcher plunged her dwindling political capital into a distant venture of whose causes and possible results few knew much.[30] A war cabinet was formed by mid April and the dogs of war began to bay.[31]

Brigadier Julian Thompson: The Right Man at the Right Place at the Right Hour

As much as Jones' actions and presence dominated all that occurred at Goose Green, the benign persona lurking behind him and all the ground operation in this conflict remained Brigadier Julian Thompson RM, Commander, 3 Commando Brigade. His steadfast and logical opposition to a battle at Goose Green was trumped by Northwood's venal expectation of a cheap triumph and nearly cost Thompson his job. But paradox sided with him and, as unpalatable to some of his seniors as it was, his common sense approach to combat made him the single person most responsible for the final British victory. He had served widely from Singapore to Northern Ireland to the United States. As a young officer, Thompson had chosen to take the weapons course because this move would prevent his assignment to shipboard duty and keep him on dry land with his cherished light infantry. He was a serious military theorist and scholar who, away from his books, commanded 3 Brigade, the Royal Marines ready combat and amphibious force. It had remained, by the skin of its teeth, the only military force within the British military establishment capable of projecting power onto an enemy-held shore. To keep his platoons sharp, 3 Brigade's exercises were held in the nastiest of weather in the most desolate places. Royal Marines' officers knew their boss and each other with an intimacy that grows from miseries shared over the years. When after the conflict a middle-ranking Royal Marines' officer was complemented for the Marines' success, he replied truthfully that all the officers were, after all, Julian's friends. The Marines were also used to sitting well below the salt when it came time to buy new weaponry or even to keep operational what they had. A doleful and perverse camaraderie often springs from that open wound.

MOD had spent little enough time on the well being of three Commandos (battalions) now deputed to save Britain's honor and Thatcher's job, compared to the multi-billion pound sums needed to keep the strategic deterrent fed and healthy until its final disuse.[32] Predictably, 3 Brigade's staff was a bare bones affair. Critical persons like qualified air intelligence officers did not exist either on paper or in fact. Not only did Britain lack the materiel with which to prosecute a war 8,000 miles from London, but there existed no evidence that those politicians-turned-warriors charged with obtaining victory owned the bellicist element in their corporate psyche necessary to gain victory.[33] After Suez, Britain had shied away from open warfare against a declared enemy state.

Thompson's problems with his civilian bosses began when, in April's early days, the government first laid on a vague invasion plan then withdrew it only to put the brigade to sea with undue haste. One cabinet minister stated: "To be frank, I don't see how Thatcher can survive if she shirks from a military showdown."[34] Loading ships was an arduous task. Supplies were put aboard with little regard for the priority of their use. No one thought to use spray cans of paint—red, green and white—to mark which went on top, which in the middle and which on the bottom of the holds. As a consequence, much time and labor were later spent at Ascension Island and at San Carlos to sort out the cargoes. Even then, and after further cross-decking of men and materiel, the ships' cargos had to be inventoried every evening.

As the weeks wore on, Thompson, the singular professional infantry general lodged aboard a pitching and rolling ship, had to argue petty points over a scatty communications system with men in London who had never been to war. His expository skills were sorely tried: "We were running a risk of losing a lot of people and I felt we were bashing our heads against a brick wall trying to explain this to the people back in England and they weren't hoisting it in."[35] For example, Nott, never an enthusiast for the war, taxed colleagues with his doubts about "an opposed landing 8,000 miles away without air cover."[36] In fact, the landing went unopposed mainly because of Thompson's and Commodore Clapp's astute planning; and air cover did exist, though not enough. Nott and some of his colleagues knew as little about the Argentine military establishment after sending a force to defeat it as they had before Port Stanley fell.[37]

Neither Thompson nor his successor as Commander of Land Forces, Falklands Major General Jeremy Moore, ever received a document well used in NATO named "Concept of Operation" that spells out in a detailed and very precise fashion the final purpose of a great military operation. On the advice of counsel from the Foreign Office, Thatcher did not declare war but instead relied on Article 51 of the UN Charter, which provides for the right of self-defense. How did Thatcher get away with it? Richard Crossman, in his Godkin Lectures delivered before a woman Prime Minister existed, wrote: "the Prime Minister can define consensus as what he thinks fit. Even though a majority of opinions were expressed against him that would not necessarily prevent him from deciding as he wishes if he can get away with it. How much he uses this power is up to his own discretion . . . he does not rely on formal voting, written resolutions, or amendments."[38] Thatcher had consumed much political capital by sending the fleet south, and badly needed to restore her diminishing supply of that essential element of governance and survival. A defeat would empty the cup; a dramatic victory would fill it to overflowing.

Inside the British leadership, hope never completely dimmed that settlement would occur before combat. Indeed, a negotiated peace without an Argentine surrender remained the distant and fantastical hope of the new Foreign Minister, Francis Pym, and his slender but fussy following in Thatcher's cabinet.[39] Britain was set to win this war absent a disaster like HMS *Canberra*'s sinking or a major military blunder. It was against this backdrop that Thatcher sought a military victory that could be publicized widely, understood thoroughly by the middle classes whose sons were being killed and put a thumb in the eyes of those timid souls who doubted her.

The brigade staff that Brigadier Julian Thompson's 3 Commando Brigade owned was intended to fight in Europe under NATO's guidance and umbrella. Thompson's men were not trained or equipped to project power ashore 8,000 miles from home, but rather to land on and protect vital ground in NATO's north.[40] The brigade lacked its own air cover, large helicopters to carry troops ashore and armor. It did have its own light artillery, a few light helicopters and some of the best trained infantry men in the world. Not surprisingly, Lt. Col. H. Jones lobbied MOD, as the invasion force was loading, to change his 2 Para's assignment from Belize to 3 Commando Brigade and to Julian Thompson. It was a wise military move—in the doing he insinuated himself into good company.

Most elite units are exercised to nearly terminal boredom, and assignment to Thompson's force offered a chance to put theory and practice into play.

The structure established and agreed upon for commanding the Falklands task force was drawn from NATO's doctrine that encompassed: the amphibious force of landing and supply ships with escorts, the battle force meant to secure and maintain air and sea space and the landing force of troops to seize and hold land. Commodore Michael Clapp, Rear Admiral Woodward and Brigadier Julian Thompson headed these three distinct groups (see Figure 3.1).[41] They had never worked together. Woodward had no experience in putting troops ashore and in the myriad tasks associated with that very complicated and changeable-by-the-minute job.[42] Clapp, a professional aviator though not a pilot, had some knowledge of amphibious matters, and Thompson, a Royal Marine, had spent a good part of his adult life conjuring with such affairs. All these commanders are equal according to NATO's doctrine and practice with respect to their part in the amphibious landing, whatever rank each holds in his own service. Woodward was senior to his colleagues, barely, but equal to them as regarded the command structure established to recapture the Falklands. He spent much time and effort trying to overcome this reality and the friction—not to say the bitterness—that he spawned lasted throughout the war and influenced its conduct and duration. "You are my soldier" was not the best introduction from Woodward to a Royal Marine, a veteran of the struggles in Northern Ireland and elsewhere, and a master of his craft, light infantry warfare. Condescension from an equal who knew next to nothing about one's (Thompson's) life work was not the best way to set out on a messy business whose end no one then knew. That social blunder and factual untruth was all of a piece with the war's unfolding.

British Admiral Ramsay of long ago was quoted as saying: "Once the army have decided how they wish to fight the land battle, it is necessary to examine how the troops can be put ashore to give effect to the army plan. In general it is the responsibility of the navy to land the army as they require, but as the plan develops naval considerations will arise which must be discussed and agreed upon."[43] Amphibious landings are difficult under all circumstances. Certain trouble looms when the landing troops and their commanders have little or no experience in such matters. The American navy has, and the Soviet Navy had, differing classes of ships and helicopters that are built and operated solely to put troops ashore under any conditions. The ships and their tasks are not elegant or cheap. The British task force that was cobbled together to retake the Falklands had

Figure 3.1: Falklands British Command Chain, 1982

Before May 20, 1982

Commander Task Force
CTF 317
Admiral Sir John Fieldhouse
HQ at Northwood

Air Commander   Land Deputy (advice)
Air Marshal Sir John Curtiss   *Major General Jeremy Moore*

		Commander
Commander	Commander	Landing Force Task Group
Carrier Task Group	Amphibious Task Group	[3rd Commando Brigade (+)]
CTG 317.8	CTG 317.0	CTG 317.1
Rear Admiral John Woodward	*Commodore Michael Clapp*	*Brigadier Julian Thompson*

After May 20, 1982

Commander Task Force
CTF 317
Admiral Sir John Fieldhouse
HQ at Northwood

Air Commander   Land Deputy (advice)
Air Marshal Sir John Curtiss   *Lieutenant General Sir Richard Trant*
                                        GOC South-East District

Commander	Commander	Commander
Carrier Task Group	Amphibious Task Group	Land Forces Falkland Islands
CTG 317.8	CTG 317.0	CTG 317.1
Rear Admiral John Woodward	*Commodore Michael Clapp*	*Major General Jeremy Moore* *

3rd Commando Brigade (+)   5th Infantry Brigade
CTG 317.1.1   CTG 317.1.2
Brigadier Julian Thompson   *Brigadier Tony Wilson*

* Note: General Moore joined the liner Queen Elizabeth II off Ascension Island on May 20, but was out of touch with events, and 3 Brigade in particular, because of comms problems on the ship until he came ashore at San Carlos on May 30, 1982.

precious few ships built for amphibious operations and almost no officers, staff, equipment or men permanently assigned to amphibious duty. Enough helicopters to put the brigade ashore in tactical shape were simply not there. By 1982, the Royal Navy operated only two major ships designed for amphibious work, HMS *Intrepid* and HMS *Fearless*, and these were shortly due to be scrapped or sold. British forces had not put a full brigade of 3,000 men ashore since Suez in 1956.

Quietly and out of the way, the Royal Marines themselves completed battalion-sized exercises annually and kept themselves aware of U.S. amphibious doctrine. Major Ewen Southby-Tailyour RM nurtured a small raiding squadron that kept effective landing practices alive. In fact, no career pattern for amphibious officers existed in the Royal Navy as in the U.S. and Russian navies. Rear Admiral Woodward, a nuclear submarine officer and now the battle force commander whose frigates and destroyers would protect the fleet, had never conducted a landing on friendly, let alone hostile, shores. Few Royal Navy officers operated from the precept that ships, in this case, were simply taxis to put fighting units ashore. In the course of designing a method to get the marines and paras from the United Kingdom to Port Stanley administrative blunders sprouted like weeds. The knowledge gap among senior commanders was enormous. Fortunately, Thompson and Clapp—the two who knew most about over-the-beach operations—enjoyed immediate rapport.

It is well to remember that so distant from Whitehall's musings was any problem involving military action on, around or over the Falklands that no contingency plans had been drawn up to defend them or to retake them if captured. Plans for the islands' repossession and Standard Operating Procedures for all the military operations involved were not pulled off the shelf; they were formulated, amended or put aside hastily as the task force sailed south. Incredibly, this lacuna existed in an era where major powers' staff colleges plan exercises for every possible contingency in just about every part of the world. Thompson and Clapp bore no responsibility for this deficit, for they operated at the bottom of the food chain and were not headmasters of military schools. As a consequence, they and their too-small staffs had to start planning from scratch. Perhaps that annoyance turned out all for the better because, far down the command chain, the marines and sailors worked together very efficiently, unburdened by yesterday's school solutions. Straightaway, a practice began here, for the junior echelons got the job done in the face of their betters' gaffes. A "mounting meeting" was convened at which it was decided what equipment units would carry and thus a rough estimate was prepared of the tonnages to be brought south. Neither Jones nor 2 Para could accomplish much at this gathering because their gear was on its way to Belize for the unit's regular and long-planned tour there.

Woodward had never presided over a "mounting meeting" and his statement to Thompson invoking his own primacy was, of course, incorrect, even though he may have believed it himself. Woodward led the battle force and no other. Admiral Fieldhouse, the overall commander of the task force, had laid out his command structure on April 8, as illustrated in Figure 3.1. In accordance with NATO and U.S. doctrine, all of Fieldhouse's subordinate commanders held equal status in the Falklands operation, regardless of their service rank. True, Rear Admiral Woodward was senior by time in rank in to his colleagues Thompson and Clapp, but this fact was intended to make no difference in the way that decisions for the invasion were made. Clapp, Thompson and Woodward were equal. They had to get along. That was what NATO's rules contemplated. Yet, even after the war, Woodward wrote inter alia: "Where should we deploy our recce Special Forces?" That was Clapp's, Thompson's and CO 22 SAS' job, not Woodward's.[44] It was only on April 9th, a full week after the completed Argentine landing, that the British Commander in Chief, Admiral Fieldhouse, assembled a staff to deal with the land-side of the operation, but not the strictly naval and amphibious aspect of the war. Administrative confusion mounted. For example, the CO of 40 Commando, one of three commandos in 3 Brigade, was ordered on April 30th to get his troops to the Falklands, but no one told him how to get there, on what ships to load his gear or what he was to accomplish after his arrival.[45]

As the amphibious force loaded out from England's southern ports and moved south, Commodore Clapp found his task force suffering from two deficits. First, the ships were loaded in the order that the materiel arrived at the docks and not in the order that they would be unloaded onto the beaches or used. Later at Goose Green, 2 Para's Land Rovers, normally used to bring mortar shells to the firing pits, remained aboard ship as did critical medical equipment. Second, Clapp had to cobble up on his own a new staff, rather than put to sea with one that had existed and worked together. His ordinary staff consisted of eight officers and eight ratings, sufficient in MOD's eyes to administer an unopposed landing, but woefully inadequate in practice. Good men all, they had no experience in administering a Brigade plus landing (5,000 men) with all that it entailed, especially if the bullets had begun to fly. They had not the man hours to fight the turf battles that invariably and rightly arise in such complex doings. Clapp lacked, for example, a senior air officer to order and to coordinate logistical operations that used helicopters. Even worse, his intelligence officer lacked the necessary clearances to communicate with Northwood about intercepted Argentine order of battle data. This particular failure contributed to Jones' lack of specificity on the forces opposing 2 Para at Goose Green.

Before the junta's invasion of Stanley, all British forces planned and exercised for a war against the Warsaw Pact's forces in Northern Europe. Army, Marines and Air Force knew one another well for combat there. In the event of war, the Royal Navy had assigned tasks outside the Eurasian land mass and scarcely ever worked with or understood the soldiers who would defend the North European plain. The sterile world of the submariner, where everything lay in its place, where well ordered day followed well ordered night and no one knew the difference and watches were stood to the minute, had little in common with the mud, blood and sweat of the places where wars are won. Former sub skippers, and there were many, who participated in the sea war around the Falklands came to be appalled when, after the air and ground action started, almost nothing occurred as had been hoped and planned.[46] That view is barely understandable. Submarines leave port with a full load of food, medicine, ammunition, spare parts and creature comforts to last a cruise of say 90 days. They are manned by technicians who wear clean clothes and have full stomachs. The key difference is movement. Ships at sea always go somewhere, usually on a predetermined course at a predetermined speed and, similarly, return whence they came. Their schedules and consumption of supplies can be calculated very finely. The Infantry's position changes willy-nilly, often without warning, then to wait in one place wet and hungry, sometimes to get killed or wounded. Food, ammunition, medical supplies and fuel arrive late, in the wrong place or not at all. Thompson, in his buildup for the campaign to retake Stanley, lacked sympathy even from his co–task force leader, Woodward, who complained to his dairy: "The land force will always bog down because they always do. They've been here for five days and done f. . . all."[47]

As the force sailed south, Thatcher's war cabinet still had not gotten MOD to issue a document called the Initiating Directive. This instruction from NATO's bible may be brief or lengthy, but it does tell the commanders what they must prepare themselves to accomplish, e.g., protect fisheries, keep open the Panama Canal, stop piracy in the Arabian Sea. In this case, the CINC (the overall boss for the entire operation of recapture), Admiral Fieldhouse—who knew little about the seizure and holding of distant lands—had simply told his three task force commanders to get to sea and go south. Minister of Defense Nott had been pessimistic about Thatcher's chances of winning a war and he lacked both the theoretical and practical knowledge to put together an organization suited to winning wars. His lack of grip on the entire operation was manifest. He wrote later, in describing the recapture of South Georgia, that the SAS and SBS had been involved, but not that the force that captured Gryvtken, South Georgia's capital, was composed principally of and commanded by Royal Marines.[48] It did little for the tactical planners that their task was open ended, especially because war had never been declared and was never to be. Additionally, no Concept of Operations had emerged from a conference held just before the latter two's departure among Fieldhouse, Clapp and Thompson. No one knew how many ships, planes and troops would be assigned to whose command to do what. This particular omission caused reluctance in some British quarters, especially in the army, to release war stores that are held expressly to defend the British Isles.

Because there had been no Initiating Directive, there could not be a "load and stow" order, reasoned in its timing and substance, that tells sailors and marines how and where to stow what gear to achieve their military purpose. This last was especially necessary because merchant ships rented from commercial enterprises and unfamiliar with naval procedures—40-plus as it turned out—brought most of the war supplies south. It was not until the amphibious task force arrived at Ascension Island that Clapp, the amphibious force commander, knew what a serious problem orderly loading was to be. The rearrangement of stores into any reasonable order of unloading took days, which put the landing back and consumed helicopter and ship wear, contributing, in turn, to the haste with which the War Cabinet later pursued the campaign.[49] By the time the ships, planes and helos arrived around the Falklands, they had accumulated more hours of wear than anyone wanted. Neither had Clapp and Thompson received a document stipulating what the Amphibious Objective Area was to be.[50] Taken literally as they left Plymouth, the task force and its oddments of war could have attacked Buenos Aires or the Argentine holdings in Antarctica.[51] This omission, coupled with an indefinite command structure, was to create havoc among Clapp's and Thompson's sensible and very professional efforts to restore British sovereignty to the Falkland Islands.

On April 9, 1982, Admiral Fieldhouse finally issued the command structure with which he wanted to win the war. It established three task groups: battle group, Woodward; amphibious group, Clapp; landing force, Thompson. He, Fieldhouse, headed all three as CINC. Woodward, by virtue of his naval rank, was to coordinate assets and their use when necessary, but not to command them. This order violated NATO and U.S. doctrine upon which British amphibious moves were supposed to be made, and confused its recipients for the rest of the war. Woodward took advantage of this pustule despite his ignorance of the complex air, ground and logistical operations that were about to occur.

Clapp and Thompson took it upon themselves, as no Initiating Directive had been issued, to begin planning for an opposed landing on the Falklands. As it turned out, Fieldhouse did issue a vague document about Sea Control that stated the staffs that were afloat with the task forces sailing south were meant to plan for a landing on the Falklands with a view to their repossession.[52] Jones was not present then nor was it necessary that he should have been. He had no knowledge of amphibious operations and he was supposed to do as his brigade commander Julian Thompson wanted anyway. Clapp and Thompson had certain constraints: they did not have enough helos to make a feasible landing behind the beach. This deficit required that the troops would land at water's edge by boat. The landing force would not storm the beach at Stanley. Because Thompson lacked Amtracs (vehicles that carry troops from ship to shore), the Argentine opposition would exact very high and unacceptable casualties during any operation that involved their use, and the Royal Navy would most likely have successfully vetoed the idea because their ships would have been in vulnerable positions too long.

It is useful to recall that U.S. Marine Corps' doctrine would have made such an attack onto East Falkland, probably at Stanley, with water and airborne transit to the beach and accepted heavy casualties in order to end the war quickly. The Argentine General Staff, much influenced by USMC doctrine, at least with respect to over-the-beach operations, had estimated that the British landing would occur at Stanley and had considered stationing *Belgrano* in that harbor as a fortress ship. The Argentine Navy prevailed and kept that ship at sea, where its sinking caused much hand wringing in both the British and Argentine press.

The British task forces heading south, with all their military expertise and paraphernalia, knew next to nothing about the Falklands, but Heaven intervened and assigned to Thompson's staff, as minister without portfolio, the one Royal Marine who knew more about the Falklands than anyone else anywhere else. A brilliant navigator and yachtsman, Major Ewen Southby-Tailyour RM had visually inspected what seemed to his listeners every rock, beach and kelp bed in the islands and recorded them both in print and in fine watercolors. The materials were his private property and he made them available to his commander, Julian Thompson, with the proviso that he, Southby-Tailyour would accompany the task force back to the islands where he had recently been the RM Officer In Charge.

This major was an unusual man and he sailed his own course. While stationed in the Falklands as the Officer Commanding (OC) of its Royal Marines' detachment, the marine had been ordered by the Governor "not to mix socially with Councilors, the Medical profession, the Education Department, the Falkland Island Company executives and a few named individuals."[53] In May 1982, the Kelpers behaved differently from their Governor and he was welcomed with great joy upon his return to the islands that he had come to love.

But there was much more to this artist, bon-vivant writer than his appreciation of the Falklands' beauty. Selection of a landing beach is the amphibious commander's most daunting task, and Southby-Tailyour's expert and farsighted handling of the landing craft before and during the landing at San Carlos and all during the war shortened the conflict and saved lives. All of a military lifetime's experience goes into deciding what troops to land, over which beach, at what time and in what order. It was the most portentous and the riskiest decision of the war.

In fact, all Thatcher's plans, hopes and fears depended on getting the troops ashore in such numbers and so equipped that the march on Port Stanley could begin. A botched landing with many casualties or destroyed equipment would put paid to the Falklands' recapture and ultimately destroy England's reputation as a reliable military partner. An election would have been called and Thatcher would have lost. Defeat at the beaches of the United Kingdom's best elite forces during the execution of a plan designed by professional military and approved by the war cabinet would sunder the NATO alliance. Many at MOD knew this too; "[there was] still a high degree of caution and skepticism in the Ministry of Defense."[54]

Criteria for picking a landing beach are known to every junior officer in the U.S. Marine Corps, many in the U.S. Navy and some in the Russian navy. This sort of in-your-bones knowledge had lapsed in the British military, except for a few devoted souls in the Royal Marines. By way of example, but not of limitation, the criteria for a successful beach landing on the Falklands are:

- A beach wide enough to get a force ashore in mutually defensible locations
- Easy egress inland from the beaches for the breakout
- Distant from possible enemy reinforcements
- Out of Argentine 155mm range
- No sea or beach mines if possible
- Easily defensible from ground counter attack and hostile patrol activity
- Adequate protection from weather
- Little or no swell for the Roll On/Off ships
- Protection from hostile SS and room and depth of water to conduct ASW ops
- Safety for ships as they unload the initial landing force, and more important, as they resupply the troops ashore
- Beach gradient that allowed landing craft to pull up close ashore
- Predictable and low surf
- Sand compaction that allowed vehicles to land and to operate
- Distance from hostile reconnaissance
- Protection from hostile air attacks
- Good arcs of fire for own AA missiles and guns
- Safe run-in for the ships that disgorge the landing craft

Each stipulation is fairly easy to satisfy, and experienced amphibious officers will add their own. It is the judgment made about all these factors acting on each other that makes matters difficult.

On April 16th, Woodward landed unannounced on HMS *Fearless* to begin discussion on what data they, the task group commanders, would present to Fieldhouse at Ascension Island. Rather than a discussion with his equals, each of whom knew far more about amphibious operations than he, Woodward ordered his colleagues to research his own options. He posed three.

First, Woodward suggested Carcass Island as a supply dump whence forces could mount their ground attack. Landing twice, first at Carcass Island and later at or near Stanley, would have doubled the shipping requirements as well as the wear on already worn ships and lengthened the time needed to retake Stanley. Carcass Island was well within the range of Argentine A-4 attack planes, but it is 115 miles, as the crow flies, from Stanley.

Next, Woodward proposed construction of an airfield in a valley off Stevelley Bay, again on West Falkland. This, he viewed, would take Hercules and Phantom jets. Never mind that 3 Brigade lacked, and probably could not obtain before winter, heavy construction equipment and that a substantial ground force would be tied down protecting the field and its workers. All the while, the builders, their ships and equipment would be subject to air attack from the mainland.

Last, Woodward suggested a feint by several ships of the amphibious force towards the Argentine mainland to draw out the Argentine Air Force and presumably to destroy it. Since the destruction of HMS *Repulse* and HMS *Prince of Wales* off Singapore in January 1942, it has been dogma for all navies that their ships do not stray inshore without parity or supremacy in the air. Woodward had neither.

If put into effect, any one of Woodward's suggestions would have lost the war before it began. Woodward's overbearing attitude and his bizarre proposals created rancor and bitterness that lasted throughout the war.[55] The Royal Marines and the amphibious group knew, at least, what to expect from their Battle Group Commander once combat began. 2 Para would fight its battles with a modicum of sympathy and little understanding from the Battle Group Commander. Commodore Clapp recorded: "All this was seen on board *Fearless* as an unnecessary attempt to dominate and it acutely embarrassed the naval members of my staff, while infuriating the Royal Marines and, more particularly, the Army members who were new to the Royal Navy and its quirks. Trust was broken and it would be a long time to repair."[56] Woodward lacked Shakespeare's "wicked charm," that trait of character that fosters generosity toward one's comrades and lethal hostility toward one's enemies. While the battle commander's narcissism throve, 2 Para had joined up with its equipment and its CO on Ascension Island.

Admiral Fieldhouse, the CINC, presided over the conference held April 16th on Ascension Island. He gave notice that the War Cabinet had approved that Jones' 2 Para would join 3 Brigade and would sail south on *Norland*. He emphasized the command and control structure that he had established, yet it was clear that the three task group commanders were not as one. Repossession of South Georgia and landing with a view to repossessing the Falklands were the stated goals on the ground. Beyond that, Fieldhouse himself and/or his staff were pregnant lodes of misinformation. The following italicized fragments paraphrase Fieldhouse's comments.

Not enough ground forces. Not true! Thompson recalls: "The ground force composition was . . . in my eyes capable of what I thought I might have to do when I set out from the UK. . . . The later additions to my brigade . . . enhanced its capability."[57]

The United States' Attitude was awkward. American aid from the outset was immediate and copious. Fieldhouse flew back to the United Kingdom in a plane that used not-yet-paid-for American fuel. While at Ascension, he used American communications and his air crew performed their ground checks with American tools. Fieldhouse had only to look through his window to see the American help that flooded over to his welcoming men and fleshed out his vague plans. From Ascension Island south, the British fleet sailed on American fuel. (See Appendix B.)

Be wary of U.S. and Soviet satellites. Fieldhouse and his staff used American communications very frequently. What could Fieldhouse have wanted to hide from the Americans? He himself did not yet know how, when or where the landing would go. Besides, American forces helped British forces load and reload their equipment. (See Appendix B.)

Chile's attitude was cooling. Chile gave active and passive assistance to the United Kingdom from the start. A failed SAS mission whose men found their way into Chile was covered by that country's military and foreign office.

Brazil was sitting on the fence. This conclusion was accurate, as Brazil's foreign office gloated over the Argentine misfortunes that were sure to happen.[58] Brazil had a disputed border with Argentina and did not wish military intrusion by Argentina to become a behavioral norm in that part of the world. Brazilian officials cheered American assistance to the United Kingdom.

Fieldhouse's conference did little to specify what the force afloat and the additions destined for the Falklands should accomplish. There was still no well-defined mission. If a clarion call to war existed anywhere, it was muted. There was no CINC's visit around the fleet to boost morale. Fieldhouse, no Montgomery rousing the men on the eve of battle, even abstained from visiting the flagship and the officers and men who had to prosecute the war from there. Upon being taxed by Clapp, Fieldhouse reiterated his command structure and assured Clapp that neither he nor his force would operate under Woodward's command and that: "We would be totally separate when the amphibious phase came. Sandy [Woodward] would be required to support the amphibious task force and its needs."[59] Still, at the end of the conference he stated: "Neither Julian nor I felt that we had had a totally fair hearing in *Hermes*."[60]

The complications that arose then and later, and the awkward decisions that had to be taken on the way south, exceeded expectations. Woodward's staff and task force seemed not to understand that the navy was a taxi service to the beaches, that ships must go in harm's way and that sailors can get killed just as readily as infantrymen. Britain's Minister of Defense Nott noted just before the landing at San Carlos: "Plans were being made at Northwood in consultation with Admiral Woodward about the timing and place of the amphibious landing."[61] Weeks into the war, Nott did not know that the timing and place of landing were essentially none of Woodward's business and certainly beyond Northwood's competence. The decisions related to them belonged to Clapp and Thompson. The muddled thinking that led to Goose Green and its deaths was the illegitimate offspring of confusion begotten well up the chain of command.

Fieldhouse left Ascension Island with one pressing task undone, which remained so for the war. No single unifying jurisdiction had been established at the site of the war. Fieldhouse, the task force commander, remained 8,000 miles from the war in Northwood. Nott's "short chain of command" was 7,900 miles too long. Petty decisions complicated by untried logistics, Woodward's assumed primacy among the task group commanders and the undecided combat use of a second brigade made life unnecessarily difficult for Thompson, who had to refer vexing issues and more than a few of his lesser headaches, to Fieldhouse in Northwood for time-consuming resolution. Distance did not make Northwood's heart grow fonder for the entire operation of recovery, and few in England sympathized with Thompson who was charged with getting the brigade ashore in one piece and, at the same time, fighting the political battles.

By April's end it was clear that negotiations with the junta had failed—there had never been much hope, at bottom, that they would succeed. Yet hard military realities had not set in. There seemed too little acknowledgement that a safe landing by 3 Commando Brigade was an absolute condition precedent to Thatcher's goal of regaining sovereignty over the islands. In reality, all else was dross.[62] Yet during Fieldhouse's two days on HMS *Hermes*, no Cromwell rose up to inspire his audience with fire and brimstone, no MacArthur with a brilliant plan, no Montgomery with correct sub paragraphs, no bombastic Patton, but only a porous command structure and little understanding of what the middle ranking officers, who were charged with completing the staff work, had to accomplish. It was a little like Mr. Gladstone and his mule in Sicily whose services he respected but for whom he felt no affection. At Ascension, all agreed that restoration of British sovereignty to the Falklands was good, but few had any ardor for the beast. At the top, military administration had even at this early stage become sloppy. Clapp, by military assignment and law, was responsible for the use and protection of his assets, the amphibious force, but retained incomplete say in their use. For example, he had lost precious helos on South Georgia's Fortuna Glacier during an imprudent operation by the SAS over which he had no control. Even worse, as the three task groups left Ascension, few there knew the location and later importance of Darwin Hill and Goose Green.[63]

Thompson was several steps ahead of the politicians, the diplomats and his senior commanders and their staffs. Thompson knew what he did not want to do, as well as what he did want to accomplish: "I did not land into Stanley because to have done so would have been very costly in casualties to us. We had no Amtracs etc." Goose Green did not figure in either of these calculations. As he stated:

> The outline concept of ground operations for my Brigade after we landed had been in my mind before we arrived. That is, we would take the high ground around Mt. Kent, but include in our plans the seizure of Teal Inlet which would enable us to bring LSLs [small landing craft] into Port Salvador and shorten the logistic line of communication. Also I wanted my axis of advance to avoid the obvious route of the Fitzroy-Stanley track. In the event, I don't think the Argies realized which way we were coming.[64]

Before he could accomplish that, Thompson had to put 3 Brigade and 2 Para ashore in safety.

Contrary to Woodward's belief that Haig's diplomacy postponed military action, the amphibious force itself needed a five-day interlude at Ascension. The political necessity of sending the fleet away with undue haste had turned it into a floating flea market. The ships carrying the impedimenta of war were loaded with no priority of usage. Ships carried the right gear by and large, but its location afloat was not easily fixed. As Clapp wrote to Fieldhouse, his boss at Northwood: the force needed restow of 1st line ammunition; recalibration of the 105mm guns; amphib training for the soldiers of 2 and 3 Para; armament modifications on the Brigade's aircraft; bore sighting for the light armored vehicles' guns and many other tasks not known to a submarine commander, but all too familiar to the marines and soldiers who would slog across the islands.[65] But, down the line, small blessings were bestowed. Major Jonathan Thompson RM, head of the Special Boat Service, set up a small arms firing range on Ascension Island so that marines and others could sight in their personal weapons that a rough sea or air passage had jarred out of kilter. Meantime, the ships suffered several scares, as though they might be marked and attacked. These were needless alarms because any seafarer would know that the ships pictured in the British newspapers as having left the southern ports would touch shore somewhere south en route to the Falklands and because not even the Argentine navy would attack Royal Navy ships in an American roadstead. On May 7, the amphibious task force and its troops cleared Ascension Island and headed south.

Even though the British mission remained unclear, and even though some, especially on the British army side, believed the entire venture profitless and probably calamitous, several Falklands beaches presented themselves to Clapp and Thompson as feasible landing sites: Cow and Volunteer Bays, Berkeley Sound, Salvador, North Camp, Egg Harbor, Darwin and San Carlos. It took weeks of considered thinking by very experienced RM officers and their naval counterparts in Clapp's amphibious staff to select San Carlos as the landing site, to avoid Woodward's interference and to convince Northwood that their choice was the best available. Landing 3 Commando Brigade remained the problem at hand, but in the back of many minds there remained a nagging rumination that Thatcher's War Cabinet had not decided on the need for an additional brigade to invest Stanley. Finally, on May 12th, Fieldhouse published a specific mission, or as specific as it was liable to get: "To repossess the Falkland islands as quickly as possible."[66] The beachhead was to be on East Falkland. Still, no mention of Goose Green, but it can be taken as certain that the additional brigade was intended expeditiously to land on the Falklands and to assist militarily in their repossession. 5 Infantry Brigade would fight, not merely garrison. In the event, it suffered substantial casualties through its own imprudence and recklessness.

By April 30th, Woodward's battle force had reached the Falklands with orders to enforce a total exclusion zone; that is, sink anything Argentine inside it. In the meantime, another unforced error erupted, not of Thompson's doing. Woodward sent two precious Sea Harriers to bomb Stanley airfield, where only low value targets existed, when his overwhelming task for his very few Harriers was air defense of the fleet and of the landing beach to come. The mission promised high risk for the small gain that it achieved. Despite all the British efforts, that day and later, Stanley's airport never closed. At 2200 on May 7, 1982, the amphibious task group departed Ascension, loaded with 3 Commando Brigade and its attached 2 Para, and headed for a beach yet to be determined.

Shortly after departure from Ascension, the Amphibious Objective Area was fixed; San Carlos was the target beach. Mention should be made here of the lack of British intelligence and its use by those who needed it—the landing force and the ship captains and pilots who transported and protected it. Almost no one got it right. The absurd desire for secrecy started well up the line. Nott, Henderson, the British Ambassador to Washington and the FCO spent days pondering electronically whether to tell Haig that South Georgia was to be invaded, while, simultaneously, Argentine reconnaissance air craft and Soviet satellites had marked the RN task group that headed for that frozen outpost.

Meanwhile, Commodore Clapp, at the sharp end of the stick, lacked an intelligence cell manned by trained intelligence persons who possessed the clearances needed to deal with sensitive traffic. Thompson had an intelligence group inside 3 Brigade, but depended almost wholly on Southby-Tailyour's notes, the Commandos' patrols, the SAS and the Mountain and Arctic Cadre for tactical data. Even when good intelligence was gathered, it was fed back to Fieldhouse's staff at Northwood for time-consuming redistribution to the appropriate user. There was little lateral dissemination. The delay was vexing and unnecessary. In consequence of this deficit, very odd episodes played out. Rear Admiral Woodward considered that mines laid in Falkland Sound might threaten the amphibious task group. The specific target and the timing of said threat was not clear then or now. Falkland Sound is a significant stretch of water, it would have demanded a major naval effort to mine it coherently and it was far off the beaten track of military operations actual or proposed. No Argentine combat ships or ships capable of laying a mine field had been noticed in or near those waters—in fact, they had fled to home waters. It is difficult to understand how even several hundred mines there would have affected the ground campaign and the recapture of Stanley.[67]

Woodward selected a Type 21 frigate, HMS *Alacrity*, "cheap and cheerful" to steam up and back from the Sound. The logic here is difficult to understand. If *Alacrity* had hit a mine, that would not have proven the absence or presence of any other mine or mines. *Alacrity* would, of course, sink. If *Alacrity* returned without hitting or seeing a mine, her uncertain outing would not have proven the presence or absence of mines because *Alacrity* did have mine sweeping or detection gear—it was a single ship covering a limited bit of water. Again, this was a perilous venture that risked loss of ship and crew, against a militarily useless outcome. While on this mission, and by sheer luck, *Alacrity* sighted and sank the *Isla de los Estados*, an Argentine supply ship. Its cargo of fuel exploded and caused greater loss to General Menéndez, the Falklands' military commander, than the discovery of his mines might have been.

Planning, reconnaissance and training continued more or less uninterrupted in the first weeks of May.[68] A few exceptions occurred. Rear Admiral Woodward suggested that the landing take place at Low Bay because it gave his ships better arcs of fire against Argentine attackers. Not one beach there could handle landed troops and their vehicles, and the option was dismissed but not before precious staff time had been wasted in its refutation.[69] But good things were happening all the while. The merchant ships taken up from trade (STUFT) were organized and their holds filled with the paraphernalia of war. At Northwood's request, troops were distributed about the fleet rather than keeping the bulk of them in HMS *Canberra*, whose damage or sinking might have ended the whole affair. Wisely, *Canberra*'s skipper kept his ship close ashore so that in the event of its possible sinking it could have been beached and at least some equipment saved.

Filing through a darkened ship's narrow passageways is not a para's way of going to war. Neither was sailing 8,000 miles from home to recapture a foggy island far distant from the North European plains, where the staff colleges had stipulated that the next conflict would occur. The 100 lb. loads could be expected, but when it came time to buckle up, they were always just a little more than could be carried with ease. The risky step from *Norland* to the pitching side of the landing craft that would deposit them on the beach was new.

At 0630 on May 21, 1982, 3 Commando Brigade landed at San Carlos Bay. 2 Para and its Commanding Officer, Lt. Col. H. Jones, came ashore at 0715, waist deep at Blue Beach Two, Bonners Bay, turned south and crawled up Sussex Mountain.[70] By then, British and Argentine ships had been sunk and men had died. The exercise mentality disappeared almost completely and the Royal Navy relearned, at least partially, the business of steaming in harm's way. Like most others in this venture, Jones had difficulty switching into wartime habits of command.

2 Para was scheduled to land on the beaches at 0340. Its emptied landing boats would then, it was planned, return to pick up the second wave in order to put the entire brigade ashore in darkness. During 2 Para's transit to the beach, one young para fell from his landing craft and broke his leg. Jones insisted that all the landing craft delay landing until the soldier was recovered from the water and his safety assured. All the while the troops waiting off shore remained vulnerable to attack from the air and from Argentine shore fire. Normal wartime procedures stipulate that the safety of one man does not jeopardize the other 600 men, let alone a brigade's landing. 2 Para and the follow on battalion who were to use the stalled LCUs went on to land, vulnerable, in the daylight. Neither was firm ashore by first light in order to repulse the expected Argentine counterattack. In the event none occurred, but Jones' unilateral decision was taken against NATO's rules and against common sense, while putting Thompson and Clapp's plans, to say nothing of Thatcher's job, in needless jeopardy. No one aboard any landing craft knew that the landing would be unopposed. In fact, only one shot, a negligent discharge, was fired and 2 Para waded ashore before first light into freezing water and began a five-hour, five-kilometer snake up to defensive positions on Sussex Mountain. Jones' hard training paid off at this early and crucial moment. On Sussex's slope, 2 Para dug in and held their ground against the Argentine counterattack that military logic demanded but that never occurred.

By darkness on May 21st, the Argentine Navy had retreated to inshore waters and Lami-Dozo's air force, after having inflicted grievous damage on British ships, would be broken within a few days. The real purpose of war was about to begin: the seizure by British infantry of land from which they could not be removed.[71] Yet at least a few politicians lagged behind events. John Nott added to the pages of error about the Falklands War when he wrote that "Colonel Julian Thompson, a Royal Marine, . . . had been in charge of the amphibious landing and had handled it brilliantly."[72] Commodore Michael Clapp RN had been in charge of the landing until 3 Brigade, under the command of Brigadier Julian Thompson RM, had established itself securely ashore. At that time,

Thompson took over. The only accurate and operative word in Nott's citation is the adverb brilliantly. The lack of accuracy here in the most important military operation of Nott's and Thatcher's career is all too characteristic of the manner in which the senior commanders far from the war conducted its moves and set its tempo.

The British paras, whom Piaggi (the Argentine commander) faced those two terrible days at Goose Green, existed in a direct line of descent from Winston Churchill. Though a Grenadier Guardsman in his younger days, Churchill became sufficiently impressed by German parachutists' success in the Blitzkrieg war of 1940 that he ordered the establishment of a corps of at least 5,000 airborne infantry. The Parachute Regiment came into formal existence on August 1, 1942. This despite the fact that in May 1941, German airborne forces, after their initial successes in Norway, Holland and Belgium had blundered catastrophically in Crete, where a landing force of 22,000 men under Colonel-General Lohr suffered 30 percent casualties and consumed resources all out of proportion to its accomplishments. This debacle caused Hitler to order all German airborne forces sidelined and airborne operations struck from the German tactical repertory. Colonel-General Kurt Student, the progenitor of the German airborne enterprise, received a backwater job until put back into the line during one of Hitler's panicky shifts of senior commanders late in the war.

Nothing daunted, the volunteers of the 2nd battalion's C Company under Major J. B. Frost dropped on February 27–28, 1942, into Normandy, near Le Havre. Their mission was seizure of German radar equipment at a station near Bruneval. The raid accomplished its chancy purpose and then some. Important equipment and several technicians who manned it were ferried back to England by the Royal Navy with a loss of only three dead, two missing and several wounded. A thread of history began that dark night on the French coast. The paras completed an odds against airborne attack into enemy territory; they throve in adversity; junior officers and NCOs executed a very complicated operation and their dramatic success bucked up public morale when it was most needed.[73]

The Paras' success in several drops and in conventional infantry actions led to a major increase in their strength. Before the invasion of Normandy, American and British parachute divisions had been formed and trained. Rommel feared their use as strategic instruments that would prevent his reinforcements from getting to the landing beaches and ordered two million mines to be placed on the probable landing grounds for paras and glider borne infantry. Fortunately, he placed his order just two days before

June 6, 1944, and the airborne soldiers accomplished their bloody tasks just as that brilliant general had predicted.[74] Rommel had died before John Frost, and his men wrote the legend of the bridge at Arnhem.

Realities of War

"War Is the Father of Us All" [75]

After Thompson's battalions had established defensive positions around San Carlos Water, Galtieri's hope of winning a military victory on East Falkland vanished. He had not defeated the British landing forces, when at their most vulnerable they struggled ashore in fragile landing craft.[76] The battle that never happened in San Carlos Water was the most important military event of the war.[77] The Argentine soldiers who manned the artillery post on Fanning Head, and whose guns could have wreaked havoc on the landing boats, had fled or been killed or captured without engaging the force afloat. A competent Argentine defense there could have held off the SBS for several hours while Menéndez's three 105mm Italian pack howitzers kept the British landing force in their arc of fire, about 10,000 yards. Had these guns been properly manned—one direct hit on an LCU would have drowned 150 men—scores, if not hundreds, of paras and marines, their boats plodding past Fanning Head and Chanco Point, would have died and the invasion would have been stopped or severely derogated. The only British guns that could have engaged the Argentine artillery position at Fanning Point were 4.5" naval guns from British ships at sea.[78] Their rounds needed a direct hit to be effective against dug-in positions. Menéndez's last possibility, to have met the British force as it disembarked with Argentine 155mm artillery that outranged the naval guns firing from off the beaches, demanded contingency planning, complex airborne positioning and resupply and aggressive troop leadership. Menéndez's forces lacked all these military skills.

Nott expressed unnecessary concern that an Argentine counterattack would menace the just-landed forces.[79] No company-sized forces existed within striking distance of Thompson's beachhead, and Argentine helo lift (Argentine helos could not lift heavy guns to firing positions over the British lodgment) was minimal—175 men—and daytime only. In a fit of almost comical perversity, Argentine logistics officers had imported 56 Mercedes trucks for the twelve miles of Falklands' roads, none of which approached Goose Green or San Carlos. Even after Thompson's men were ashore, Menéndez had not lifted small Argentine fighting patrols to San Carlos to sting the landing force and keep it off balance.[80] The Argentine Air Force had not lengthened the field at Port Stanley to handle the attack planes that could have hit the amphibious fleet as it lay virtually motionless while unloading artillery and supplies. The Pucará ground attack planes based on East Falkland, at Goose Green and at Stanley, had not jumped into the attack as first light illuminated targets. Neither had Anaya's sole carrier closed the British fleet to harry it with iron bombs from the short range A-4s. The Exocet-equipped frigates never steamed within range of the British amphibious force, either during its approach or while it unloaded. Nor had the two modern diesel subs erected a barrier north of the Falklands through which the task force would have had to fight its way in order to arrive at a beach.[81] No Argentine warship of any sort attempted to stop the British landing. Admiral Anaya, a schemer and not a warrior, reached where he could not grasp. British ships would sink, planes would fall and fighting men would die in the following days, but by noontime on May 21st Galtieri had begun to lose the war. But first, a few bloody nails were needed for his military coffin.

By evening on May 22nd, even as Menéndez's military options had contracted, so, too, Galtieri's diplomacy had lost its comfortable options. Thompson's and Clapp's brilliant plan had succeeded. Thompson's brigade held the beaches and a secure enclave above and around them. That astutely chosen lodgment was never threatened. Thompson's patrols had to search out Argentineans who, when found, showed a marked reluctance to engage. Soon would come the patient slogging by British troops and the awful casualties on both sides. True, Argentine units would stoutly defend some jagged hills, but Argentine ground forces never counterattacked in battalion strength, instead they sullenly awaited defeat around Fortress Stanley. Menéndez and his fresh-from-their-desks colonels were to relearn a hard lesson: that troops who remain nested in their trenches will lose to a tactically agile enemy who dominates the air and whose logistics permit movement. When Galtieri forced the negotiating site from the UN's faux elegance to 2 Para's trenches on East Falkland's Sussex Mountain, he changed his country's destiny in ways little understood then or now.

On May 21st, Argentine planes struck the British fleet, but not the landed brigade, with a bravado and verve that few had expected. Too late, Lami-Dozo attempted the task at which he and Anaya had earlier failed, destruction of the British landing force. Clapp's amphibious ships, virtually motionless as they unloaded, were sitting ducks. The LCUs and Mexifloats remained vulnerable the entire day. An Aero Macchi from the Argentine Navy's detachment at Port Stanley attacked first in midmorning and hit HMS *Argonaut* with cannon fire. Although 26 Skyhawks and 19 Daggers sortied from mainland bases, only 26 planes arrived in the amphibious area and completed runs on British ships while twelve were lost. The air attacks were never coordinated with ship-to-ship or sub-to-ship attacks.

That only 60 percent of the Argentine Air Force's planes leaving the Argentine mainland completed attacks, made two dramatic points. First, the Argentine Air Force had not prepared well for war and, second, basing all these aircraft on Port Stanley, Goose Green or Pebble Island would have altered the shape of that critical first day's battle.[82] Lami-Dozo had not lengthened Stanley's runway, though he had six weeks to complete the task. His logisticians had brought over the useless trucks, but not enough construction equipment to lengthen the strip or to repair bomb damage. Keep in mind that each aircraft based from Stanley could have sortied two or three times per day. Argentine Air Force pilots, aided by their excellent observation points ashore, could have targeted the British ships better and carried greater bomb loads because of shorter trips to San Carlos. But the reverse happened. The Argentine Air Force carried light loads for long distances. Scatty blunders surfaced too. A-4 Skyhawks flying from the mainland were painted a bright white that made them stand out to the Sea Harrier pilots who shot down nine of the attackers.

In this devastating but ultimately failed attack lay harbingers of the Argentine Air Force's final defeat. Lami-Dozo's pilots attacked in waves and, because of that, they failed to saturate the defenders ashore with one massive strike that would almost certainly have overwhelmed the just-landed British air defense system. The Argentine Air Force's planners misunderstood war, whose essence remains the seizure and retention of contested ground. Argentine pilots targeted neither troops nor their supply ships, but concentrated instead on the British warships that Admiral Anaya's navy had failed to challenge.[83] *Canberra*, the largest and most obvious target, whose sinking or beaching would have altered the war's complexion if not its outcome, was not hit. Later, partly unloaded and stationed well to the northeast of the Falklands, it would never again be the profitable kill it was that bloody day. However grave the damage British ships suffered, the ground units, once ashore, never had their tactical integrity compromised. 3 Brigade's supplies were always jeopardized, but never stopped. By day's end, Clapp had landed Thompson's brigade of 3,000 men, an artillery regiment of 24 × 105mm guns and eight armored vehicles. An entire town of fighting men had been picked up and landed 8,000 miles from home, at great risk, and none the worse for it.

In the days after the British landing, Thompson's force built up its stocks of artillery ammunition, patrolled aggressively and prepared a balanced offensive force for the push on Stanley.[84] Troops ashore became habituated, as well as anyone can, to the Falklands' winter weather, its bogs and its tufted grass that reduced even the hardiest to a speed across country of one kilometer per hour. A world away from the comfortable efficiencies of shipboard life, logistics and living conditions abruptly became nightmares.[85] Still, Thompson's bold landing gave his splendid infantry momentum they never lost.

3 Brigade's secure position ashore allowed the second part of Moore's May 12th directive to Thompson to come into play:

> You are to secure a bridgehead on East Falkland, into which reinforcements can be landed, in which an airstrip can be established and from which operations to repossess the Falkland Islands can be achieved. You are to push forward from the bridgehead area so far as the maintenance of its security allows, to gain information, to establish moral and physical domination over the enemy, and to forward the ultimate objective of repossession. You will retain operational control of all forces landed in the Falklands until I establish my headquarters in the area. It is my intention to do this, aboard *Fearless*, as early as practicable after the landing. I expect this to be approximately on D + 7. It is then my intention to land 5 Infantry Brigade into the beachhead and to develop operations for the complete repossession of the Falkland Islands.[86]

This cleverly crafted document gave Thompson the option to bear failure if the landing aborted, but not to stake out his own strategy once his men got ashore. Moore remained at sea on the *QE2* far from the landing site and without direct communication to his subordinate Thompson, CO 3 Brigade. Oddly, Moore's order omitted direct mention of Port Stanley, whose possession was the essential point of the landings. It is clear from this document that 5 Brigade was intended to be a fighting formation and not, at least at first, a garrison force. Deficient radio communications prevented Moore even from knowing immediately how the landings had pro-

ceeded. After May 22nd, he, Moore, had only to take over as land commander after Clapp and Thompson performed the very difficult military
and administrative feat of getting 3 Brigade ashore in one piece. In the
event, Moore did not land on the Falklands until May 30th, just in time
to preside over the burial rite for 2 Para's dead at Goose Green when he
took command of all land forces. His arrival then let Thompson get on
with the familiar task of directing 3 Commando Brigade.

However Northwood judged the event, Thompson's successful landing by itself gave him moral and physical dominance over his enemy. Well
after the war, at least a few Argentine generals admitted off-the-record
that Clapp's and Thompson's successful landing *per se* crushed them into
a realization that their defeat was certain and imminent. No Argentine
ground force ever tried to eject Thompson's brigade from its moldering
enclave. His military problem thenceforth was, on its surface, simple. He
had to take Stanley, and the line of march thither was straight. It remained
only for the Marine Brigadier and his staff to decide upon the axis of
attack—the line on the map along which attack forces, logistics, communications, anti-air defense and artillery support would center. His most
irksome enemies, as he planned the breakout, were not Argentine infantry
and artillery, but the Falklands' awful weather, hamstrung logistics and
Northwood's ignorance of the difficulties posed by these two. Even
adding the helos that he possessed to those nearly arrived aboard *Atlantic
Conveyor*, Thompson could leapfrog only one maneuver battalion with its
supporting arms per day.[87]

A technical aside is needed here. Thompson's brigade consisted of five
light infantry maneuver battalions. Such units are called "light" because
they do not carry the ponderous impedimenta of modern warfare such as
tanks, heavy artillery, armored personnel carriers or sophisticated air
defense weapons. Nor can they long hold a position against an adversary so
armed. Light units are intended to seize discrete objectives by shock,
stealth and momentum and hold their ground until reinforced or relieved
by heavy forces. They are hard trained to walk rather than to ride to war.

The adjective "light" in its military context remains unclear to many.
Light battalions consume tonnages of beans and bullets unthought-of
during World War II. Out of a 600 man light battalion or commando,
about 125 officers and men, the bayonets, will charge an enemy position.
The rest are support or reserve. All use copious amounts of command,
control, communications, ammunition, food, air defense, POL and medical supplies. For example, a battalion in the attack owns a platoon of 8 X

81mm mortars. They are the heaviest weapons that belong to the battalion; bigger guns are assigned to it from other units. The battalion's commanding officer is responsible for the men who man them and their use in battle. Each mortar platoon fires 8 × 11 lb. rounds per minute, or about 480 rounds per hour. The platoon fires, when fully committed, a theoretical 3,840 rounds per hour. Assume that changed fire missions, casualties, destruction of targets and adjustments to the base plates reduce that consumption to about 1,000 rounds, or about 12,000 lbs. of ammunition. That equals 2+ Sea King loads or 1/2 Chinook load. Clearly, a full battalion attack with mortar section's participation demanded logistical support that 3 Brigade lacked. The standard machine gun, the GPMG, has a rapid fire rate of 100 rounds per minute and barrels must be changed after 400 rounds. The Toms went into battle threaded with chains of GPMG ammo. The crews and their trucks or helicopters that carry this ammunition to the fighting platoons must in turn be fed, protected, fueled, medicated, etc. The logistical effort needed to support 125 men in a battalion attack is enormous. As we shall see, the absence of sufficient helicopter lift to keep 2 Para's mortars, machine guns and rifles supplied during the attack on Goose Green kept 50 paras hauling rounds on their backs to the firing positions, to the exclusion of any combat assignment.

Thompson knew his military objective, Stanley, and how to get there. He knew, too, that he was about to fight battles where no roads existed and that his transport would consist of men's feet and helicopters laboring over bogs through sleet.[88] True, he owned the Royal Marines' logistics regiment that had exercised with the three commandos and knew how, when and where to deliver what the combat marines needed; but the addition of two para battalions to the three commandos stretched Lt. Col. Ivar Hellberg's capabilities almost beyond their limits. "It's a logistical nightmare for the British. They have paid the price for letting their conventional forces deteriorate."[89] Two pervasive problems bedeviled Thompson as he planned to break out of the San Carlos beachhead and march to Stanley: one was human and the other concerned materials of war. Neither ought to have occurred, at least to the extent that it did.

The British Choice and Unintended Consequences

The British Army of the Rhine's mission against Warsaw Pact forces had dominated the British Army's and Royal Marine's thinking since the Cold

War's birth. Movement of a Brigade or Division and its gear to a shore 8,000 miles from London without roads was not considered. Defense against the Slavic hordes was the essential intent.

No overall commander of army, navy and air forces existed on or near the Falkland Islands where the combat occurred. His absence prevented timely solutions to the vexations that arise even among well-intentioned commanders. Despite the fact that he was not the commander of land forces, once ashore, Rear Admiral Woodward could and did send in for offload ships of his choosing that did not meet the land force commander's needs. Conflicting logistical priorities for the different battles were often settled by Northwood, 8,000 miles from the scene. By the time the problem was resolved, the harm was done. The Royal Navy and the STUFT ships moved supplies from ship to ship without keeping accurate records of what was where. Logistic Regiment's men had virtually to inventory each ship's contents as it arrived each evening in San Carlos.

Northwood decided after the first Argentine raids on the ships in San Carlos that stationing *Canberra* and *Norland* there presented unacceptable risks. These ships were ordered away to the East under the carrier task force's close protection. They carried supplies like a Surgical Support Team and the unit stores of two commandos and both para battalions. The land forces did not see these vital people and artifacts until war's end.[90]

MOD had not thought to mobilize the Commando Brigade's fuel handling troop, a reserve unit, and as a consequence other marines and soldiers had to fill in and learn on the job. The Royal Navy had no recent experience in complex operations outside NATO's umbrella. Woodward, the battle group commander, had no experience in amphibious operations. Only a close and mutually respectful relationship between Michael Clapp, the amphibious force commander, and Julian Thompson, the landing force commander, made the overall planning and execution work. Commodore Clapp was the amphibious force commander whose helos unloaded ships owned by the naval task force commander that, in turn, fulfilled the land force commander's logistical needs. Even so, helos could be, and were, removed in the middle of a mission for the land force commander, Thompson. A naval captain "Air Boss," a commander of all flying assets, assisted by appropriate deputies who would order and coordinate all airborne missions, was not written into the British Table of Organization and did not exist for the entire war. Clapp lacked a trained, experienced and senior air intelligence officer who could advise him and Thompson on the parlous state of Argentine air capabilities.[91] 29 Commando Logistics Regiment did not have an air officer attached to Hellberg's staff to give him guidance on helo missions that, beyond the strained backs of the men, provided the bulk of logistics support. Then, too, 3 Brigade had been trained in logistics principally by truck. These were not available on the Falklands.[92]

Limitations in Materiel

Eleven Sea Kings and five Wessex helos arrived with the task force. These could not lift 3 Brigade to the beaches in the short time needed to land a balanced force. This deficit necessitated a landing by boat, a dark and perilous trip at six knots. Four Sea Kings, their pilots just issued with Passive Night Goggles (PNG) that allowed excellent vision in the dark, were permanently allocated to the SAS and SBS for their nighttime insertions. One Sea King did nothing but supply fuel to the Rapier anti-air missile sites that guarded the beachhead. These missile sites consumed vast quantities of fuel.[93] No roads existed on Thompson's axis of attack.

Because landing craft were scarce, and because not enough landing spots existed on the off loading ships, helos could not always refuel when and where they wanted. Want of prompt refueling for the helos meant fewer resupply missions than would otherwise have been possible. Fruitless hours of hard use piled up on the hard-used engines and pilots.

The Emergency Fuel Handling Equipment was mistakenly dispersed among several STUFT ships, in fact lost, for several days. Ingenious solutions by the Royal Engineers to the problems thus caused reduced delay to the breakout. Back-breaking work was the theme here. Men handled jerry cans a la World War II to keep the tracked vehicles and raiding craft functioning. This evolution was critical because no tracked vehicles meant no charged radio batteries for the brigade's and battalions' radios. Mexifloats, unarmed and underpowered rafts, ferried supplies from ships offshore to the beaches. Designed to carry 125 tons, they often carried 250 tons ship-to-shore with their decks awash.

Far many years and budget cycles, war in Northern Europe, and to a lesser extent in Northern Ireland, had permeated MOD thought and practices all the way down to the purchase of boots. For example, the standard British Army boot worn in 1982 was the DMS, direct molded sole.[94] It shod all the troops that were to land on the Falklands, except a Royal Marine Commando that used an experimental model and a few daring souls who wore mountaineering boots, Wellingtons, ski boots and cherished hiking boots. The DMS had a hard, durable and nonporous sole. Water, perspiration or even heavy dew, once inside, could not leave. Getting inside was not difficult, because the uppers were made of permeable leather and had eyes for laces that opened onto the socks. Thus, any fluid that got inside the boot remained there.

MOD's planners envisioned that the British Army would fight its wars in Northern Ireland, mostly sidewalks, alleys and streets and in Northern Germany, a few streets and many potato fields. They were half right, but the common denominator remained: combat over mostly dry terrain. Of course, in the one-boot-fits-all procurement scheme it happened that troops debarking from landing craft into three or four feet of icy Atlantic Ocean wore the same footwear as an office-working quartermaster at Aldershot.

In fact, most of 3 Brigade landed off the ramps into the wet, some above their waists. For most, their boots never dried out completely. The best that could be hoped for was a change into dry socks that were carefully husbanded under armpits. Some gave up on that and merely squeezed water out of socks before putting them back on. Because the ground water level in the Falklands rises in most places to within a foot of the surface, digging foxholes only heightened the men's discomfort because they took their little rest in the ooze. Standard British practice called for slinging a poncho between trees to shelter resting troops from the elements, but there were no trees as we know them in the Falklands. Tramping about in the wintry mess of sleet and mud made matters worse. Few of the fighting men ever got inside an undamaged building for any length of time and completely dried out themselves and their kit until war's end. The truth was that the fighting platoons of 3 Commando Brigade ate, rested and fought cold and wet until the Argentine surrender.

Casualties from trench foot began soon after the landing. Feet swelled and boots once removed could not be replaced. More than a hundred men from the fighting companies had to be evacuated from the line. They did not suffer from the normal shrapnel and bullet wounds as might be thought, but they were as unable to perform their military duties as those who had lost limbs. Some could not walk. All the line companies' personnel were afflicted to a greater or lesser extent before combat ceased. 3 Brigade's rear echelon did not endure such miseries by virtue of its proximity to rudimentary shelter and warmth. Damage to tissue was neither severe nor permanent, but, once evacuated, very few of those afflicted returned to duty in the battles ahead. The Geneva Convention also forbade the return to combat of those treated in a designated hospital ship.

There was yet another side to this quandary. For want of good boots, Thompson's parlous logistical situation worsened because the evacuees took up scarce helicopter space and strained the resources of medical facilities, both at Ajax Bay and on board nearby ships. By contrast, the footwear worn by the average Argentine soldier or marine held up far better than the British boot and many Toms made strenuous efforts to acquire them from the captured, dead or wounded. Argentine officers' boots were especially prized.

A Subtle Change

It is fair to say, though it cannot be proven, that shortly after May 22nd, the Argentine high command—the junta—and its entourage on the mainland and principally in Buenos Aires decided to fight a defensive war based on Fortress Stanley, Darwin Hill and Fox Bay (details are contained in Appendix C). This delaying action was designed to gain time for a diplomatic settlement and specifically to bring America in on Galtieri's side. No evidence suggests otherwise. The lack of offensive action against the British before, during and after their landing, the Argentine failure to risk high value ships against the British landing force and the bloodless British recapture of South Georgia suggest that keeping the Kelpers in line, minimizing their own casualties and saving face while the diplomats talked had assumed implicit primacy in the junta's thinking.

What did not happen in the few days after the landing constituted a passive victory for Thatcher's forces and this should have obviated the need for the show case victory that Goose Green was meant to be. Brave though its pilots were, the Argentine Air Force's mission planners knew little about the art of war. Their pilots did not damage, let alone sink, *Canberra*, the *sine qua non* of a successful British landing. After their first day's defeat, they did not return the second day with changed tactics. When, on May 23rd, they struck, it was not a saturation attack that could have overwhelmed the overworked Sea Harriers, but rather the same piece meal commitment of fighter-bombers that led to their earlier defeat. The Argentine Daggers, French built, could not refuel in mid air and, therefore, had but one pass over San Carlos before heading home at a speed and altitude not best suited for avoidance of the Sea Harriers. Argentine combat planes, except for the dismal Pucarás and a few Navy Aero Macchis, were never based on the Falklands and few staged from Port Stanley. By day four of the war, even with several British ships on the bottom, the

Argentine Air Force, its best pilots dead or confused about how to beat the Sea Harriers, could not win the war.

Thompson's actions before, during and after the landing had been logical, prudent and successful. He had not moved, because vital transport helos went down with *Conveyor* on May 25th, because 3 Brigade needed a logistics buildup and because Moore's not especially precise directive of May 12th had strongly implied that Thompson should do naught but preserve his lodgment's integrity until he, Moore, and 5 Brigade arrived. Over all these, Thompson had no authority. Thompson's logistical base was 8,000 miles distant; he could not replace a ruined battalion with two fresh units, as could the commanders at Normandy. But in the end, Northwood yielded to Thompson's correct logic; Stanley remained the only nearby military objective and Thompson would remain as CO 3 Brigade as long as he accomplished something. And that something was an action against Goose Green.

Notes

1. Vice Admiral J.J. Lombardo, written correspondence intended for the author, December 1999. Carlos Busser, the head of the Argentine Marines, also voted for immediate invasion.

2. At the war's outset, Argentina had but five Exocet missiles and 14 serviceable A-4s. An Argentine mission was sent to Israel to procure their stored A-4s. The planes were paid for in part, but none was ever delivered.

3. Woodward's battle force and logistics train behaved as though under constant threat from Argentine submarines. In fact, these menaced very little. Out of a fleet of four subs, two were ancient American models of whom one was captured earlier in South Georgia while the other remained in port and inoperable. Of the two German coastal boats, one had lost two engines and was not deployable. It was used as a battery pack for its twin, which had lost one engine. This submarine had excellent Dutch electronics, but the crew was not trained to NATO's standards in their operation. One source claimed to the author that the submarine in question had penetrated the British battle force, but that its fire control system had failed and that as a result the skipper ordered the boat home. No second and third sources substantiated this report and it is, therefore, omitted from the main text of this book.

4. It should be noted that the loss or crippling of Thompson's one remaining Chinook helicopter would have necessitated substantial changes in his plans for investing Stanley and perhaps in the war's outcome.

5. See Jackson Diehl, "Falklands Move Planned Early," *Washington Post,* August 15, 1982, p. A17.

6. Leslie H. Gelb, "U.S. is Expected to Support British if Haig Mediation Proves Fruitless," *New York Times,* April 25, 1982, p. 1.

7. Secretary Haig in a particularly trying moment with General Galtieri during negotiations in Buenos Aires. Quoted in Edward Schumacher, "Falkland Mission," *New York Times*, April 21, 1982, p. 1.

8. Senior Argentine official quoted in the *New York Times*, May 2, 1982.

9. R.W. Apple in the *New York Times*, May 20, 1982.

10. A small but nettlesome crowd in Washington, not necessarily connected to one another, opposes any person in power as a matter of habit. Ideology, political party, race, religion, color, etc., play no role in their sniping. A modest living can be found in this gray and shabby existence.

11. Argentine economic policy blundered just as famously as its military. Argentina sold 80 percent of its grain crop to the Soviet Union for a soft currency, the ruble, to pay its debts in a hard currency, the dollar.

12. Tony Benn, *On The Falklands War*, NEC Resolution, April 28, 1982.

13. Benn, *The Benn Diaries*, (London: Arrow, 1996), p. 531.

14. Ibid, p. 531.

15. Ibid, p. 532.

16. "Why U.S. Decided," *The Guardian*, May 6, 1982, p. 4.

17. Ibid, p. 532.

18. Percy Craddock, *In Pursuit of British Interests* (London: John Murray, 1997), p. 21.

19. Bernard Gwertzman, "Peru Peace Plan," *New York Times*, May 5, 1982, p. A17.

20. John Lehman, secretary of the Navy during the Falklands War, letter to the *London Daily Telegraph*, March 30, 2002, p. v. Lehman had attended a British university.

21. Caspar Weinberger, *Fighting For Peace* (New York: Warner Books, 1991), pp. 214–215.

22. Senior British civil servant to author, May 1983.

23. Weinberger, *Fighting for Peace*, p. 215.

24. Ibid, p. 216.

25. Secretary Weinberger ended several discussions on the Falklands War by saying to the author: "It was the right thing to do."

26. "Tell the CINC that I can hold the political arena. There will be no political meddling in the war. It is up to him to conduct the operations as he thinks best though I would be grateful if he does not delay things longer than necessary." Margaret Thatcher, after *Atlantic Conveyor* had sunk, to Brigadier Christopher Dunphie, letter to the *Daily Telegraph*, January 17, 2002, Opinion.

27. 40 Commando and the Air Defense Troop were stood down on March 31, 1982, and were told: "no units are required." Michael Clapp and Ewen Southby-Tailyour, *Amphibious Assault Falklands* (London: Cooper, 1996), p. 14.

28. R.W. Apple, in the *New York Times*, May 6, 1982.

29. "John gave the MOD's view that the Falklands could not be retaken once they were seized." Margaret Thatcher, *The Downing Street Years* (London and New York: Harper, 1993), p. 179. Galtieri's junta agreed.

30. Thatcher herself erred when in her opening statement to the House of Commons on April 3, 1982, she mentioned the "Falkland Islands and their

dependencies." South Georgia is a dependency of Great Britain itself and administered from the Falkland Islands. Thatcher, *The Downing Street Years*, p. 183. Dr. David Owen corrected Mrs. Thatcher in the House.

31. The War Cabinet consisted of: Margaret Thatcher; Francis Pym, forced on her by the House; John Nott, who supported Thatcher against Edward Heath for her occupancy at No. 10 and who was the very warranted scapegoat for much that had gone wrong; Willie Whitelaw, the ubiquitous gray man of conservative politics without whom nothing significant in the Conservative Party could occur; Cecil Parkinson, narrowly defeated by Thatcher for Prime Minister and ready to assume that job when Thatcher stumbled; Sir Terence Lewin, Chief of the Defense Staff, needed to pull Thatcher's fat from the fire; and the Attorney General Michael Havers, ready to offer legal fig leaves for military action. Whitelaw's presence was useful because, as Thatcher is believed to have said, "everyone needs a Willie." Later, Parkinson took himself out of the running for No. 10 Downing when he admitted to having fathered a child out of wedlock. From time to time, sundry FCO and military persons attended, like Brigadier Peter de la Billiere, head of the Special Warfare community and a firm believer in the coup de main to solve the knottiest of problems abroad. Quite properly, Geoffrey Howe, the Chancellor of the Exchequer, was excused because Thatcher wanted no niggling about the war's costs. Thatcher had only a tenuous control of her cabinet and wanted no insufficiency of loyalty or will to cloud thinking about the war. Howe became Foreign Minister after the Falklands, just in time to suffer "humiliation" at not being forewarned about the U.S. invasion of Granada. He remained a major figure in Conservative politics until 1990, when he split with Thatcher over their differing views on union with Europe. Denis Healey likened Howe's subsequent parliamentary attack on Thatcher as "being savaged by a dead sheep." At least one meeting about the war was held each day. Thatcher, *Downing Street Years*, pp. 188–189.

32. As noted in Chapter 2, John Nott had been installed as Minister of Defense with orders to cut spending. He had nearly eviscerated the Royal Navy in the doing.

33. John Nott, Thatcher's Defense Secretary, whose resignation after the Argentine invasion Thatcher refused to accept, implied an unlikely motive for going to war when he wrote, "Sir Henry Leach, the First Sea Lord, joined our meeting—dressed in full naval uniform. The sight of a man in uniform always pleases the ladies, and Margaret was clearly impressed." John Nott, "Heading for War," *Daily Telegraph*, March 20, 2002, p. 2.

34. Cabinet minister to R. W. Apple, in the *New York Times*, April 7, 1982.

35. Julian Thompson in Michael Bilton and Peter Kosminsky, *Speaking Out: Untold Stories From The Falklands War* (London: Andre Deutsch, 1989), p. 224.

36. Nott, "Heading for War," *Daily Telegraph*, March 14, 2002.

37. Nott's connection to his own military seems always to have been frayed. He stated that air strikes had rendered Stanley's airport unusable by heavy transport aircraft. Quoted in Nott, *New York Times*, May 5, 1982. In fact, Argentine C-130 flights into and out of Stanley continued unabated until the very end of the war.

38. Richard Crossman, *Godkin Lectures at Harvard 1970* (Cambridge: Harvard University Press, 1972), p. 33.

39. Pym, never close to his Prime Minister, failed to forge a trusting relationship with Secretary of State Haig, who with clarity remarkable for a diplomat is widely believed to have called Pym a "duplicitous bastard." The day after the *Belgrano*'s sinking, Pym stated: "Today I have come back to consult with him (Haig) as an ally." Caspar Weinberger, *Fighting For Peace* (New York: Warner Books, 1991), p. 209. Pym was later dismissed from Thatcher's circle, allegedly for muttering that too large a majority was bad for either party. Thatcher disagreed.

40. The author was surprised to learn that he, a desk-bound functionary, had made more amphibious landings—no shooting—than had almost all RM and RN officers of similar rank.

41. Besides the dead and wounded, this war had many heroes and displayed very competent military men. Vaux's attack on Mt. Harriet with his 42 Commando was brilliant in plan and in execution. Sheridan's taking of South Georgia was of a different stamp, but equally courageous and well timed. There were many others. The olive wreath for patience under administrative fire must go to Julian Thompson, 3 Brigade's CO, whose sensible plan gained the final victory and saved lives. He also saved Thatcher's job and place in history.

42. Woodward had insufficient knowledge of Argentine aircraft and their potential to harm his ships. He mused about the Entendards landing on and taking off from the Argentine carrier. The Entendards could barely make unsafe landings—touchy arresting gear—on that well-worn carrier, but they would sail rather than fly home because the carrier's catapult was insufficient to launch so heavy a plane.

43. Admiral Bertram Ramsay RN, who organized and led the amphibious invasion of Normandy in June 1944, quoted in Clapp and Southby-Tailyour, *Amphibious Assault Falklands*, p. 26. For the word army in this passage substitute Royal Marines because: "the army wished to have little to do with what they thought would be humiliation and the area of operation was too far away for any sensible RAF involvement." Southby-Tailyour, *Reasons in Writing* (London: Cooper, 1993), p. 103. Clearly, Jones disagreed.

44. See Admiral Sandy Woodward, *One Hundred Days* (London: Harper, 1992), p. 78.

45. Clapp and Southby-Tailyour, *Amphibious Assault Falklands*, pp. 13–14.

46. Admiral Fieldhouse, the CINC, had also been a submarine officer. Few in the naval chain of command knew much about defending Royal Navy ships from air attacks. HMS *Ardent, Antelope, Coventry* and *Sheffield* were lost straightaway.

47. Woodward, *One Hundred Days*, pp. 300–301.

48. See Nott, *Here Today, Gone Tomorrow* (London: Politico's, 1992), pp. 301–303.

49. Nott stated that the "Royal Navy['s] . . . logistics were brilliant," Ibid, p. 476. Not so. They were back-breaking and ultimately successful. Logistics ashore under Lt. Col. Hellberg RM and his 29 Commando Logistics Regiment were very efficient under awful circumstances. Until the war's end, ships had to reinventory their cargoes very frequently. The sailors, through no fault of their own, did not know before departure from the United Kingdom where to stow combat gear that was to be off loaded first, against that of lesser importance.

50. The Amphibious Objective Area (AOA) is a box, defined by the operation's high command and delineated on a map or chart, inside which amphibious operations are meant to occur. Hence the military expression: "thinking outside the box." Planning centers on this area and, because the military goal in this case was simple, Clapp and Thompson could reasonably define the AOA on their own.

51. Upon setting out from Ascension Island, Woodward headed on "a course which might suggest we were approaching Buenos Aires rather then the Falklands." Woodward, *One Hundred Days*, p. 93. Military action, real or imagined, against Buenos Aires was off the table in both London and Washington. It is not inconceivable, however, that Woodward considered a real or threatened invasion of Buenos Aires by 3,000 men to constitute a feasible military option.

52. Clapp and Southby-Tailyour, *Amphibious Assault Falklands*, p. 53.

53. Southby-Tailyour, *Reasons In Writing* (London: Cooper, 1993), p. 67.

54. Clapp and Southby-Tailyour, *Amphibious Assault Falklands*, p. 54.

55. When the author asked one of the participants about the events of that meeting, he replied: "It was worse than that." Officer A in conversation.

56. Clapp and Southby-Tailyour, *Amphibious Assault Falklands*, p. 57.

57. Thompson, letter to author, June 5, 1997.

58. OAS staff conversations, 1997–1998.

59. Clapp and Southby-Tailyour, *Amphibious Assault Falklands*, p. 65.

60. Ibid, p. 70.

61. Nott, *Here Today, Gone Tomorrow*, p. 309.

62. In the section of her autobiography that deals with the Falklands War, Thatcher passes over with little notice the utter competence that went into Clapp and Thompson's planning and execution of the landing at San Carlos.

63. None of the several persons present at or on the periphery of those sessions and interviewed for this book remembers Goose Green being mentioned.

64. Thompson letter to author, June 5, 1997.

65. Clapp and Southby-Tailyour, *Amphibious Assault Falklands*, p. 70.

66. Ibid, p. 85.

67. Woodward claims that Argentine notions of British landing sites would have included San Carlos, and that demanded sweeping the entire area. His supposition had no basis in fact. SAS and SBS reconnaissance had found no beach defenses at San Carlos, only a few watching patrols that were evident elsewhere as well. Argentine staffs had concluded that the British would follow the American practice and land at Stanley, take casualties and end the war quickly. San Carlos was not densely covered by Argentine artillery as were possible landing sites around Stanley. See Woodward, *One Hundred Days*, pp. 302–304, for his discussion of this matter.

68. Woodward's frequent mention in his book, *One Hundred Days*, of his speculations on possible landing sites was superfluous. That selection was not his affair. He commanded the battle force only. Clapp commanded the amphibious force and Thompson the troops. See Woodward, *One Hundred Days*, pp. 186–187, passim.

69. Woodward's attention had by now turned to air defense. This may account for his erroneous statement in *One Hundred Days* that the amphibious

ships sailed down San Carlos Waters in order to launch their landing craft. Woodward's statement of the ships' position is inaccurate. The ships launched their landing craft behind and south-west of Chanco Point out of sight of the beaches. The landing craft were led thence to the beaches by Southby-Tailyour and his stalwart RM color-sergeants as coxswains.

70. Woodward commented: "The Royal Navy had planned and carried out one of the most successful landings in military history." This hyperbolic statement is not factual. The landing had been planned jointly with the Royal Marines, whose Commander, Brigadier Julian Thompson RM, in concert with Commodore Michael Clapp RN, had, in principle and in fact, decided upon the time and place of the landing. Omitted from Woodward's comment was the fact that two battalions of paras had landed alongside the marines. The craft that put the men ashore were manned by Royal Marines. The astuteness of the day-to-day planners of whom Woodward was not one led to the landing on an undefended beach. Most of the troops' gear remained aboard ship. See Woodward, *One Hundred Days*, p. 263.

71. In debarking from their landing craft the paras did not answer the marines' fabled command: "Troops Out." A young para officer remedied that misunderstanding with: "Paras Go."

72. Nott, *Here Today, Gone Tomorrow*, p. 313.

73. Student had advocated using airborne troops only in mass, and not for raiding. Perhaps by some transference of thought, this doctrine accounted for Bruneval's fairly light protection against the obvious.

74. Liddell Hart, ed., *Rommel Letters* (New York: Harcourt Brace, 1953), pp. 47–48, passim.

75. Heraclitus.

76. A retired Argentine general, Carlos Della Larroca, was placed under arrest after he stated in a post war TV interview that his army erred in not meeting Thompson's brigade on the beaches. *Washington Post*, June 29, 1982.

77. Goose Green's commander sent 80 men to guard San Carlos' beaches, a possible landing site, while busily fortifying Goose Green's beaches, which could not accept and deploy a useful amphibious force.

78. These guns, the heaviest carried by the Royal Navy, fired a 46 lb. round that kept opposing forces' heads down, provided illumination, and devastated troops in the open but required a direct hit to demolish a bunkered gun position.

79. Nott, *Here Today, Gone Tomorrow*, p. 312.

80. Argentine Air Force's 601 Aviation Battalion, stationed on the Falklands, had 2 X Chinooks, 3 X Augustas, 5 X Pumas, and 9 X Hueys. Almost certainly no crews were certified for night flying and it is doubtful that all helos could lift off simultaneously. One-time troop lift by helicopter was at most 175 armed troops without crew-served weapons.

81. *Santiago* was not operational during the war. *Santa Fe* had serious technical difficulties that kept her out of ship to ship combat. Argentine Navy Vice Admiral J.J. Lombardo's reply to author's questions, December 1999.

82. A loss rate of 20 percent per day is unacceptable. A force engaged in a sustained campaign may suffer no more than 3 percent daily attrition. Above that figure, tactical integrity and unit cohesion fragment fatally.

83. The Rapier air defense missiles had not yet been positioned on the hills above San Carlos. Landed troops lived without their AA protection that day.

84. Author's interviews with Major-General Thompson, 1996–1997.

85. Finding potable water ashore was a problem. In many cases, soldiers stamped out a depression in the turf and let it fill with water, which was then scooped up and purified by the addition of a pill. The taste was awful.

86. Julian Thompson, *No Picnic* (London: Cooper, 1985), p. 73.

87. In "Falklands Chief," *Daily Telegraph*, March 26, 2000, p. 1, Thompson chides himself for not attacking Goose Green with two battalions and for not moving his HQ near there in order to direct the battle. His lament is questionable in the extreme because at that moment he had the logistics barely to run only one battalion in the attack; he could move only one half battery of 105mm guns at once and scarcely had the logistics to move his endangered HQ before the attack. Goose Green had room to maneuver for only one battalion.

88. Because Operation Corporate was a "Light" military evolution, Thompson did not have construction battalions to build roads, storage facilities and airfields as the Americans did in Vietnam.

89. Former Chief Of Naval Operations, Admiral Elmo Zumwalt, in the *Washington Post*, April 6, 1982, p. 6.

90. Julian Thompson, *Lifeblood Of War* (London: Brassey's, 1991), p. 271.

91. When quizzed about the Pucará and its capabilities, a USAF Colonel and a licensed aeronautical engineer accurately predicted, after ten minutes' study, the Pucará's operational characteristics and why it would fail as a military asset.

92. It should be noted that when British troops arrived, Kelpers' tractors and Land Rovers that had been inoperable during the Argentine presence suddenly got fixed and provided, as they did at Ajax Bay under Alan Miller's direction, invaluable assistance in getting the troops' gear inland and off the beaches.

93. Rapier was credited with only one confirmed kill, a small payback for the effort expended in keeping it operational. Jeffrey Ethell and Alfred Price, *Air War South Atlantic* (New York: Jove Books, 1986), p. 276.

94. Some British troops stationed in Northern Ireland wore a model that was lighter and better suited for streets and sidewalks.

4

Goose Green

Goose Green, the most storied battle of the Falklands war, had no military purpose and only delayed the conflict's final resolution.[1] "Why go to Goose Green? That's a question that needs answering."[2] This forlorn outpost contained fewer than 200 Kelpers and was not connected to any other settlement by a paved road. It commanded nothing and was a bridge to nowhere. It is a cartilage of land connecting two parts of East Falklands on a northeast-southwest axis. Apart from its isolation, Goose Green was notable as the final resting place for *The Vicar of Bray*, a 122-foot barque built in Whitehaven, England in 1841. Meant for the coal trade, it finally carried its intended cargo of coal to Valparaíso in 1870, 30 years after the keel was laid. Needing repairs, it put in to Port Stanley where it stayed until its removal to Goose Green. The Falkland Islands Company bought the *Vicar* in 1873, but, even now, the coal's disposition remains a matter of interest. The ship ended its life as a hulk, and served as jetty and pier for such few ships and boats as made Goose Green.

Each end of the land bridge can be sealed off by an entrenched platoon. Sixteen British were killed and sixty-four wounded at Goose Green, the number of men that, divided in two and placed at either end of the isthmus, could have masked the Argentine Garrison for the war. That option in fact risked little because, after British infantry had dug in ashore, the Argentine army had adopted a passive and defensive role. The Falklands garrison possessed no tactical mobility beyond a one-time daylight lift into Goose Green of about 175 men without crew-served weapons.

Yet, had Argentine defenders formulated a normal plan of defense for Goose Green, they would have retained some advantages. Killing zones were easily established. Had they been professionally emplaced, mines and wire would have made for even more miseries than Jones' men ultimately suffered. Shallow draft ships can approach it by sea on both sides only at high tide, and combat ships would, in any case, be plugged inside narrow waters with no room to maneuver. On the debit side, the isthmus is not easily defended from artillery fire, air strikes or naval bombardment. Goose Green did own a muddy 450-meter air strip which was not ever lengthened to take heavy attack planes or even improved to assure safe operations by the Pucarás based there.[3] Fueling of aircraft was done from drums; maintenance was scanty. Tactically, Goose Green provided a trap for any who fought there because little room existed for maneuver by attacking forces. Both sides were scorpions in a very small bottle. Ironically, the battle was won in the end not by massive firepower, but by junior officers and NCOs who made clever use of what little space they had. Remember that Goose Green was not vital ground in Stanley's defense nor, therefore, was it necessary for Thompson to seize it before going on to Stanley. Goose Green was off the British line of march, as any Lance Corporal could see.[4] But the Argentine staff and junta were just as misguided. No reason, military or political, existed to nominate Goose Green as one of Galtieri's three fortresses.

At bottom, the battle at Goose Green resulted from the disingenuousness that snaked through wartime discussions around Thatcher. In London, it was tacitly held that one artfully publicized victory, if a military success at Goose Green could be so styled, might convince Galtieri to leave the Falklands adorned by a fig leaf of discussions about sovereignty in order to redeem his gaffes and to perfume his relations with a fickle electorate. A victory by Thompson's force would satisfy those British military and civilians alike who demanded movement of 3 Brigade at any cost in the face of contradictory military logic.

The smarmy self-interest that clouded discussion in the cabinet about the war led to Thatcher's hectoring her subordinates during May's last days on Reagan's and Haig's alleged reluctance to support her position, not withstanding the American aid that had flowed to British forces before she sent the task forces south.[5] Thatcher's war cabinet should have known better. After all, it had never fought a war and never engaged Galtieri as a hostile principal. For Galtieri, he had by this time too much invested in his misadventure to hang himself with so slender a thread as defeat at Goose Green would offer. Sheridan's seizure of South Georgia had not toppled Galtieri's regime, but only got it to stumble around in its own black hole from which no recovery was ever possible, however long the drama took to play out. Thatcher's minister of defense, John Nott, wrote that "We, as politicians, expressed our collective view to the Chiefs of Staff that the length of time between establishing a landing and total repossession of the Islands was a matter of concern to us all. . . . International pressures were bound to mount. . . . Speed was of essence to this whole operation."[6] Not for Thatcher was a long Churchillian summer of blood, sweat, toil and tears.

Nott misread international opinion after the war began, just as acutely as he had misjudged Argentine intentions before April 1st. The few international pressures that had mounted against her majesty's government dissipated as the British task force steamed south; besides, prudence, not speed, was the order of the day. Not a few South American chanceries, some have suggested, managed polite smiles as their neighbor began to twist in winds from the north. All said, Thompson's goose was cooked; against his will, he would put a military drama of some sort into play. By this time, too, it was clear that Admiral Anaya, who had lobbied for seizing the Falklands on the premise that the British would not fight, declined to sacrifice his small navy in defense of Port Stanley. The Argentineans and the British had misjudged each other again.

Both had underestimated Haig, Lehman and Weinberger. Haig's health-destroying peregrinations had several benign and legitimate goals. Haig especially needed time to convince America's and Britain's partners of the validity of Thatcher's position; time and opportunity to let all view British good faith negotiations without which a jaded world might declare neutrality; time to persuade the junta that America would support a victorious Britain; and time to get the British task forces in Falkland's waters well bolstered by American military aid of every sort. These were subtle and necessary goals whose usefulness was not apparent to Thatcher and her friends for much of the war. Too few senior British officials seemed aware of Haig's unequivocal statement made on April 6th: "The President has directed that the United States will respond positively to requests for materiel support for British forces."[7]

That America propped up the UK, and for reasons that went far beyond ownership of the Falkland Islands, seems to have escaped Nott's and Thatcher's ruminations. Hear Sir Nicholas Henderson at a meeting on May 17, 1982, with Thatcher, Nott, Chief of the Defense staff, and assorted other military persons:

Right at the end of the meeting Nott protested about the American attitude. Did they realize the bitterness in the UK about them? There was
strong criticism in the House of Commons. Would it be a good idea if a
group of MPs . . . were to go over to tell their opposite numbers in Congress how unpopular they were? I [Henderson] asked him in what way
the Americans had fallen short of expectations since they had declared
their support for us on April 30. Surely they had met all our demands for
intelligence and equipment. [Nott did not answer.] . . . But the Chief of
the Defense staff demurred at the suggestion that the Pentagon had
failed to meet our request for supplies.[8]

By this time, of course, the President, the Senate and the political establishment gave public and private support to British diplomacy and military
initiatives. The Pentagon, from the Secretaries to the sergeants, were filling
ill-provisioned British military stocks at full speed and with a new-found
efficiency that bordered on delight. There were few rules. In London, the
panic induced by a failed defense policy, perhaps exhaustion or perhaps an
inability to communicate with his juniors caused this cast-by-fate protagonist to mangle his lines. Whatever it was, Nott was the least informed or the
most duplicitous senior member of the British team that ran the war.

The political exigencies of May's last days may seem flimsy, almost
diaphanous, in retrospect, but as glimpsed through the fusty fog of politics by Thatcher's war cabinet and military advisors, they demanded a military victory. In May's waning days, after *Atlantic Conveyor* and its precious helicopters had sunk, British morale, at least in Northwood and in
MOD, plunged. Admiral Fieldhouse, the overall commander of the entire
operation, lamented 8,000 miles distant from the battlefield that he had
put 5,000 men ashore, that nothing had happened since, that he had lost
5 ships to Argentine air attacks and that he would be forced to "contem-
plate lifting 3 Commando Brigade off the beaches."[9]

Fieldhouse had been a submarine commander and probably had a
tourist's notion of the North European plain where a NATO war would
occur, but he had no foot-on-the-ground knowledge of the Falklands. He
had no notion of what a ground attack by sodden British troops
demanded in the way of logistics, gun support, transport and reconnaissance. He was, from his professional experience, the wrong man to head
what was principally a ground operation. Neither did he grasp the minutiae of orchestrating the diplomatic and military aspects of this unnecessary conflict. For example, he had either not been told or acted in igno-

rance of President Reagan's letter to Margaret Thatcher that military action by the Argentineans was not acceptable to the United States and that, by inference, America would take every necessary step in order to return to *status quo ante bellum* (see Figure 2.1). The realization that in war men die, ships sink and planes fall, and that these awful events are the stuff of final victory, seems not to have entered the Admiral's calculus. Thompson, Jones, Vaux and their colleagues knew differently. The hard part had been done; only the bloody end game awaited.

To have replicated Dunkirk, as Fieldhouse conjured, when most others concerned with the war sought retribution for America's lack of support in Suez in 1956, when American aid was pouring into the British war machine, when British troops were dug in ashore, when the Argentine air force had been defeated, when Anaya's navy hugged its own shore and when American diplomatic efforts had marshaled the UN and the rest of the free world against Galtieri's junta would have come close to sundering the Special Relationship. The effect of a withdrawal on the world's opinion of Great Britain, Thatcher's disgrace and probable fall, the British army's humiliation, the broken faith with Thompson's brigade and the squandered capital of a so far successful military operation seemed absent from Fieldhouse's bizarre meditations. Perhaps it was the shock of an unforeseen war fought under an unpopular Prime Minister that rendered Northwood's cerebrations so blatantly different from the blood-bathed optimism and the crisp, if snippy logic of Brooke, Montgomery and Slim forty years earlier. John Lehman, Secretary of the Navy during the war and, with Secretary Weinberger, one of the most ardent and practical supporters of British efforts, caught a whiff of the inconsistencies that confused British war efforts when he visited London (see Figure 4.1).

Meanwhile, unsupported by any fact, Thatcher's war cabinet concluded that allies and fence sitters alike needed bolstering. A showcase victory to compensate for the Royal Navy's lost ships would suffice. Some manifest heroism and glamour would not hurt either. Goose Green was the nearest and cheapest theater for the play. It escaped Northwood and Thatcher's war cabinet that HMS *Alacrity*'s sinking of the supply ship *Isla de los Estados* on 10–11 May with 325,000 liters of helo fuel, guns and miscellaneous supplies was a far greater British victory, and damaged Galtieri's military efforts far more than the seizure of the Community Hall and muddy air strip at Goose Green ever would. Never having fought a war, Margaret Thatcher lacked much of the language of war. Sinking an Argentine supply ship inside Stanley's harbor or downing the Boeing

---

Figure 4.1: Text of Letter by John Lehman, March 30, 2002

By **John Lehman**, the Secretary of the US Navy, who helped provide Britain with vital intelligence and military equipment

In the Pentagon, there had been a massive de facto tilt toward Britain from the very first day. It was the inescapable result of the "special relationship". The depth and breadth of cultural, social and historic ties between America and Britain were overwhelming.

It is highly unlikely that even Jeane Kirkpatrick, the US ambassador to the United Nations, or anyone at the State Department or the White House understood at first the extent of the assistance we were providing, especially in communications and intelligence.

We had, for instance, sent two tankers to Ascension Island, without which the Task Force could not have made it to the Falklands.

When I visited London on May 31, I was perplexed to find that many of the civilian members of the Ministry of Defence seemed to be resentful of what they perceived as reluctance by the American government to give full support and assistance to Britain.

Jeane Kirkpatrick and, surprisingly, Al Haig, the Secretary of State, came in for considerable criticism. The Royal Navy itself, by contrast, could not have been more grateful and appreciative. I concluded that the Royal Navy had not fully shared with their ministers everything that was going on.

The two navies had developed a substantial integration of doctrine, weaponry, operations and logistics. Perhaps even more important, it provided a system of very active exchange of personnel between the two navies, building bonds of friendship and familiarity.

This common framework proved decisive in the Falklands. Because there was a system in place for sharing communications and intelligence, and liaison officers to handle the sale, loan and other transfer of weapons and equipment, there were no hard decisions to be made in the first days of the crisis.

Requests through these channels for such things as Sidewinder missiles began to flow in April. At first, before the Task Force arrived at the Falklands, the requests were handled routinely, without reference to higher authority.

As the requests began to involve more substantial logistical assistance, communications equipment and intelligence, we kept the Secretary of Defence, Caspar Weinberger, informed, and he then required us to submit a daily report to his deputy, Frank Carlucci.

There was little doubt where Weinberger's sympathies lay. But, because of the deep divisions in the administration, we did not want to raise the level of consideration or increase the flow of assistance to the Royal Navy. We made sure that Cap Weinberger knew at every step what we were proposing to provide.

Source: Letter to The Telegraph, March 30, 2002, p. v.

reconnaissance plane that dogged the British fleet as it headed south might have conveyed unmistakable intent and ended the war then and there. Instead, no such attempts were made. In his summation of the whole affair, Lord Runcie, the former Arch-Bishop of Canterbury, was moved to criticize: "Those who stay at home, most violent in their attitudes and untouched in themselves."[10]

While the Royal Navy lost men and ships, Britain's ground situation in May's waning days was static, simple and aimed at the investiture of Stanley. Still in play was Moore's directive of May 3rd: "To forward the ultimate object of repossession." To accomplish that goal, Thompson had first to seize and hold the vital ground overlooking the town, and this demanded the seizure of Mt. Kent, 60 kilometers from Thompson's lodgment at San Carlos. Patrols by the SAS, SBS and, most importantly, the Marines' own Mountain and Arctic Cadre had determined that no hard resistance existed on the ground between his base and Mt. Kent. Yet Thompson had come to learn what Northwood failed to appreciate, that any move outside the positions at San Carlos presented enormous logistical difficulties. He had one Chinook and five Wessex helicopters to ferry troops, artillery and supplies; wheeled vehicles could not operate on his line of march and his foot soldiers could cover only one kilometer per hour. No roads existed beyond Stanley's perimeter. Thompson's investiture of Stanley and his tactical options were limited by a logistics situation not studied in NATO's war colleges.

While Thompson built the stocks needed for the run-up and final attack on Stanley, a dispute, over whose resolution he had little control, festered. "Operation Corporate was planned to fight the land battle with one brigade (3 Commando Brigade) reinforced by two infantry battalions and one air defense battalion."[11] Thompson was meant, at least at the war's outset, to seize Stanley alone even if few of those far from the battle knew that such a victory would take time. En route to the Falklands, 5 Brigade still nurtured the notion that it was to be a garrison force after Stanley had fallen, but in time Northwood's slothful dithering mutated that mission into a combat role. Even so, Brigadier Tony Wilson's brigade arrived on June 1–2 in East Falkland without a logistics organization, adequate ground transport,[12] or a staff capable of handling combined operations in a non-NATO environment. Few considered its pre-embarkation training exercises satisfactory.[13] Decisions made at the conference held by Fieldhouse on April 17th at Ascension Island set a more limited role for Thompson's brigade: "Landing with a view to repossessing the Falklands," as opposed to: "Repossession of the Falklands." A logical interpretation of these words meant that Thompson must wait for 5 Brigade's arrival and settle in before marching on Stanley. On its face, Fieldhouse's decision simplified Thompson's job but left open the question of who would fight the land battle and on whose timetable.

Confusion about how the landed 5 Brigade would conduct its part of the war permeated the battle commanders' thoughts as they remained dug in at San Carlos. Aggressive patrolling confirmed the view that the 3 Brigade's landing had forestalled any immediate Argentine ground attack by battalion or larger forces. Suddenly and contrary to the notion that 3 Brigade would not fight the land battle alone, Thompson was ordered, against his strenuous and valid objections, to conduct military operations against Goose Green or to lose his job.[14] Once ashore, Thompson had planned Stanley's investiture from sound military logic; 8,000 miles away in England, Northwood spoke from perceived, if tawdry, political necessity. Northwood had ordered Thompson to acquire physical and moral domination over the enemy by risking 20 percent of his ground strength in an unnecessary diversion, but also to await 5 Brigade before proceeding with Stanley's investiture. The contradictions in these two directives were clear.

Thompson knew that, 5 Brigade or not, Stanley was defended by three rings of mountains. Of these, Mt. Kent was the highest peak and dominated the terrain around it. It was the most vital ground on the march to Stanley. Mt. Kent lay 50 kilometers from the British beachhead; in between, an unfortified no man's land was probably mined but irregularly covered by Argentine 155mm artillery. At this distance from his tactical objective, Thompson lacked the helicopters immediately to conduct a full-scale attack on Mt. Kent. Surprise was necessary, and a clandestine approach march of 30 kilometers was out of the question. He could not carry his 105mm guns and their ammunition forward for an attack on Mt. Kent and conduct the raid on Goose Green simultaneously. Men can carry ammunition, but they cannot porter guns. In the absence of discreet military victories, Thompson's methodical buildup for the operation on Mt. Kent riled the clean-shirted staff officers at Northwood as dilatory behavior unacceptable to politicians and to their military subordinates.

Prudently, Thompson persisted in his opposition to any move that diverted men and materiel from the march on Stanley. From his position as commander on the ground, careful haste was imperative; after all, his logistics remained scanty and vulnerable to raids and bad luck. If the Argentineans reinforced Kent, if they moved their 155mm artillery either to it or in support of its garrison, Kent's seizure, essential to Stanley's investiture, would be a very difficult and bloody affair. Logic dictated that reconnaissance of Kent, with the necessary allocation of helicopters and patrols, claimed first military priority. In second place came the forward movement of 29 Commando Regiment's guns, ammunition and equipment. These tedious but necessary actions did not capture the public's imagination or the politicians' favor. Of course, Thompson's immediate commander, Major-General Jeremy Moore, remained at sea with no communications possible to Thompson, who had therefore to fight the political military battle with Northwood while still performing as the tactical commander ashore. In the run-up to Goose Green, Thompson was more sorely tried by his own side than by his nominal enemies.

By May 22nd, the dander was up, at least for Thompson's political masters. A successful raid on Goose Green would satisfy "the moral and physical domination over the enemy," part of Moore's directive; boost home front morale; strengthen Thatcher's position inside and outside her own party; lessen the misperception that the navy bore the brunt of combat; and perhaps convince Galtieri to quit. In Thompson's words, "The aim of the raid would be to cause as much damage as possible to the garrison and its equipment, including air defense guns and missiles."[15]

On May 23rd, Thompson sent Lt. Col. H. Jones, CO of 2 Para, a formal warning order that 2 Para was to raid Darwin/Goose Green. It should be understood that raid means smash, grab and leave. The notion of raiding is a holdover from commandos' missions against occupied Europe during World War II, as a consequence of which the Royal Marines maintained a small boat unit called "1 Marine Raiding Squadron Royal Marines." Seizure and lengthy occupation of ground is specifically omitted from the definition. The raid's aim, as ordered by Thompson, was to damage equipment, kill or capture enemy troops and quickly to withdraw.[16]

On May 24th, Thompson held an O Group that covered the plan but not the orders for a raid on Goose Green. 2 Para was designated as the raiding force, in part because it was the maneuver battalion nearest Darwin Hill/Goose Green, because, after five days in Sussex Mountain's soggy trenches, Jones' men and their CO itched for action and because use of any other battalion would burden the helicopter lift unnecessarily.[17] 2 Para's CO, Jones, faced an immediate problem: How to get his paras to Goose Green unscathed and, if possible, undetected. Southby-Tailyour and Jones investigated the use of Brenton Loch to ferry troops part of the way, but this option was rejected out of fear that landing craft could not safely navigate the Loch's treacherous sand bars at night. Sufficient lift by helicopter for the fighting platoons was not available. That meant an approach march of 25 kilometers from the battalion's position on Sussex Mountain to Darwin Hill, its military objective. Twenty-five hours of plodding through wind and rain was scarcely an optimal way to prepare unbloodied troops for a next-day battle in strange territory against a well-prepared foe. Yet Jones was not deterred. Even more troubling, the absence of cover from hostile fire necessitated a silent night attack with no artillery support until the attack began. Worst of all, with *Atlantic Conveyor* sunk, enough helicopters to lift the battalion and all its equipment in one evolution simply were not there. If disaster struck and the attack failed, the battalion would in all likelihood be forced to walk out.

On May 25th, miserable weather prevented helicopters from flying in the 3 X 105mm guns with 300 rounds each to Camilla Creek House. A raid without even this minimal support was not possible, and Thompson cancelled the operation once and for all, he thought.[18] He returned to his immediate goal, the seizure of Mt. Kent and provision of the reconnaissance and helicopter lift needed for that attack. Yet Northwood continued to tax Thompson for a lack of picaresque military success: "The people back in the UK started getting impatient and asked me what I was doing. I replied, 'recce-ing Mount Kent, and I can't move the guns to support 2 Para, so the raid on Goose Green is cancelled.' They said: 'You don't need recces for Mount Kent and you don't need guns for Goose Green.'"[19] Northwood heard, but did not heed. Clearly, Northwood still considered the attack against Goose Green to be a raid, a chilly walkabout with shots fired, and not a seize-and-hold action.

Not for the first or last time did Thompson's seniors, out of ignorance about his logistical difficulties and about the exiguous ground mobility for his troops, attempt to force on him unsound military solutions to problems of which they had no direct knowledge.[20] Hardliners from Thatcher's own party wanted action too.[21] Thompson knew in his gut what the desk officers at Northwood ignored. Clausewitz put it best: "The first duty and the right of the art of war is to keep policy from demanding things that go against the nature of war, to prevent the possibility that out of ignorance of the way the instrument works, policy might misuse it."[22] In his defense, it was not that Thompson wished to omit Goose Green from his military plans, but only that he gave it low priority compared to his principal task, the seizure of Stanley. "We had planned to raid Goose Green before 5 Brigade arrived—a battalion raid by 2 Para, with gunfire support, wellie in, duff up the garrison and bugger off, . . . but I couldn't move the guns because we were short of helicopters, so I called the raid off."[23] Throughout the entire war, the loss of *Atlantic Conveyor*, its three Chinooks, five Wessex helicopters and their spare parts and manuals remained the all too nettlesome sub-theme of Thompson's military logic.[24]

On May 25th, a black clad Thatcher announced to the House of Commons that HMS *Coventry* had been attacked and sunk with great loss of life. *Atlantic Conveyor*, carrying Thompson's much needed Chinook helicopters, had also fallen victim to Exocet fire that day. Thenceforth, incompletely understood military facts, adulterated with the need to win the war of public relations, informed Thatcher's cabinet and its decisions. As one minister stated, "We were losing a ship a day and nothing on land was moving."[25] Masters at winning elections in England's shires and cities, Thatcher's circle sunk into near despair at losses that in Britain's other 20th-century wars were the accepted stuff of struggle. According to Alan Clark, "There was a school recommending that all the military commanders be changed, including Woodward."[26] A quick compensatory victory was needed more than it had been a few days earlier. During the dark days of World War II, Churchill muttered to his physician, Lord Moran: "When heads of state become gangsters, something must be done."[27] So it was to be. On May 26th, Thompson was called to the Satellite Communication Terminal at Ajax Bay and told: "The Goose Green operation was to be remounted and more action was required all around."[28] Thompson's 3 Brigade was the sharp end of the British stick and 2 Para was to be its point. No one has ever claimed that Jones wanted to call off the mission.

For Brigadier Thompson, the raid was a politically motivated sideshow extraneous to his mission, but brief and cheap; for Jones, it was a full scale attack, the consummation of an infantry commander's career, even if replete with unknown risks. The possibility of immediate personal satisfaction and ultimate secular reward portended. Yet, from the start, Jones and Thompson decided, planned and executed under a wholly different set of assumptions. Thompson stated: "I decided we would do a raid in order to cause the maximum damage and harassment to the enemy. We weren't actually going to stay there, in accordance with my direction to hit any enemy close to the beachhead prior to the moveout."[29] By contrast, Jones wanted a winnable battle—2 Para standing triumphant on Darwin Hill. That, after all, was what his training and career had been all about.

Even Thompson's small affair, a quick attack and withdrawal, strained his logistical formulations. For example, in order to preserve surprise for the mission against Goose Green, the half battery of 105mm guns and 300 rounds each had to be lifted at night. Only four helos had the necessary PNG glasses needed to fly at night, and these were needed to fly in the recon teams for the very necessary attack on Mt. Kent. Moreover, these four helos were barely adequate to lift the ammunition needed for the raid's noisy phase and to assist the battalion's withdrawal after the smash and grab had ended. Adequate for a well executed raid, they did not suffice to support a full battalion attack, especially one that might find itself in unforeseen and lengthy difficulties. According to a Royal Marine NCO, "[There were] only 2 mortar tubes at Goose Green. . . . I did not realize that they had so little fire support. Fire support is god. With Guns in support they would have soon suppressed those trenches. The 29 Cdo Artillery guys were brilliant."[30]

On May 26th, Thompson's brigade still had received no Concept of Operations, a formal instruction about the war's goal and conduct. 3 Brigade's HQ remained under the impression that further offensive action awaited the arrival of 5 Brigade and the divisional commander Major-General Moore.[31] Nonetheless, acting on Northwood's order of May 23rd to Thompson, his staff had set about the tedium of arranging a boggy march to the ring of stone-riven hills that constituted the Argentine defense of Stanley. A bare three days later, on May 26th, radical change occurred: Northwood, bypassing the divisional commander, Moore—who remained incommunicado at sea aboard *Queen Elizabeth 2*—insisted to Julian Thompson that Goose Green be taken without 5 Brigade's help or even presence. Then there was uninformed caviling from Thompson's reluctantly equal task force commander, Woodward, who wrote in his diary; "The land force will probably bog down (because they always do). . . . They've been here for five days and done f. . . all."[32] This meddling caused enormous disruptions at 3 Brigade's HQ.

Woodward's departure might have hastened the war's end. He is perhaps the only commander during Falklands whose behavior recalled the sad tales of Robert Graves or the savage comedy of Evelyn Waugh. All within 100 days, he acted as though the military arts forbade accuracy and good judgment. After he had insulted his fellow task group commanders, he schemed to land troops on beaches that could not sustain them, to build an airfield with construction equipment that he did not have, to find mines with but one ship that could do so only by sinking and to defend his battle task force against poorly manned Argentine diesel submarines that stayed in port. In Woodward's defense, it must be said that he had reached the rank of Rear Admiral without having participated in a war.

Military plans like those formulated for Thompson's proposed investiture of Stanley have an integrity, a coherence and a rhythm that, once alloyed, contaminate every subsequent event they touch. Even though Jones and 2 Para were more than competent to mount such an operation, the injection of an attack on Goose Green into Thompson's military administration derogated all his subsequent efforts, as the battle's outcome will show. Nonetheless, with his job in the balance, Thompson reiterated 2 Para's mission for the raid that he had cancelled on May 24th: "2 Para is to carry out a raid on Goose Green isthmus to capture the settlements before withdrawing in reserve for the main thrust in the north."[33] A 2 Para junior NCO stated, "We were told that it was in and out. Leave our bergens behind and carry as much ammunition as was possible."[34]

Either the politicians and Fieldhouse's staff were at odds, or Nott, the British Minister of Defense, misspoke when he announced to Parliament on May 24th: "Our forces are now established . . . with their heavy equipment. . . . There can be no question of pressing the force commander to move forward prematurely—the judgment about the next tactical moves must be his and his alone."[35] Whether this statement resulted from the usual political duplicity or honest error must await the frank discussion— that we are unlikely to get—by the parties involved. Here, Nott erred again, for Commandos and Para battalions do not, by definition, carry heavy equipment. What is clear is that Thompson's sensible and simple military plan had been corrupted by forces over which he had no control and were 8,000 miles away.[36]

While Thompson prepared for battle, he fell victim to yet another petty intrigue. "Adm. Fieldhouse spoke to Brigadier Thompson, commanding the brigade in the Falklands. Thompson submitted his plan—to move three units up to the hills west of Stanley while 2 Para 'raided' Goose Green. Gen. Trant took this plan to Adm. Fieldhouse, but advised one change—delete 'raid,' insert 'destroy' the enemy at Goose Green. The CINC agreed."[37] The word "destroy" does not turn up in the plans for Goose Green, and no length of time or assignment of resources is specified. Destroy has quite different meanings to a ground force commander who need only take prisoners to destroy a military capability, and to a naval commander who must sink ships or render them hulks to fulfill the definition. The word inserted another layer of vagueness into Thompson's plans. British Command and Control had left a mission open-ended and confused again, and the monkey fell on Brigadier Thompson's back.[38]

Night relief of an encircled force is the infantry commander's most challenging task. Perhaps next was Jones' mission, a night attack by unbloodied troops on prepared positions, without cover, in wretched weather.[39] The weather was so unpredictable and so awful, in any case, that Jones could not be assured of air support, naval gunfire or even 3 Brigade's 105 guns. Like all commanders since the dawn of warfare, he had to convince his officers and men that the operation would succeed.

The information available to Jones about opposing forces, their equipment, positions and fighting spirit varied widely in quality, quantity and timeliness. Jones' two patrols from C Company reported enemy positions on Darwin Hill, but hostile fire prevented these patrols from approaching near enough to Argentine positions to obtain militarily useful information.[40] From its diversionary raid by forty men during the main landing on May 21st, the SAS had concluded that perhaps one company of Argentine infantry remained on the Isthmus.[41] After being ordered to remount the raid on Goose Green, 3 Brigade's staff gave Jones its very different and grander estimate of enemy forces that he would face on Darwin/Goose Green. Throughout the entire war, Thompson never had good aerial photography, and all used recon data were collected the old fashioned way, by eyeball.[42]

The Argentine order of battle at Goose Green included: two infantry companies of 12 Infantry Regiment; one company of 25 Infantry Regiment; one platoon of 8 Infantry Regiment; one platoon of engineers; and possibly one amphibious platoon. Argentine artillery was thought to be plentiful: as many as six 35mm dual role guns and six 20mm guns plus two 105 pack howitzers.[43] Patrols from 2 Para's C Company had also reported Argentinean positions on south of Boca House and on ring contour 50 in the northwest part of the isthmus.[44] Major Chris Keeble stated: "We reckoned they were about a battalion, so it would be one for one."[45] On the day just prior to the attack, a patrol from 2 Para's C Company captured, by accident, the CO of Goose Green's Argentine reconnaissance platoon, LCDR Morales, who disclosed that the garrison there was far stronger, at least in sheer numbers, than the weak battalion first estimated by the SAS.[46] It is doubtful that any intelligence on Argentine forces would have deterred Jones from executing the attack on Goose Green. Italo Piaggi had known that the British would attack; now C Company's patrol and his own recon team's disappearance told him when.[47]

At that early stage of the war, 3 Brigade owned a patrol master, Major Héctor Gullán, who coordinated all such activity. Yet SAS patrols around

Goose Green had taken priority over 2 Para's own patrols; well and good if the data gained thereby were passed to Jones' infantry companies, but they were not.[48] MOD in London had intercepted Menéndez's communications and constructed an accurate order of battle for Task Force Mercedes, the Argentine group assigned to Darwin Hill and Goose Green, but failed to inform Thompson.[49] Their reasons were trivial and bureaucratic, for, at that moment, the Brigade's intelligence staff lacked the necessary clearances to read intercepted communications. As Jones faced his O Group at 1600 on May 27th, he lacked sufficient intelligence to mount an attack at night on an enemy he had never faced over terrain he had never traversed. Jones thought what he wanted to think about his enemy without knowing what he had to know. In his own words: "If we hit them hard, all evidence shows that they'll crack."[50]

Jones' tension before the attack turned to fury after the BBC announced his forthcoming action against Goose Green. His wrath was understandable but unjustified.[51] His ultimate boss, Margaret Thatcher, had already announced that a breakout from the beachhead was imminent. Bernard Ingham, Press Secretary to Thatcher, added: "We are not going to fiddle around."[52] Remember that the Chief of the Defense Staff, Admiral Lewin, had opined to the press: "We are going to move and to move fast."[53] All this in the face of Thompson's knowledge that 3 Brigade could not move fast on Stanley and had no nearby military target, except Goose Green. Even earlier, the SAS' diversionary attack on Goose Green during the main landings at San Carlos had marked it as an area of military interest. It had a primitive airstrip, fueling from drums and an ill protected ammo dump. Sea Harriers from No. 800 Squadron on HMS *Hermes* had successfully bombed the strip into disuse and, by May 26th, no serviceable Pucarás were based at Goose Green.[54] Why risk very valuable aircraft against an Argentine target unless it had military significance to the British attacker? Given the junta's assumptions that war should perdure until a diplomatic settlement was reached, it was natural that the overall Argentine defense plan for the Falklands should include Goose Green (see Appendix C for the Argentine defense plan for Goose Green/Darwin Hill). It was, after all, the Islands' second largest settlement and the headquarters for a 400,000 acre farm.[55] Indeed, Major Neame, OC D Company, had Camilla Creek House shelled prior to his seizure of that ramshackle structure the night before the main attack.[56]

Keep in mind that, early in April, the Argentine staff and field officers alike posited that the British would attack Stanley, Darwin Hill and

Fox Bay; but they did not know when, which or in what order. A British attack on Darwin Hill was much on Menéndez's mind well before May 27th. Jones' opponent, Lt. Col. Italo Piaggi, the Argentine ground force commander, had spent five weeks digging trenches and defensive positions against an amphibious landing that never occurred.[57] The sixteen or so trenches dug on Darwin Hill were the well designed work of 25th RIM's service company. Although prior to the battle Lt. Roberto Estévez's three dozen men who fought A Company on Darwin Hill had been stationed at the schoolhouse, they had never manned or exercised from the empty trenches. The extent of these positions, the placement of valuable artillery pieces, extensive mine fields, ample stockpiles of ammunition, a garrison second in size to Stanley's and the herding of Goose Green's civilians into the community hall should have tipped any would-be attacker that the settlement's defenders considered military action there to be imminent and inevitable. All said, Goose Green had been openly designated a military location from which, in the Argentine staff's mind, British forces might be disrupted and destroyed. Clearly, only two areas of military interest existed on East Falkland: Port Stanley and Goose Green. Goose Green was the nearest to Thompson's brigade. In another giveaway to scrupulous British coverage, Galtieri's visit to Goose Green, just before the battle, constituted a blessing of sorts that rendered that wretched land's loss of major significance to its defenders, even if Thompson and Jones had not measured the approaching combat there in those terms.

Argentine reasons for fortifying Goose Green were just as improvident as the British reasons for attacking it. The garrison's nominal commander, Brigadier-General Parada, did not participate in the minutiae of planning for Goose Green's defense and remained in Stanley before and during the battle. It is almost certain that Generals Joffre, Menéndez and Galtieri for the chain of command of the Argentine forces decided on May 21st to defend the Falklands principally from Fortress Stanley, and that, thenceforth, Goose Green had the least military significance in what was envisioned as the three fortress notion (Stanley, Darwin Hill and Fox Bay). It was a gimpy lamb sacrificed to gain time for diplomats who failed to find agreement during the conflict, just as they had failed before it. Yet on May 26th, SubLt. Zanela continued the reinforcement and brought in two 105mm pieces by Chinook helicopter.[58]

Suspicious of an impending attack on Goose Green well before the BBC broadcast and the event itself, Menéndez had ordered two 105mm guns from San Carlos to Goose Green and a further two to be shipped from Stanley to Goose Green. These latter departed Stanley on May 22nd, before first light, aboard the cutter *Río Iguazú*, which was promptly discovered by Lt. Martin Hale RN, whose Sea Harrier's cannon fire raked the unfortunate ship and caused it to beach. Later, a rescue party from Goose Green, led by Lt. Centurión, hoisted the two guns from their straits and brought them thither by helo. By May 26, 1982, the day before Jones' O Group arrived, Piaggi had four 105mm guns of which three were reliable.[59]

Argentine defensive efforts were scatty at best. The Argentine staff never did calculate their assets and liabilities on Goose Green. After their victory, paras found extensive heaps of 155mm artillery for the guns that had never arrived to support troops that often dug their foxholes with their helmets. Indeed, 2nd lieutenants just out of school found themselves there commanding line infantry units of uneven quality. Goose Green's retention did not assist Stanley's defense, and drained resources from that effort. Goose Green could be shelled from seaward with no means of reply. It could not be reinforced in size, because the Argentineans had a one-time lift by helicopter of but 175 infantrymen without crew-served weapons, and that only during daylight hours. The garrison could not be evacuated, nor did it have a route over which it could retreat. Simply by being there, the Argentine garrison became a prisoner of location, weather and 3 Brigade's tactical mobility. Piaggi's infantrymen had no place to go but death or British POW cages. No reasonable military man would have sought to take or to defend Goose Green. Right down to the village's sad burial ground, it was a politicians' war.

In forced retirement, Piaggi has argued that he faced 2 Para "in his shirtsleeves." His protests ring hollow. He had many advantages. The bad weather that kept Lami Dozo's Pucarás on the ground also inhibited Harriers' attacks. High winds made spotting fall-of-shot chancy, soft mud diminished the explosive effect of British point-detonated 105mm rounds and, with gusty winds, air burst rounds that are good against men caught in the open were not very useful against dug-in or emplaced troops and guns. By contrast, the Argentine Air Force's 20mm and 35mm direct fire weapons caused the paras considerable distress.[60] Piaggi had adequate time and space for reconnaissance on Jones' approach march, but watching patrols seem never to have formed part of the Argentine military vocabulary. From the isthmus' neck at Low Pass, it is a seven-kilometer march over open ground to Goose Green settlement. A mere two hills over 100 feet in height and slight undulations in the bare ground made cover impossible in daylight.[61]

Yet Piaggi failed to string barbed wire and to lay mine fields covered by artillery fire in order to establish kill zones. Oddly, Argentine infantry did not man Darwin Hill in strength from the outset, although Piaggi had in defense what Jones lacked in the attack—much time to prepare.

Jones' Battle

"There is no such thing as conversation. It is an illusion. There are intersecting monologues. That is all."[62]

Jones had been a successful instructor at the School of Infantry's Directing Staff; his very correct plan was one of scholastic complexity, undue length and, under the circumstances, very nearly incomprehensible.[63] Never a fore-lock-tugging junior officer whose deference toward his seniors barely reached the military minimum, for this, his first battle, Jones shrouded his energetic brilliance in the dusty format of a staff college solution. In elevating Goose Green to the repository of his unfulfilled military dreams, Jones had concluded that the various ganglia of his battle plan would unfold sequentially and on time, as written in his Mission Orders (see Appendix D). Jones craved the correct execution of a brilliant plan, as normal people want air. It is very clear, especially from John Wilsey's fine book, that Jones, although very much in this world, was of a different stamp from most. Jones never knew about targeting by satellite, but he would have at home, defending an Afghan pass in the 19th or 21st century. This time Thatcher was lucky; vanity, ambition and competence all rode the same horse.

All military commanders struggle with uncertainty. Jones' plan posited that little of that existed, or at least none with which he and his men could not cope. As things turned out, his training of himself and of his men and their motivation redeemed a failed paradigm. In fact, the battle was won by stubborn Toms, his Toms, fighting singly or in sections, and not by masterful tactical strokes. When an unusual man is deputed to accomplish a task that is ill-found by anyone's reasoning, very unusual events are bound to occur. Of course, Jones knew this. But the butcher's bill for 2 Para's job turned out high, and he was included. Almost certainly he foresaw that, too.[64]

As combat approached, Rear Admiral Woodward, the battle force commander, was no more prescient than he had earlier been tactful. "My fleet is properly formed. There is the run-up to the big match which, in my view, should be a walkover."[65] 3 Commando's fighting platoons would have disagreed. 2 Para had moldered in its soggy emplacements on Sussex Mountain for five days before yielding them to the marines of 42 Commando. The paras' 14 kilometer slog to their lay-up positions at Camilla Creek farm was not much more comfortable. The farm's out buildings, well outside hostile artillery fire and Argentine outposts, gave a little comfort, but not much. It was not a warm, dry and fully rested group of officers and senior NCOs that Jones convened at 1600 hours on May 27th in Camilla Creek House. Jones had two options for his action against Task Force Mercedes: design and execute a plan of his own making; or advance to contact, i.e. disable, capture or kill the enemy wherever found. Under the latter option, Jones would send his companies forward to seize designated targets and to fight their battles as they found them, while he orchestrated from behind the advancing troops artillery fire, naval gunfire, casevac, ammo resupply and deployment of his battalion's reserve. Jones elected the former. His plan stipulated a six-phase night/day, silent/noisy attack, an elegant formulation that left him control of the operation at the expense of his company and platoon commanders' initiative and discretion.[66] That neither he nor all but a few of his unit commanders had experienced live combat, did not deter him from this unusual complexity.[67] Battles' inadvertencies test the finest and most stable minds. It was as if Jones had thought through the entire battle and concluded that none of the variables, like weather, poor going under foot, enemy capabilities, own casualties or plain bad luck, could alloy the purity and linear unfolding of his elegant construct. Jones never acceded to the suspicion that on the subject of Goose Green there was any wisdom greater than his own. Mud, blood, pain and the grim attentions of British surgeons seem not to have invaded his speculations; he was not a man of nuance. Jones' plan contained a purely military error, too. He stipulated naval gunfire support from a one-gun Royal Navy ship whose fall of shot, because of poor weather, could not be guaranteed to be noted and corrected. An experienced commander would have put that combat asset on his wish list because experience has very frequently shown that single guns do little good on a protracted fire mission. As Jones and his men would soon discover, the devil was in the details.[68]

Jones had one asset coveted by many commanders but enjoyed by few. He commanded a superbly trained battalion of infantry, as well prepared by him and Keeble for the awfulness of war as any group could be.[69] Jones had trained them for 18 months; they were his men and they fit his mold. In spring 1982, 2 Para had been headed for its deployment to

Belize, and its personal weapons were en route thither when its mission changed. The weapons were hurriedly redirected to Ascension Island, unpacked and zeroed in there.

On the trip south, Jones brought his men to the highest state of readiness. Jones did not join his battalion until it arrived at Ascension Island, and Keeble used the interval as acting CO to formulate his command relationships and to put a final edge on Jones' fighting platoons. He equipped his sections with two GPMGs, rather than the usual one, thus giving each section two fire and maneuver units. The Toms had run miles around HMS *Norland*'s deck each day in full packs and boots; each platoon had several men trained to the level of combat medic; Captain Steve Hughes, 2 Para's doctor, acquired a thousand drips to keep the wounded in fluid, and a very realistic, if artificial, arm was bought upon which to practice insertion of needles.[70] As described by Rick Jolly:

> Steve Hughes was a young tiger of an Airborne medical officer. Inspired by the Israeli experience of 1967 and in the 1973 war, he trained his regimental combat medics of 2 Para relentlessly, inspiring them with his personal enthusiasm. He split his medical stores up within the rifle companies as well, ensuring that each man carried a half-litre bag of saline with him—in addition to the extra ammunition and mortar bombs that were part of "first line scales" for combat troops. He also distributed intravenous giving sets throughout these front line troops so that critically important resources would be available to him at the front despite the appalling terrain, lack of any roads and vehicle-based logistic support—and the probability of a battlefield environment in which air superiority was by no means certain.[71]

As a direct result of his pre-planning and innovation, the 64 or so men badly injured at Goose Green survived, despite long delays in getting them to surgery at Ajax Bay. Of course, that resuscitative 'meatball surgery,' so wrongly derided elsewhere, was critical for morale and heroic in itself, but the accolades for this brilliant track record must rest with 2 Para's splendid young medical officer. "The battalion loved and trusted him. They were content to fight (uniquely) a second action (Wireless Ridge) just as long as Doc Hughes was with them."[72] Keep in mind that it was Jones, 2 Para's CO, who put all these measures in play, and that it was Keeble, every bit as much a military intellectual as Jones, who ensured that such prudent preparations got done on the trip south.

For 2 Para, war stores were invaded; new and reliable radio sets were issued and practiced upon. For the voyage south of 8,000 miles aboard *Norland*, small arms exercises, medical training and map reading filled the little time left after physical workouts. The superfluous ornament of Jones' first days in command in Northern Ireland, a 50 mile hike, had been followed in 1981 and early 1982 by hard efforts aimed at building the practices and structures necessary for war. All exercises have a certain artificiality about them, but Jones' and Keeble's were grueling and close to the real thing. Junior and senior NCOs knew their men and their jobs. Jones and Keeble determined that, in the bloody confusion of war, their men would have the soldierly skills to survive and to win. Later in the day, this reliance on military fundamentals prevented defeat and saved lives, too. That the wounded men who arrived at 3 Brigade's surgery, some terribly afflicted, all survived, was due to Jones' insistence on their medical preparation as well as to the unusual fitness they had acquired on the voyage and before.

Jones had assumed command of 2 Para just after 18 of its members had been killed in a terrorist attack on August 27, 1979, in Warrenpoint, Northern Ireland. After taking command of the battalion, he assembled his unit in their gymnasium and promptly ordered the now fabled 50 mile march—almost certainly to impress his men that the new regime was a stern one. Their reaction amid the perspiration was one of quiet indignity that professional infantry, such as they, needed any such show of authority, especially from a CO who was not a badged para officer and who came from a fashionable "county" regiment. Much to his credit, Jones also announced that: "If any member of my battalion retaliates [for the Warrenpoint massacre], I'll have him court-martialed."[73] Jones spent the 18 months before Goose Green injecting a fighting élan that brought his men to a fine edge from their slough of humiliation and loss.[74] It was after his death that his successor Keeble drew from this impalpable substance to win the battle. But make no mistake, the men who triumphed at Goose Green were Jones' men.[75]

Jones from Eton, from a prosperous family and from the directing staff of the British Army's School of Infantry, was not only the commanding officer of Britain's most famous para battalion, but also a candidate member of the British establishment. His father's family had been American, and Jones père had graduated from Princeton.[76] After long residence in Europe when he wrote passable verse and sailed competitively, Jones' father renounced his American citizenship in 1948 to become a British subject. James Bayley, a distant and direct American ancestor, received a degree from Harvard College in 1672 and became a minister loyal to The Book of Common Prayer and later a physician.[77] The first preacher in Salem Village, he was replaced because of his opposition to the hysteria surrounding the Salem Witch Trials.[78] From the later discovery and subsequent sale of a zinc mine in the American mid-west, the family acquired great wealth and played a substantial and unselfish part in Woodrow Wilson's political life. Jones' American ancestors included a famous Roman Catholic bishop, James Roosevelt Bayley, who built churches for Irish immigrants in New Jersey, and several wealthy businessmen who helped to finance President Woodrow Wilson's private life when the fame and glitter there had gone. Jones had no immediate family in the British Army whose alliances in the jungle of service politics might have guided his climb to any military pantheon. He made his own success. Orchestrating the actions, indeed the lives, of 500 professional soldiery grants a supreme satisfaction that only a privileged few can know.

Jones came to 2 Para from the Devon and Dorset Regiment, a heavy infantry unit. Earlier, he had served as Brigade Major with 3 Para, though he was not a badged member of the Parachute Regiment. He was an unusual man by any standard. Brash, forceful and intense, he would not have lacked well-paid employment in any profession. There was nothing pinched about Jones' public or private life. There was the Lotus-7 for racing at Brand's Hatch and the family's boat *Romanel* for maritime excursions. He had the best the world has to offer close at hand. Nothing indicates that he made his career by toeing the army line and no one has ever claimed that Jones played to the mob. That this half-American chose British infantry as his life's work, despite his family's wealth, seemed, at first, an eccentric choice, but was all of a piece with his barely restrained flamboyance. Yet no evidence suggests that he was other than a serving officer more or less content to spend his forty years in the wilderness of military affairs—well armored, of course, with life's richer pleasures. Truth to tell, his high intelligence and enormous energy had found in early life its natural outlet in the study of the military arts and in the practice of his profession. His was a rare spirit, an over-exuberant one in the eyes of some. The mortmain of modesty never fell on his shoulder.

Jones' early years in the army, dotted with petty inadvertencies, did not show promise. One classmate (later a general) judged his beginnings inauspicious and some wondered if he were suitable for a military career. Later, as a middle ranking staff officer, he was not remiss in pointing out his peers' and superiors' inadequacies in a variety of circumstances. Jones did not sniff many flowers; he dispensed his energies to the army and to his family.[79] Jones was not an elusive man; he wore few, if any, masks. This tale concerns the face his men saw on May 27–28, 1982.[80]

While merit and vigor recommended him for high position, his command of so-celebrated a unit as 2 Para seemed inevitable, as much from his birthright as from his talents. Jones was an opportunist, but not in the pejorative sense. His uncompromised core was service to state and family. He beheld a moral code, which stipulated that service to the state by way of the army's combat arm was of the greatest worth. A doctor might do one thing, a teacher another. His kind of service was bashing the Queen's enemies. It is inconceivable that Jones should avail himself of the right to send men into battle without assuming the duty to die at their head. Jones turned on its head Kant's belief that all worth comes from the state. Jones' death and the manner of it gave glory and validity to Queen and country. It takes little imagination to conclude that, at some point in his life, Jones would have faced high drama and little speculative energy to believe that he would have died in the doing.

Jones did not govern 2 Para with serenity. Nothing equivocal or languid invaded Jones' instructions to his men. His great drive, his insistence on meeting the highest standards, his compulsion to involve himself in detail and his reluctance to delegate authority to his officers, made duty for his juniors in 2 Para a desirable, if arduous, assignment. On the slog up Sussex Mountain, just after 2 Para's landing, one young soldier fell out exhausted by the 120 lbs. that he carried. Keeble and the RSM prevented an angry Jones from creating an unnecessary disruption of their primary mission. Compassion for his men seemed never to have matched his own technical excellence. "He ruled with a bull whip," is how Keeble described Jones' reign.[81]

The Culmination

"Life is a trap for logicians. . . . It looks just a little more mathematical and regular than it is. Its exactitude is obvious, but its inexactitude is hidden; its wildness lies in wait."[82]

O Groups (Orders Groups) are spoken military rituals with their own conventions. Commanding Officers add or subtract pieces from this military liturgy according to their own style and the problem before them. O

Groups specify to their audiences of officers and senior NCOs military goals, and describe the assets and methods used to achieve those aims. Some commanding officers shout their plans, while others intone them. If one were to read 100 such at random, it is unlikely he would be rewarded or improved. O Groups normally herald exercises or pantomimes of war. These are periods of intense boredom designed to sharpen military skills, and are usually punctuated by rain, snow, mud, lack of sleep or any combination of the foregoing. They are meant to shore up tribal cohesion and purpose. The astute participant will note who gets things done and whom to avoid when war comes.

At O Groups during combat, COs state to their subordinate commanders their units' goals and the methods, as well as those of the, this time, real enemy. COs' plans, as dispensed at O Groups, are not devised to show cleverness or to satisfy seniors, but to deploy human and materiel assets and to establish procedures for their use. At such times, O Groups become of critical importance. Clarity and intensity of purpose are requisites. The peacetime notions of routine must disappear and there is no room for multiple subordinate clauses or strained metaphors. Lives hang on what is understood or omitted. Always arid, not intentionally sanguinary, sometimes a grim elegance emerges. Repugnance at the prospective bloodletting is not done because, in most cases, the listeners are professional soldiery who have volunteered to be present. Implicit in any CO's O Group are a bet and a promise. A bet that he can win the fight, and a promise to his men that he has done everything possible to ensure the mission's success with the fewest casualties.

Jones' O Group, his first in combat, was a brusque and scanted affair as he stipulated his intentions for the attack on Goose Green. Jones had never set foot on Goose Green nor even seen it. He had no aerial photographs of the area and poor maps. Neither he nor his men had ever marched at night into the attack across the troublesome tufted grass, where a careless step could break an ankle. He knew less about his axis of attack than Wellington at Waterloo or Grant at Vicksburg. He had never seen a jumble of scattered limbs and disemboweled bodies.[83]

Jones had scheduled his O Group at 0900L on May 27th, but set the time forward to 1500L out of his rage at the BBC for its lightly veiled disclosure of his intentions. "If any of my fucking men die, I'm going to personally sue him [John Nott] and the Ministry of Defense."[84] However likely that Jones' remarks may have stemmed from honest exasperation as well as genuine rage, his administrative armory did not contain habits of cool moderation nor did he understand that, under the law, stupidity, however egregious, does not provide grounds for legal action. Besides, the Admiral of the Fleet had stated: "We are going to move and move fast. You can expect a great deal of activity in the next few days."[85] An Argentine recon team had been captured, and its debriefing gave Jones the best hard data yet on his target. Jones' anger at his leaders' leaks and whatever else may have suggested a British attack on Darwin Hill was unjustified; nothing of the sort forewarned the Argentine ground forces that an attack would occur specifically on May 27th. The conglomerate of Argentine generals who sent Piaggi his marching orders considered the BBC's disclosure a *ruse de guerre*, and that is certain.

Nonetheless, unbeknownst either to Jones or to Thompson, Argentine staff appreciations had determined, after the passage of UN Resolution 502, that the British would fight on the ground, that Stanley, Darwin Hill and Fox Bay would be attacked and that they should be fortified against British military efforts.[86] Nothing that Thompson, Jones, Northwood or Thatcher's war cabinet did or said changed that view or the Argentine military decisions that sprung from it. After the garrison's buildup was completed on April 21, 1982, Galtieri himself visited the base. To convince the Argentineans further that British ground action threatened that base nearest 3 Brigade's lodgment, two RAF GR-3 Harriers had attacked Goose Green and, on a second run, Squadron Leader Iveson's Harrier was shot down by the 35mm Oerlikons that were later to cost the Toms so much blood.

It was only at this late time that Jones learned the approximate size of his fighting opposition: roughly eleven platoons and three guns, about the size of his attacking force. Few of 2 Para's officers dared ask questions in the face of Jones' obvious impatience. Just as well, because Jones had few answers beyond the stern insistence of his own plan. Several officers felt it necessary to remain after the briefings to secure vital details from Jones' Operations Officer, Major Miller. Jones' Intelligence Officer, Allan Coulson, was made to hurry his own brief into near incoherence.[87] Jones' plan reads clearly after twenty years, but to the cold and wet officers and NCOs drying out for a few hours in that primitive farmhouse, his clarity and precision were not so apparent. Pulses did not quicken at this verbal display of Jones' tactical brilliance.

No evidence exists that Jones' subordinate commanders were told or knew that, unless they fulfilled the tight schedule laid out in the O Group, their troops would face, without cover, artillery fire from at least three guns. Jones had not, prior to that time, discussed his plan with his subordinates or, as far as is known, taken counsel with anyone else.[88] No fractious junior officer asked questions whose answers might have troubled; no fever swamp of discussion had offered alternative approaches to the attack. No sullen mutterings counterpointed Jones' certainty. It was a one-man construct and there was nothing pallid in his orders or in their presentation. No heretical emendations clogged Jones' composition. Commanding officers risk all in their plans, for nowhere else is an idea reified as quickly and as plainly as in combat. Jones was to maintain control over the flow of information and of movement at the expense of his officers whose units did the fighting.[89] The single known exception to Jones' reticence was his proposal to Southby-Tailyour that 2 Para be ferried up Brenton Loch, thus saving half the foot march. Uncertain navigation there at night and the grave risks to Southby-Tailyour's boats foreclosed this option.[90]

On May 27th, Jones would send his unbloodied men over unknown territory against poorly calculated opposition in order to fulfill a plan that few others, if any, understood.[91] Commanding officers do more than manage human and materiel assets; they must inspire. Even here, a fine balance exists between Cassandra and Pollyanna. In this critical matter, Jones did not excel, even if his men did admire and respect him. He drained this capital boldly. Neither did Jones proffer the possibility of diminished returns: "All evidence shows that if the enemy is hit hard he will crumble."[92] The bravado was sincere and real enough, but the facts to support it were absent. Jones never mentioned, for example, that the Rapier Missiles that were meant to protect his troops and the beachhead were sighted optically and not by the Blindfire radar. In action, the missiles proved ineffective. Jones' plan, precious in its detail, milked dry the sterile Warminster format of battle. Absent was a stipulation to his men of what he did not know.[93] In fact, as the briefings drifted down to the sections, the men in A Company, at least, were given to understand they faced about two infantry companies and that 2 Para would be plentifully supported by mortars, artillery and naval gunfire.[94]

A dramatic victory at Goose Green would have whisked Jones onto the front pages as no young officer had been since World War II, and he knew it. Yet he did not seek public accolades in the conventional sense; he already had most that any man could want by way of family, position, education and wealth. He was not a would-be General on a white horse. Indeed, nothing heritable inclined Jones toward a military life. His soldier's life could almost be said to have gotten in the way of his family life, and not vice versa. He annoyed many, but his unfeigned exuberance kept him and those around him safe from boredom. Almost certainly, Jones craved the chance to meet or to exceed the high standards that he had set for himself, and to fulfill a destiny or to achieve a myth that had vexed him all through his career. Affection for army life, an obsession for order and unabashed self-interest made for a commanding officer around whom unusual events were bound to happen once the firing began. Jones had suggested, at least to one fellow officer, that he might not survive this, his first battle. Perhaps, as the true warrior that he was, he had keened the fates and they had tapped him on the shoulder. After all, in Beowulf, the earliest poem in the English language, the poet writes: "no easy bargain would be made in that place by any man. . . . He was sad at heart, unsettled yet ready, sensing his death. His fate hovered near, unknowable but certain."[95]

Most troubling of all, Jones' mission statement to his company commanders departed from Thompson's orders to him and said: "2 Para is to capture Darwin and Goose Green."[96] Goose Green was ancillary to the push on Stanley. No one, from 3 Brigade's staff to the dimmest Lance-Corporal in the Logistics Brigade, believed that Jones' management of a battle at Goose Green and a victory there would be, in Clausewitz's words, a "culminating point of victory," or, in 21st century language, a "war winner." On the other hand, it is difficult to avoid concluding that Jones understood that his defeat at Goose Green would almost certainly stop the war. He also knew that the victories on Mt. Harriet, Mt. Longdon and Tumbledown, bloody and brilliant as they turned out, still had to be won before Stanley was to be taken. The differences among Northwood's order to Thompson, his directive to Jones, his orders to his men and what the Toms knew as their mission seem, even at this remove, enormous. One junior NCO remembers: "It was to be an advance to contact. . . . A silent night attack, in and out. No mention of capture, raid or sustained battle. We dumped bergens and went in battle order, carrying as much ammo as possible."[97]

No evidence has since been brought forward to show that Jones informed his superior of changes that he made from the orders given to him. Adkin stated: "I have seen an extract from 3 Commando's situation report for the afternoon of the 27 May, which makes it plain that it was the intention of 2 Para to withdraw after an attack on Goose Green and Darwin airfield."[98] How Jones' assignment got repackaged without Thompson's knowledge and approval remains hidden. This transparent deviation from Thompson's stated intentions metamorphosed a simple, if chancy, ground operation into high drama and the stuff of military legend. A slim possibility exists that the mission order was renegotiated with Thompson, on the flimsy basis that "Raid" is not included in the Parachute Regiment's lexicon as it is in the Royal Marines' vocabulary and practice. Yet nothing baroque emerged from Jones' plan itself; in it, he reverted to the pedestrian lines of a well-trod school solution. At that moment, there was no artifice about Jones and none about his plan either. A few have criticized Jones as an unprofessional hothead. In fact, Jones showed himself as a most conservative by the book infantry officer, sorely tried when a critical part of his plan went awry through no fault of his own. After Jones' death, one of his NCOs, Staff Sgt. Phil Collins, commented: "He was the best, the very best."[99] He followed a received creed—seldom a useful idea for the very intelligent—and he paid up.

Blood Time

"A victory is very essential to England at this moment."[100]

Each para company had multiple tasks to execute within each phase of Jones' plan. Note that the entire battle was to occur before first light at 0746, and that any combat after that hour would take place without cover and within visual range of Argentine guns. After Jones' plan was briefed in its diluted and hurried form to the troops who would make the attacks, they knew little more than that they were to find and kill as many of the enemy as possible and as quickly as possible. And that was just the way it would turn out.

A word here about Piaggi's plan and estimate of the situation.[101] Jones' anger at the BBC's alleged disclosure of the attack was needless because, as noted earlier, Piaggi considered it a *ruse de guerre* and made no moves to counteract it.[102] John Nott credited Thatcher's staff with the leak, a bit of spin, perhaps, to show the British public that the unseen military hand was tirelessly at work. Four Argentine 105mm howitzers of little utility did arrive before the combat began. Their delivery had been planned weeks before the battle, had nothing to do with the imminent British attack, and did not prove that Piaggi knew that the British were about to attack. Task Force Mercedes did receive some troop reinforcements before the impending battle, but not because of it. Keep in mind that the Argentine High Command had already designated Darwin Hill as one of three strong points that the British were certain to attack, and circulated a staff appreciation to that effect well before Jones' attack.[103] The paras lying up around Camilla House after their miserable stumble from Sussex Mountain did hear Huey and other helicopters flying about, but none threatened Jones' platoons. On that frigid evening, an even moderately competent attack would have found the exhausted paras "cold, stiff and switched off."[104] It can be flatly stated that no military event occurred before May 27, 1982, at Goose Green that could be ascribed to the BBC's ineptness. The War Cabinet's desire to show a hungry public that flamboyant success lay just around the corner is another matter.

Here, it is helpful to recapitulate Argentine reasoning and the actions derived therefrom. The passage of UN Resolution 502 had convinced the junta that military action was inevitable and, as a consequence, the junta ordered the islands fortified.[105] Gen. Daher's order of April 7, 1982, established three strong points: Stanley, Darwin Hill and Fox Bay. Thatcher's inflammatory rhetoric and the tumultuous dispatch of the British task forces incited both the British public and certainly the Argentine military staffs. Reinforcements began to flow into the islands and, by April 15th, Goose Green, now Military Air Base Condor, housed Pucará ground attack planes and Chinook transport helicopters. A small contingent of Argentine troops was meant to garrison Goose Green air field, but, by May 27th, the entire 12th Infantry Regiment (in numbers a large battalion) had landed along with an anti-aircraft artillery unit, three 105mm pack howitzers and the usual superfluous persons who have seemed, since the dawn of warfare, to have attached themselves to bodies of fighting troops. Two of the howitzers had been rescued from the wrecked *Río Iguazú* that Harriers had strafed and disabled on May 22nd.

Before the landing at San Carlos, Piaggi had built an ill equipped and undermanned defense against a British attack from the sea. Mines were laid on the beaches against ships whose draft would have prevented their approach, let alone their landing. For all this, for defense from an attack by sea or by land or against an assault on the air strip, Piaggi had 111 Brigade, a few well trained infantrymen from various parent units commanded by their inexperienced junior officers, no heavy equipment and a rickety command and control system that would not have allowed sound deployment of more troops in any case.[106] Piaggi's fighting troops numbered no more than 700 men.

The misshapen conglomerate designed to man and to defend Goose Green was named Task Force Mercedes. Piaggi had no ground transport or helo lift integral to his unit. Just as well, because he had no room to maneuver. He had already stored plentiful supplies for the weapons on hand, but few experts in their use, and stacks of 155mm rounds for the big guns that were never delivered to him.[107] On the other hand, Piaggi's 30mm Oerlikon anti-aircraft guns and 20mm Rheinmetal guns, anti-air artillery pieces from A Battery of the 4th Parachute Artillery Group, were well manned. Firing over open sights, they caused havoc among the paras from the start. In total, he had 11 fighting platoons from different regiments, perhaps slightly more than he faced in 2 Para.[108] Approximately 1,000 others, most non-combatants from the Argentine Air Force whose planes had flown off or been destroyed, consumed food and attention to their military deployment.

Like Thompson, Piaggi received inane orders from his seniors. Just before 2 Para attacked, Headquarters Stanley ordered Piaggi to move his defense line north to the isthmus neck beyond the mine fields that he had installed, thus removing any hope of a well prepared killing zone. He had but two radios, an absurdity in any combat; such messages as were sent arrived by runner.[109] Piaggi's platoons did have some excellent night sights, snipers who took a substantial toll of paras and a number of .5 MGs that outranged the British GPMGs. He built roofed trench lines, impervious to all falling shot, even from *Arrow*'s 46 lb. rounds that gave his troops admirable shelters from which to engage British attackers. He had opted, perhaps out of necessity, for a static defense, but had not established Darwin Hill, the highest point, as a wired and mined position covered by his three 105 pack howitzers. A fourth howitzer was not operable and Headquarters Stanley declined to fix or to repair it. That main line of Argentine resistance came into existence almost by accident as the battle began.

Oddly, Piaggi had earlier failed to install any mine fields ringed with wire and covered by his plentiful artillery that would have diminished 2 Para's already limited capability to maneuver. Neither had he planned a mobile defense. After the fight began, Piaggi's defense lost what little coherence it had, as platoons and companies moved willy-nilly in response to British fire and movement. In the end, the Argentine platoons had nowhere to go except to slouch toward their ever-shrinking perimeter around the community hall and airfield. In the confusion, approximately 35 of Lt. Estévez's under strength C Company from the 25th Argentine Infantry Regiment, mostly 18- or 19-year-old conscripts, stumbled into the prepared but empty positions on Darwin Hill. Those men, present since April 3rd, had seen the trenches built, but had never exercised from them or the covered positions on that low mound. Ironically, it was the lack of Argentine tactical integrity approaching chaos that in no small way induced the dispersion of 2 Para's fighting units and set the stage for A Company's travail on Darwin Hill.[110] It was a motley and undertrained but very expectant crew that would face 2 Para.

It is also well to recapitulate the British situation as it existed above Jones' level of command just before he made his attack on Darwin Hill. It was clear that his own government did not lend him unanimous support, even if the cities and shires cheered on their men at arms. America, in the persons of the U.S. Senate, Lehman, Weinberger, Haig and the working military supported him, and in a real way sheltered him from the bleatings of Benn, Hart, et al. At least a few of his own army's nabobs in England considered the war a losing proposition. Woodward, the battle force commander, showed little understanding of the logistical needs of the troops ashore and of workable defensive measures against an air force of the second rank. *Canberra*, with its 90,000 meals, surgical supplies and tons of the oddments of war, was stationed most of each day and night far from the fighting. As the war wore on, *Canberra*'s positioning offered a classic case of diminished returns. 3 Brigade's main supply dump had just been bombed, but beyond the materiel destruction, five British had been killed and seventeen wounded. HMS *Fearless* and its handy refueling spots for the Sea Kings left San Carlos early each day for ultra safe lodgment northeast of San Carlos, despite the evaporation of the diesel sub threat and the defeat of the Argentine Air Force.

Jones' CO, Julian Thompson, and his close professional friend Lt. Col. Michael Rose of the SAS, opposed the attack, each for different and valid reasons. Jones had never seen combat, he knew next to nothing of the terrain over which he would fight opponents, whom he did not know, and worse, his troops arrived at the start line exhausted and wet, as they would remain until war's end. His support from heavy guns did not exist. And, as it turned out, his opponent had dug well-sited positions with good fields of fire that were proof, except for a lucky shot, against all the guns at Jones' disposal. At least in his own mind, Jones was playing loose with his mission's orders from Thompson. If 2 Para got in trouble, there were not enough helos to pluck them from harm. A defeat at Goose Green would almost certainly stop the war and end Thatcher's premiership.[111] His own career would languish if not die. Jones knew most of these facts and sensed the rest. He could have been excused for questioning the utility of the job; instead he showed a zest for battle that resonates even today. Cold, hungry and wet, Jones stood as the military virtuoso, pitted against the constraints of fate and the flawed humanity of those above and beneath him. It was a very secure and confident officer who faced his men that dreary afternoon.

The night of May 27, 1982, began clear, cold and dry. C Company departed its position near Camilla Creek House at 2200 to secure and fix the start line for the rifle companies. Awful weather, absence of decent maps and lack of familiarity with the terrain delayed fixing the start line, and it was only Lt. Connor's three very wet and frustrated paras who finally, and by luck, secured that line at about 0100 on May 28th. Confusion struck straightaway when Neame's D Company found itself forward of Jones' TAC HQ, and received corrective advice from 2 Para's clearly offended CO. Mortar section remained well back on the Isthmus, machine guns and snipers on the western edge and Milans at the neck, well behind, and of no immediate use to the fighting platoons. A half battery of 105mm guns with nine hundred rounds remained near Camilla Creek House.

A Company had, under Jones' plan, three physical objectives: Burntside House, Coronation Point and Darwin Settlement. The first was Burntside House. Direct fire onto that target from HMS *Arrow* was tardy, and compelled A Company to set off at 0635, 35 minutes late. At 0727, after intense fire from the paras and no casualties of its own, Major Farrar-Hockley's company secured the position.[112] As it turned out, Burntside House had never been a permanent Argentine defensive outpost, only a stopping point for patrols; its normal inhabitants were four Kelpers and a dog. A few Argentineans were probably hit as they fled the immediate area. Indeed, two were later found dead nearby. This first assault cannot be considered a military success, because A Company had not overcome any hostile fire. One thing was certain: the bombardment from HMS *Arrow* destroyed any illusion of the "Silent Attack" posited in Jones' mission order.[113] Piaggi and his men were certainly alerted many hours before first light on May 28th.

Before the attack on Burntside House, Jones asked A Company for a sitrep, but, finding no officer for 15 minutes, ordered the officer responsible for this lacuna, the 2 i/c of A Company, Captain Dent, to carry the radio himself.[114] Why Jones demanded a sitrep when A Company was about to engage, rather than waiting until after the attack, seems premature and unnecessary. Why Jones humiliated an officer in public, rather than waiting for a private moment to vent his spleen, seemed needlessly petulant, as that officer was about to enter what all present believed would be hard combat.

B Company, under Major John Crosland, the sole troop leader in 2 Para to have had combat experience, pushed off just after 0700 for Burntside Hill. His briefing to his men was short and limited. Crosland's platoons were implicitly ordered to fight the enemy wherever found, and to maintain momentum even at the expense of a pristine orchestration of their advance.[115] The physical target remained seizure of Burntside Hill.

Crosland's platoons found empty trenches during their initial advance. HMS *Arrow*'s fire and the certainty of a British attack had induced Argentine Lt. Manresa to remove to safety his A Company, plus part of the 12th regiment's recon platoon. Shortly, though, Crosland's 5 and 6 platoons encountered effective fire and dug out the Argentine positions one by one in section attacks that became the hallmark of the war. By the time that Burntside Hill was taken—with no British casualties— Crosland had lost contact with his scattered platoons.[116] Yet the momentum achieved by the section and platoon leaders carried B Company well beyond its primary objective, Burntside Hill, and onto Coronation Ridge. With the aid of a strobe light and flares, Crosland reunited his men and got them and himself back onto the axis of attack.[117] Crosland's ability to yield control of the action to his fighting platoons stands in marked contest to Jones' insistence that every turn in the action demanded his specific approval. By dawn, neither A nor B Companies had met serious opposition, but no British unit was closer than three kilometers—or three hours of travel across country—from Goose Green settlement. Jones' unrealistic timing had fallen two hours late. The sun rose at 0746 and set at 1559 that day. No sheltering darkness, only fog and rain remained and the Argentine artillery began its work.

D Company, under Major Phil Neame, saw the first hard fighting and took the first casualties. At about 0700 Jones visited Neame, and himself reconnoitered forward of D Company. After being fired upon, Jones returned to Neame and ordered him to attack enemy positions on a hill of whose precise location neither had a firm idea. The dark and rain precluded Neame from estimating distance and form: "I had very little idea as to exactly where this hill was or where the enemy were on it."[118] Because Jones had given an order outside the scope of his plan, Neame simply ordered an advance to contact. 12 Platoon cleared the Argentine trenches in section attacks, but not before taking fire from B Company. Quite unexpectedly, Neame's rear right 10 Platoon under Webster took intense fire that pinned down the entire unit. Darkness and the confusion of battle prevented Webster from contact with his sections. Nevertheless, when the fire slackened, Webster and one found section cleared enemy trenches by grenades. Webster later stated: "I'd like to say it developed through clever thought and training, but it just kinda happened. . . . We just knew what needed to be done. . . . We had no alternative but to go forward."[119]

In cresting the hill, 11 Platoon, under Waddington, came under very heavy machine gun and rifle fire from a hitherto unmarked Argentine position. Here, Neame's D Company suffered its first casualties: 1 wounded and 2 killed. The Argentine positions, many well found and roofed, others mere hollows in the ground, were probably planned for a two platoon defense, although, after the engagement, Waddington estimated the opposition at under that number. Some Argentineans, a minority, fought well; others cowered in their holes or fled. That was understandable; they were mostly recalled conscripts. It should be emphasized that from first light, many Argentine infantry, as opposed to those who manned the guns, wandered about the battlefield, some to fight, some to nest in whatever deep holes were empty. At least 20 lay dead in this small part of the battlefield after the shooting stopped. In this instance, Neame's outnumbered infantry fought a section leader's war, trench by trench and grenade by grenade, without their officers' lead and unencumbered by Jones' plan. Precise control of the battle by Neame, the OC, proved impossible. Unity of purpose and hard training compensated for this deficit.

By 0730, all of 2 Para's companies had seen action. About 0645, Corporal Camp's section had advanced into the reentrant that was to pen up much of A Company that morning. It came under very heavy fire, but in the gloom the Argentine infantry fired high and Camp's men went to ground. Hardman's section followed, and a few Royal Engineers joined them. Farrar-Hockley's TAC HQ arrived and, at sunup, approximately 60 men of A Company found themselves in the reentrant where steady Argentine fire from Lt. Estévez's men—probably no more than 35 at the scrap's beginning and, as the stragglers drifted in, about 90 when the position fell—stopped the paras' advance. Jones' plan was now at least two hours behind schedule, first light (about 0746 that morning) had passed, and his fighting platoons were kilometers away from Goose Green.

Notes

1. "Darwin and Goose Green did not lie on the route I intended to take and any effort in that direction would be a diversion from that aim." Julian Thompson, *No Picnic: 3 Commando Brigade in the South Atlantic, 1982* (London: Cooper, 1985), p. 78. More accurately named "The Battle for Darwin Hill," the term Goose Green will be used here. The stop in London is called Goose Green.

2. Then Major Chris Keeble, 2 i/c 2 Para, in The Sunday Times Insight Team, *The Falklands War* (London: Sphere Books, 1982), p. 219.

3. The Pucará has a tricycle landing gear. At full load its nose tends to burrow in soft going. Several Pucarás crashed on takeoff.

4. This battle has given rise to significant contention; even the facts are not agreed upon. Frost claims 250 Argentine dead. John Frost, *2 Para in the Falklands* (London: Buchan and Enright, 1983), p. 100; Max Hastings and Simon Jenkins, *The Battle for the Falklands* (New York: Norton, 1983), p. 251; and Mark Adkin, *Goose Green* (London: Orion Books, 1992), p. 55, had difffering figures. A distinguished Argentine historian has given the author a figure of 55 dead and that is probably low.

5. See Sir Nicholas Henderson, *Mandarin* (London: Weidenfeld and Nicolson, 1994), pp. 461–475, for the self-interested dithering that characterized British Ministerial discussions about the war and America.

6. John Nott, *Here Today Gone Tomorrow* (London: Politicos, 2002), p. 311.

7. Richard Halloran, "British Supplies," *New York Times,* April 30, 1982, p. 1.

8. Henderson, *Mandarin,* pp. 462–263.

9. Quoted in John Wilsey, *H. Jones VC: The Life and Death of an Unusual Hero* (London: Hutchinson, 2002), p. 248.

10. Lord Runcie, "Special Report, The Thatcher Era," *The Guardian,* Nov. 29, 2000, p. 1.

11. Major-General Moore, Lecture by British Commanders on "The 1982 Falklands Campaign," National Defense University, Washington, DC, November 19, 1982.

12. "Wilson wanted my BV 202s, I wouldn't give them to him." Author's interview with Major-General Thompson, November 1997.

13. See comments by the participants of "Exercise Welsh Falcon." *Honor Regained,* in *Britain's Small Wars,* www.britains-smallwars.com.

14. Major-General Moore, Thompson's legitimate senior, was incommunicado aboard *QE2.* Northwood gave Thompson his orders in violation of the chain of command it had established and of military common sense.

15. Thompson, *No Picnic,* p. 74.

16. John Wilsey claims that, from the outset, a raid was not intended. His evidence almost convinces to the contrary. On May 29th, Keeble received an order from Brigadier Thompson to keep 2 Para in Goose Green once it was secured. This order would not have been necessary if Thompson's original intention had been: "To seize and hold." See John Wilsey, *H. Jones VC: The Life and Death of an Unusual Hero* (London: Hutchinson, 2002), p. 255 et seq.

17. To this day, several of 3 Brigade's staff believe that from the start Jones had pestered Thompson for orders to attack Goose Green.

18. On hearing of the cancellation, Jones remarked: "20 years I have waited for this and now some fucking marine has gone and cancelled it." Frost, *2 Para*, p. 54. Jones had apparently forgotten that it was the f... marine who had gotten 2 Para unscathed to East Falkland. Whatever his deeper motives, Jones strove for a tactical victory that had no immediate military relevance to the seizure of Port Stanley.

19. Robin Neillands, *By Sea and By Land* (London: Orion, 1996), pp. 398–399. 2 Para's infantrymen would probably not have been amused to learn that their personal weapons and two mortars could, in Northwood's view, take Goose Green against Argentine 105mm artillery and 20mm and 30mm guns.

20. For example, 2 Para's mortar platoon saw its Land Rovers remain aboard ship for the war's duration. This deficit meant that their ammunition was either portered to the firing pits or took up precious space on the Sea Kings.

21. Julian Amery nudged his Prime Minister: "We must, as soon as all preparations are ready, proceed to the next step as soon as possible." *New York Times*, April 22, 1982.

22. Carl von Clausewitz in Peter Paret, *Clausewitz and the State: The Man, His Theories and His Times* (Princeton, NJ: Princeton University Press, 1985), p. 369.

23. Neillands, *By Sea and By Land*, p. 398.

24. Again, the lack of adequate staffing bedeviled Thompson. A senior air officer would have ordered all helos off *Conveyor* as soon as they were within range of land. Hitting multiple targets in the air or on the ground poses a far greater targeting problem for an enemy than destroying one ship with the targets aboard.

25. Hastings and Jenkins, *The Battle for the Falklands*, p. 254, quoting an unidentified minister.

26. Alan Clark, *Diaries* (London: Weidenfeld and Nicolson, 1993), p. 219.

27. Winston Churchill, quoted in Lord Moran, *Dairies of Lord Moran* (Cambridge: Riverside Press 1966), p. 13.

28. Thompson, *No Picnic*, p. 81.

29. Thompson quoted in Michael Bilton and Peter Kosminsky, *Speaking Out: Untold Stories From the Falklands War* (London: Andre Deutsch, 1989), p. 227.

30. Email correspondence between author and Royal Marine NCO dated February 2001.

31. Ewen Southby-Tailyour, *Reasons In Writing: A Commando's View of the Falklands War* (London: Leo Cooper, 1993), p. 232.

32. Admiral Sandy Woodward with Patrick Robinson, *One Hundred Days: Memoirs of the Falklands Battle Group Commander* (Annapolis: U.S. Naval Institute, 1992), pp. 300–301.

33. *Benest Manuscript*, a transcript written by then Captain Benest, 2 Para's communication officer, of the 3 Brigade's sitrep, 27 May 1982, p. 55, quoted in Adkin, *Goose Green*, p. 147. Two junior NCOs told the author that they were to carry as much ammo as possible and medical packs to the exclusion of all else because it was to be an " in and out" operation.

34. Email correspondence between author and 2 Para junior NCO dated February 2002.

35. *The Falklands Campaign; A Digest of Debates in the House of Commons 2 April to 15 June 1982* (London: HMSO, 1982), p. 309. Here comes to mind the fictional Lord Copper, a newspaper owner in Waugh's *Scoop*, 1938: "I never hamper my correspondents in any way. . . . Remember that the Patriots are in the right and are going to win. The Beast stands by them foursquare. But they must win quickly. The British public has no interest in a war which drags on indecisively. A few sharp victories, some conspicuous acts of personal bravery on the Patriot side and a colorful entry into the capital. That is The Beast policy for the war." Evelyn Waugh, *Scoop* (London), 1938, p. 44.

36. Thompson's UK seniors had corrupted his common sense plan. Worse, his negotiating position in the matter was awful. The "force commander," in this case Moore, Thompson's immediate senior in the chain of command, remained aboard *QE2*, unable to communicate with Thompson or Jones. Thompson had no recourse to Thatcher's war cabinet or to any other higher level, except Northwood, unlike Montgomery after the landing in Europe, who habitually whined to Brooke or Simpson about Eisenhower's and his staff's shortcomings. See Nigel Hamilton, *Monty* (New York: Random House, 1994), p. 439. As a tactician, Monty was meticulous and stodgy. "Montgomery . . . risking as little as possible." Erwin Rommel, *Letters* (New York: Harcourt Brace, 1953), p. 395. He was without peer as a trainer of men. Prior to the British evacuation from Dunkirk in June 1940, Montgomery moved his 3rd division of 13,000 men 25 miles laterally at night, on back roads, 2 miles from German lines in order to plug a gap left by the Belgians. Montgomery's hard training enabled tactical brilliance. Here, too, began a professional and protective relationship with Brooke, the best British thinker during World War II, for whom Montgomery fulfilled obvious needs with an odd combination of stingy and flamboyant military competence. As commander of 8th Army in North Africa, he corralled 50,000 deserters and malingerers who had withdrawn from war to hang about Cairo and Alexandria, and turned them into useful military assets. Later, as NATO's military commander and with George Patton dead, Montgomery turned his anti-American animosity from the general to the particular when he stated to Denis Healey: "He needed only two American soldiers under his command—one for the Russians to kill when they crossed the frontier, and the other to kill if the Russians missed the first one." Denis Healey, *The Time of My Life* (New York: Norton, 1990), p. 162.

37. Christopher Dunphie, Letter to the *Daily Telegraph*, January 17, 2002.

38. Great confusion existed among the British politicians at home on what to do and how to do it. John Nott, the defense minister on whose watch the Falklands were lost, wrote about Thatcher's Mr. Ingham: "Bernard was a constant nuisance throughout the Falklands campaign—jumping up and down and causing no end of difficulty criticizing the Ministry of Defense on trivial issues. . . . I was determined to keep the press under the tightest Ministry of Defense control and . . . away from No. 10 with its obsession for spin. . . . We had a constant problem trying to prevent Ingham from adding his largely uninformed opinion to the No. 10 spin." See John Nott, *Daily Telegraph*, Arts Section, April 9, 2002, p. 1, and Nott's *Here Today Gone Tomorrow*, p. 263. It is very difficult to judge, even at this

remove, who was the least informed in London during those days, as Thompson, Jones and their colleagues slogged over East Falkland.

39. "I couldn't very well tell them what it was like because I didn't know myself." Major Phil Neame, OC D Company, quoted in Max Arthur, *Above All Courage* (London: Sphere Books, 1986), p. 251.

40. Adkin, *Goose Green*, p. 120.

41. Frost, *2 Para*, p. 39, claims that the SAS concluded after their reconnaissance that: "Only A Company or so of infantry remained on the Isthmus." If this statement were true, the SAS had miscalculated badly again.

42. Thompson, interview and correspondence with author, 1997.

43. Thompson, *No Picnic*, p. 81. In fact, Piaggi had 3 X 35mm Oerlikon guns and 2 X twin 20mm Rheinmetal AA guns from Attack Group 25 whose Pucarás had either departed or been destroyed. The 35mm guns later caused 2 Para, especially C Company, great discomfort. These guns were well served and had plentiful ammunition, much of which remained after the battle.

44. Thompson, *No Picnic*, pp. 82–83.

45. Major Chris Keeble, 2 i/c 2 Para, quoted in Sunday Times Insight Team, *War In the Falklands* (New York: Harper and Rowe, 1982), p. 237.

46. Hastings and Jenkins, *The Battle for the Falklands*, p. 240.

47. See Appendix C for the Argentine defense plan against certain British attack.

48. "The SAS did not go and look properly." Thompson, in Adkin, *Goose Green*, p. 150. Also, conversations with author 1997.

49. Hastings and Jenkins, *The Battle for the Falklands*, p. 252.

50. Jones to his O Group, quoted in Adkin, *Goose Green*, p. 165.

51. "We knew the paras were on the way. We heard it on the BBC World Service." Gerald Morrison, a Goose Green shepherd, quoted in Martin Middlebrooke, *Task Force, The Falklands War* (London: Penguin, 1987), p. 259.

52. Adkin, *Goose Green*, p. 102.

53. Hastings and Jenkins, *The Battle for the Falklands*, p. 254.

54. Designed as a counterinsurgency aircraft for pilot and observer, its three-wheel landing gear and heavy nose made takeoffs from dirt/mud strips hazardous. It had no nighttime combat capability. Several Pucarás crashed on takeoff early in the war. To save weight, the Pucará's second crewman, the observer, was dropped. This meant that the Argentine pilot flew, observed, attacked, navigated, avoided hostile fire and found his way home through bad weather solo, all with rudimentary instrumentation. The Pucarás destroyed only one British helo, piloted by Lt. Nunn RM, the afternoon of May 27, 1982, over Goose Green. That Pucará's wingman, Lt. Miguel Daniel Giménez, flew shortly thereafter into a mountain, where he and his plane's wreck remained undiscovered until 1986. The Pucará did have two engines that let pilots get home if one were disabled. The lack of experienced air intelligence officers on British staffs probably accounted for the undue deference paid this unlikely combat plane.

55. Hugh McManners, *Falklands Commando* (London: William Kimber, 1984), p. 196.

56. Adkin, *Goose Green*, p. 123.

57. Air Commodore Wilson Pedrosa headed the air force contingent at Goose Green and was its senior officer. Many of his personnel were drafted in as ground force. Brigadier-General Parada was ordered to move from Stanley to Goose Green, whose commander he was. Parada did not arrive in time for the battle.

58. Trooper D letter to author, July 21, 2002. This move probably accounts for the helo noises heard during the run-up and reported to the author by several NCOs.

59. Letter from the Sub-Lieutenant Jorge Zanela, July 2002.

60. This Oerlikon gun had three especial virtues: a range of 4,000 meters, a high rate of fire and the ability to shoot 5 degrees below horizontal. Somewhat reminiscent of the German 88mm used in World War II.

61. Oddly, 2 Para's standard personal weapon for assault troops was the 9mm sub-machine gun, less useful in open ground than the Argentine 7.62 FN rifle that the men picked up and used wherever possible.

62. Dame Rebecca West, *A Dictionary of Quotations* (New York: Barnes and Noble Books, 1995), p. 741.

63. See Appendix D for Benest's transcription of Jones' plan.

64. Several have asked the author how the attack on Darwin Hill/Goose Green should have been planned and executed. The answer: Advance to contact; frag orders to follow. Place minimum reliance on naval gunfire as one-gun ships easily falter. Place little reliance on the 105s because their fall of shot cannot be accurately gauged. Scant ammunition exists for the mortars and their shot cannot penetrate bunkered positions. At or before first light, order up the Milans. Maintain momentum, supremacy of fire and unit integrity at all costs; we will be fighting in the dark. Remember, too, we are scorpions in a bottle. Neither of us has anywhere to go. We will walk out if the attack fails. Remember that you are the best light infantry shock troops in the world. The Argentineans have never seen your like.

65. R. W. Apple, "Britain Reported Ready," *New York Times,* April 28, 1983, p. 1.

66. Many British commanders keep their mission orders to three parts because more induces the intrusion of Murphy's Law.

67. Major John Crosland, B Company's OC, had served with the SAS.

68. For example, just before the rounds were to have been shipped forward to Jones' gun positions, an Argentine air raid destroyed the netted cargos of mortar and 105mm ammunition. Lt. Col. Hellberg and his men reacted with great expedition; scarce ammo was scrounged up, re-netted and heloed off in time for the initial fire missions.

69. 2 Para's tour in Northern Ireland was spent mainly in South Armagh with its endless patrols in good weather and bad. Setting up OPs and ambushes and practicing the basic soldierly skills glued small units together and honed their skills far better than a set training schedule.

70. Paras were trained to insert drips through the rectum if arms were mangled. This technique added a new subject to the soldiers' armory of humor, an act many had thought nearly impossible.

71. See Rick Jolly, *The Red and Green Life Machine: A Diary of the Falklands Field Hospital* (London: Century Publishing, 1983), seriatim.

72. Surgeon-Captain Rick Jolly RN (ret), correspondence with author, April 20, 2002. Jolly, the only officer to be decorated by both sides for his skillful and valiant work, labored away under bombs that had lodged unexploded in the roof of his battlefield surgery at Ajax Bay. That surgery was converted from a former refrigeration plant, that had served earlier as the storehouse for beef sold to American whalers on their trips north and south.

73. Trooper A correspondence to author, February 2002.

74. While stationed in Ireland, 2 Para was split into small fighting units, companies, platoons and sections as it patrolled the troubled towns like Bessbrook, Forkhill and Newry. Companies rarely saw each other. Shots were fired and the junior NCOs learned their trade and knew their men. By the end of the tour, morale was sky high.

75. Several paras interviewed for this book claimed that they fought for survival, to get the job done and, foremost, for each other. Of course, Jones as CO encouraged those very motivations to dominate all during his tenure.

76. See Wilsey's fine biography, *H. Jones VC*, seriatim.

77. John Langdon Sibley, *Biographical Sketches of Graduates of Harvard University*, Vol. 2 (Cambridge: Cambridge University Press, 1881), pp. 291–299. Courtesy of Sheryl Steinberg, Connecticut Historical Society.

78. James Bayley (1650–1707) was not a crank. His family arrived from England in 1635 aboard the badly battered ship *Bevis*. His was a respectable clan and not indentured. He graduated from Harvard College and accepted the call to serve as Salem Village's first minister; five of the village elders gave him 40 prime acres there. His first employment was not tranquil, for he was an educated man (Harvard MA) in what was then a rough and often violent frontier village. His reasonable opposition to the nascent hysteria of Salem, the unfairly questioned method of his selection as minister and his adherence to the Book of Common Prayer brought him unyielding enemies in his new parish, yet he was widely respected at large in the Massachusetts colony. Bayley left Massachusetts for Connecticut where he arrived just as "The New Collegiate School" now Yale was founded. Although wisely, perhaps, he appears to have abstained from efforts that would mark him for posterity as a founder of that institution. He returned to Boston, as a physician, and labored assiduously in its public life. In 1694, he was formally assigned a pew in the Roxbury Church, where he cared for orphans and strays. He helped to compose and witnessed the will of Joseph Weld, one of the colony's wealthiest citizens, and served as juror in the Ipswich court. A colleague wrote a heroic poem in his honor as he lay dying from "The Stones" in Roxbury, Massachusetts. He died impecunious and sustained with currant cake sent by his friends, perhaps the last in his line to do either. He was buried, with more than the usual pomp, during a severe storm of sleet and snow in the Elliott Street Cemetery in Boston, Massachusetts. The Governor of Massachusetts, Samuel Sewall, and several other notables attended Bayley's internment by sleigh. Sewall's diaries quote a Mr. Walter who spent Bayley's last night with him: "He answered pertinently, by Yes and No: thought he should dy [sic] that night, of which he was not

afraid." See Samuel Sewall, *Diaries*, Vol. 1 (New York: Farrar, Strauss and Giroux, 1973), p. 561, and the relevant documents in the Massachusetts Historical Society and the Boston Society.

79. Jones wrote 44 letters to his wife and family after his departure from the UK until his death on Darwin Hill.

80. Jones, the man, is best described in Wilsey, *H. Jones VC.*

81. Lt. Col. Chris Keeble, quoted in Adkin, *Goose Green*, p. 20.

82. G. K. Chesterton, *New York Times Book Review*, September 14, 2000, p. 13.

83. Perversely, many great men are risk takers and often appear disinterested in self-preservation. Montgomery worried about history and rivalries, and that concern mated to his high technical competence, consigned him to a bright spot in the British pantheon, but no more. Slim, his back to the wall and starved of resources, thought only about the battle. That habit of the mind coupled with a sensitive touch about combat, right down to his sadly diminished platoons, made him a great general and perhaps even a great man.

84. "I heard Jones rant in the dark." Trooper A, written answer to author's questions, February 2002.

85. Admiral Fieldhouse, *The Observer*, May 23, 1982.

86. See Appendix C for a detailed plan for the Argentine defense of the islands.

87. See Adkin, *Goose Green*, p. 384. Little doubt exists that, before his O Group, Jones wished no one to interfere with or even to know his plans for Goose Green.

88. The intelligence officer's job for any CO or senior is to get into his mind so as to advise him, before the plan is written, on the rocks and shoals that menace. No evidence exists that Jones accepted any such counsel.

89. A poorish *apologia* for Jones' tight control lay in the cramped area over which 2 Para was to fight. The battle was won when B and D Companies maneuvered adroitly around Argentine positions and attacked them from the side and rear. C Company attacked straight into the Argentine guns.

90. Southby-Tailyour, *Reasons In Writing*, p. 219. Jones also discussed with Southby-Tailyour the need for having one's will and private papers in order. The dark significance of this remark lies outside the historian's realm.

91. "I remember at the O group I lost track of it . . . it was very complicated." Major Héctor Gullán, 3 Brigade's liaison officer to 2 Para, quoted in Spencer Fitzgibbon, *Not Mentioned in the Despatches* (Cambridge: Lutterworth, 1995), p. 16. If Gullán failed to understand, how could Thompson and the attacking infantry tumble to Jones' intentions and methods?

92. Jones at the O Group's end, quoted in Frost, *2 Para*, p. 58.

93. The location of the three Argentine 105 pack howitzers that bedeviled British troops went unknown to the British until the battle's end.

94. As the author's discussions and correspondence with 2 Para's men wore on, a subtext emerged: that at Goose Green few cared too much who led 2 Para with what plan, and that the Toms, as professional soldiers, would complete the job even if the present CO, greatly respected as he was, were not a career para. At the end of Jones' briefings, at least one section was given to understand that it was

to be "an advance to contact in and out." Trooper A written answer to author, February 2002.

95. Seamus Heaney trans., *Beowulf* (New York: Norton, 2000), LL 2415–2421.

96. Benest Papers, quoted in Fitzgibbon, *Not Mentioned in the Despatches*, p. 191.

97. Junior NCO present at the Battle of Goose Green. Written correspondence to author, February 2002.

98. Adkin, *Goose Green*, p. 382.

99. Robin Fox, *The Guardian*, June 6, 1982, p. 4.

100. Sir John Jervis before the battle of Cape St. Vincent, February 13, 1797, in Tom Pocock, *Nelson* (London: Pimlico, 1994), p. 129.

101. Brigadier-General Parada, the nominal commander of the Argentine garrison at Goose Green, had declined to join the troops there and remained in Stanley.

102. Lt. Col. Italo Piaggi was junior to the resident Argentine Air Forces' CO Air Commodore Wilson Drozier Pedrosa, but was placed in command of Goose Green's defense anyway. On May 27th, his forces fired on and caused the withdrawal of patrols mounted up the Isthmus by 2 Para's C Company.

103. See Appendix C for the Argentine army's views on the defense of the islands.

104. Trooper A correspondence to author, January 2002.

105. See Appendix C.

106. When later Argentine reinforcements were ferried from Mt. Kent to Goose Green, they were ordered inside the defensive perimeter around Goose Green. They failed to take the offense against exhausted British infantry. Their CO remained on Mt. Kent. Their only military role was to become British POWs.

107. See Barrie Lovell, in *Britain's Small Wars*, www.britains-smallwars.com, for a discussion of inventory of Argentine arms captured after the engagement.

108. "Poor little conscripts . . . not from where I had been sitting." Jim Love, Coronation Point, in *Britain's Small Wars*. Also various letters to author.

109. Piaggi could never have put the much feared reinforcements into battle because he had no speedy way to talk to his tactical commanders and no flexible tactical plan except withdrawal inside a shrinking perimeter. Almost certainly, the only two radios available to Argentine infantrymen at Goose Green were those of Lt. Roberto Estévez, the sole Argentine officer killed at Goose Green, and his link at the battery of 105 pack howitzers.

110. The error that Piaggi's forces outnumbered 2 Para had a long life. It crept into the British Government's official assessment of the war: "by their outstanding performance against a numerically superior enemy 2 Para established a psychological ascendancy over the enemy which our forces never lost." Para. 122, *The Falklands Campaign: The Lessons* (London: HMSO Cmnd. 8752, December 1982). 2 Para was outgunned but not outnumbered.

111. If Jones had lived, not a few of his seniors would have found some cause to despise him for being right.

112. 3 Brigade Log, 28 May 1982.

113. Despite a two-hour hiatus caused by mechanical failure to its single gun, *Arrow* fired 157 rounds that morning before withdrawing.

114. Captain Chris Dent still carried the radio when he was killed a few hours later. It is impossible, at this late date, to determine if the extra weight of the radio hampered Dent as he assaulted the Argentine position.

115. More than a few military commentators have since argued that the entire battle might better have been fought in that way: advance to contact and defeat the enemy.

116. "All three platoons had vanished into the dark, and we didn't have a clue where they were." Captain Young 2 i/c B Company, quoted in Fitzgibbon, *Not Mentioned in the Despatches*, p. 38.

117. Fitzgibbon, ibid., pp. 38–39.

118. Major Neame OC D Company quoted in Fitzgibbon, ibid., p. 44.

119. Shaun Webster quoted in Fitzgibbon, ibid., p. 46.

5

Myth and Truth

Myth: Jones ordered Farrar-Hockley to halt A Company until Jones himself could assess A Company's position.[1] Jones thus yielded two precious assets—momentum and the cover of darkness—because Jones' discovery of A Company took between 30 and 60 minutes. We can never know if Jones understood that his order forewent the chance to assault Darwin Hill in the dark. All the foregoing being the truth if it is believed that Jones, not Farrar-Hockley, stopped A Company's advance.

Truth: Very compelling evidence from interviews with A Company's officers and men who either heard conversations on the command net between A Company and Jones or were present when Jones spoke with Farrar-Hockley, confirms that the opposite is true, that Jones did not stop A Company and that it had halted well before his arrival. Jones' bodyguard was quoted as saying: "They weren't going anywhere, A Company. They wouldn't have got out of that hollow. Yet once the CO got there and instilled his form of authority on them, things started to happen."[2]

It is true that Farrar-Hockley had around him 60 or so distressed paras who were suffering casualties at a fast rate and could not move without the near certainty of being hit. Still, all the verbatim testimony[3] avers that Farrar-Hockley himself had stopped A Company's advance, or what remained of it, before his communications with Jones, and that Jones rushed to A Company in order to move it out under his direct control towards Darwin before first light (about 0746 that day).[4]

Thus began the breakdown of British efforts to seize Darwin Hill, because Jones took about an hour to arrive in the open through fire at A Company's CP. As A Company halted until Jones made his own determinations, what little momentum A Company retained was lost. An NCO from A Company, who was present when Jones arrived, recalled: "The CO then turned up and in his normal, very abrasive manner, and started screaming and shouting and wanted to know why the OC had stopped."[5] 2 Para's battery commander, accompanying Jones, corroborates this story: "The company was stationary. They were all sitting down."[6] Several others, officers and NCOs, spoke similarly. An NCO remembers: "He bollicked the officers and went off."[7] This version, well attested by those present on Darwin Hill from about 0830 on May 28, 1982, contradicts Frost's version in every respect, and shifts responsibility for the halt from a dead man to a live one.[8] Then, too, few have noticed that Jones' plan did not envision taking Darwin Hill, the high ground that, with their mothers' milk, all infantry officers learn to seize and hold whatever the cost. Farrar-Hockley compounded the error by leaving that flank open (his left), while Wallis' platoon sat unengaged on Coronation Point. An experienced adversary would have seized upon this grave error and perhaps thwarted Farrar-Hockley's attack on Darwin Hill entirely. No Darwin Hill, no Darwin; no Darwin, no Goose Green, and none of the moral ascendancy that Moore had rightly craved, and perhaps no more Thatcher.

Although A Company was, just before dawn, face down in the turf a kilometer from Darwin, Jones informed 3 Brigade: "On schedule and approaching Darwin." Neither statement was accurate. Then too, Crosland's B Company, on the isthmus' western side, had fallen at least two hours behind Jones' schedule and had also lost its directions. Crosland had retained his wit, however, and when asked his position by Jones, replied: "400 yards west of the moon, for all I know."[9] B Company was intended to take two positions: Boca Hill and a position at grid 640590 that had never existed or was misidentified. Crosland's three platoons, now attacking Boca Hill in daylight, came under heavy sniper, mortar, artillery and machine gun fire and got bogged down. Some of the fire came from Darwin Hill, which A Company had not, as yet, captured. As described by Crosland: ". . . it was a fairly unpleasant time, I would say . . . 3, 4 hours now, while we were stuck in the wadi bottom, really unable to do a great deal."[10]

As B Company lay immovable in its own muddle, but fairly safe from hostile fire, A Company laid continuous fire onto two trench lines on Darwin Hill. One of these was that hill's major defensive line, and was occu-

Woodes Rogers sailed from Bristol in 1708 with two frigates, *Duke* and *Duchess*. He carried with him letters of marque and the best navigator of the day, William Dampier. In the Pacific, he rescued Alexander Selkirk, thought to be the model for Robinson Crusoe, and at first captured few prizes. Fortune struck and Rogers took the Spanish treasure galleon, *Nuestra Señora de la Encarnación*, whose cargoes were sold Thameside for ?148,000. Dismissive of the Falklands, Rogers then leased Jamaica from the Crown, made himself its governor and pirated handsomely in his own waters. On his infrequent visits to England, he set himself up as a Grand Seigneur and among other perquisites of wealth, had his portrait painted by W. Hogarth. Rogers died in 1732.

Source: National Maritime Museum, Greenwich, London, BHC 2973.

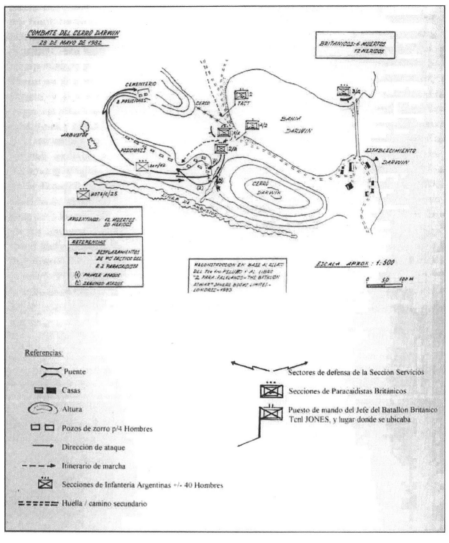

This map was drawn up by Jorge Zanela, an Argentine artillery officer present during the battle on Darwin Hill. He was captured and drew the map soon after the battle ended. This map is the only such of the Argentine view of the battle.

Source: Courtesy of Jorge Zanela.

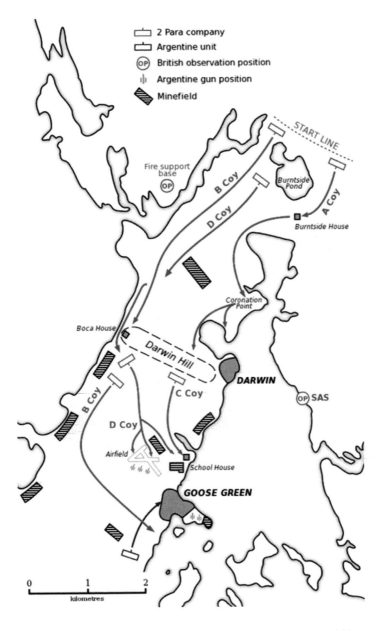

Legend:
- ▭ 2 Para company
- ▭ Argentine unit
- (OP) British observation position
- ⅰⅼ Argentine gun position
- ◧ Minefield

START LINE

Fire support base (OP)

B Coy

D Coy

Burntside Pond

A Coy

Burntside House

Coronation Point

Boca House

Darwin Hill

DARWIN

(OP) SAS

B Coy

C Coy

D Coy

Airfield

School House

GOOSE GREEN

0   1   2
kilometres

Positions and company movements during the battle of Goose Green, May 28, 1982.

Courtesy of British Small Wars.

3

Jones in his CP atop Sussex Mountain before the approach
march to Goose Green.

Source: Imperial War Museum, FKD 2797.

Major Chris Keeble took
command of 2 Para after
Jones died.

Source: Courtesy of Lt. Col. Keeble.

The sole Argentine officer killed at Goose
Green, Lt. Roberto Néstor Estévez.

Source: Photo by Raúl Alfredo Pürzel, courtesy of
Oscar Teves.

Lt. Col. Carlos Braghini, whose firing over open sights at the charging members of 2 Para's C Company might have won the war. An outstanding feat of arms on both sides.

Source: Courtesy of Jorge Zanela.

Compañía C: Depicted in the first row are 1st Lt. Esteban, Lt. Estévez, and Sublieutenants Gómez Centurión, Reyes and Aliaga (the latter of the 8th Infantry Regiment).

Source: Photo by Raúl Alfredo Pürzel, courtesy of Oscar Teves.

The schoolhouse at Goose Green before the war.

2 Para's dead arranged for burial, May 1982.

Source: Imperial War Museum, FKD 1287.

The last goodbye: A Para pauses over a mate's body before its burial.

Source: Imperial War Museum, FKD 116.

Secretary of Defense Weinberger's military department store remained open all during and after the war to supply British forces with the oddments of war that Minister Nott's armory lacked.

Source: Caspar Weinberger.

LCDR John Lehman, a reserve naval officer and later the Secretary of the Navy who opened the spigot for American aid to British forces during and after the war.

Source: Courtesy of John Lehman.

U.S. Secretary of State Alexander Haig speaks to reporters outside No. 10 Downing Street, Margaret Thatcher's official residence, on April 13, 1982, after his third session of talks with Thatcher on the Falklands crisis.

Source: AP/Wide World Photos.

Surgeon Captain Rick Jolly being decorated by Queen Elizabeth II.

Source: Surgeon Captain Rick Jolly.

Thatcher and Reagan out for a stroll.

Sir Anthony Parsons was the British ambassador to the United Nations before and during the war. His adroit management of Resolution 502 that condemned Argentine aggression and called for the removal from the Falklands of Argentine forces gave the British time to assemble a useable military force and the Americans time to gather support for British retaking of the islands.

Source: UN Photo 149,256/John Isaac.

Sir Antony Acland in full fig. So grievous was Acland's blunder in not informing his masters of impending war, that he could not be fired. Later, he became professional head of the British Diplomatic Service, Ambassador to the United States, Provost of Eton College and Chichele Professor of War Studies at Oxford University.

pied by one understrength company, probably Lt. Estévez's three-dozen or so men and some stragglers. The paras' forward movement was stopped principally by effective sniper fire that ultimately killed seven men. One man described it as "organized chaos."[11] Remember that Lt. Wallis' 3 Platoon had been sent around Darwin Pond in order to support the attack on Darwin Settlement, and remained out of the fight. Wallis saw little Argentine activity in the settlement itself and he engaged no enemy; Piaggi had wisely decided, if in fact it was a conscious decision, to let Darwin Hill be his main defensive position, but only after the battle began. Wallis asked Farrar-Hockley if he might join the fight of the now beleaguered 1 and 2 Platoons—Coronation Point was not, after all, occupied, and Wallis had no opponents—but Farrar-Hockley declined for reasons not clear then or now.[12] It should be kept in mind that A Company's left flank remained open until the battle's end.

At about 0800—full sunrise—Jones had three major options. He could do nothing as he listened to A Company's exertions. That was impossible because Jones was incapable of doing nothing. Second, he could shift his command emphasis to Crosland's B Company, which could move without intolerable harm. Third, he could hasten to the unit in the most trouble. He chose the last and most perilous course. By 0900, Jones, ever mindful of A Company's leading role in his plan, had insinuated his TAC HQ into the pinned down crowd of 1 and 2 Platoons. He found those men badly stuck and not a few dead and wounded. Why Jones chose to visit A Company—it took almost an hour dodging Argentine fire—instead of B Company, who did have room to maneuver despite being hard pressed, and why he did not bring up the Milans, who could now in daylight hit bunkered positions, will probably never be known.[13] One thing is certain: Jones did not move forward simply to assess Farrar-Hockley's plight. He knew that, against his wishes and the stipulations of his plan, A Company had been stopped. Jones went forward with one purpose, to get A Company on the move. John Wilsey has opted for Keegan's thesis that commanding officers must be seen to bear the same risk as those whom they send into harm's way. That laudable theory did not apply on Darwin Hill because everyone on that tiny battlefield bore roughly the same risks before combat ended. It is not difficult to conclude that Jones chose the wrong Company, in the wrong place, at the wrong time, to show his mettle at the spear's point.[14]

A CO manages assets in order to gain a specified objective. At the time of Jones' arrival, A Company was a decaying asset while B was still intact. Jones might better have gone to John Crosland's HQ in order to recoup the integrity of his plan. In any case, remember that Jones had not brought up the Milans that in the end broke up the Argentine bunkers, and weather prevented Harriers from accurate delivery of any ordnance. Keegan goes on: ". . . watch them [his changes] taking effect and reconsider his options as events change under his hand."[15] Jones acted as though his plan were still intact. It wasn't. And he did not know what else was happening to his other fighting companies. But clearly, he had concluded that his actions, as he then effected them, would restart the attack.

Mission Orders, especially as laid out in Jones' O Group, illuminate the proposed battle, which, as it unfolds in all its pandemonium, informs the commander's actions and intentions. Jones failed to grasp that the battle reifies the plan; that the plan does not reify the battle. A strong need to put matters right haunted his military career. The imposition of order on perceived chaos constituted a major part of his professional armory and heaven knows that he did not mind making a fuss. The calm integration of negative feedback was, however, not part of his mental equipment, the sign perhaps of a very intelligent but overly determined man who did not yet know that some obstacles cannot be breached and that some leaders, both senior and junior to him, will fail at some time. In his haste to get the plan and its timings back on track, he immured himself in a small fold of the Isthmus where he could grasp only the immobility of two of A Company's platoons. In battle, a commander's first task is to know everything about the course of the fighting. He cannot decide wisely from guesses or wishes, his own or others'. From shortly before sunrise on May 28th until his death perhaps 90 minutes later, Jones knew only what he could see and hear among the 60 or so men stuck with him in the reentry. His other units could as well have been fighting on the moon. Worse, he refused to hear information proffered to him that, properly used, could have altered the battle's outcome and perhaps preserved his life. Clearly, Jones had no Plan B. He sought elegance and perfection in the hurly-burly of combat where neither could exist. Nor did Jones credit the old saw: "Plans only get you to the fight; they don't tell you what to do after you get there."[16] And readers must know the elegance of written words lives in the recounting of a battle, not in its palpable unfolding.

No incontrovertible evidence shows that Jones ordered a halt to A Company's advance before it got stuck. Rather, the weight of evidence suggests to the point of certainty that Jones and his TAC HQ moved forward to prod A Company, which had already stopped, into taking Darwin

Hill. There had been trouble in the offing for A Company all morning long. Hear Keeble, then waiting at Main HQ: "I'm sitting back at main headquarters, and I'm trying to understand what is happening out of sight from where I am. And I'm trying to get information from Dair Farrar-Hockley, who commanded A Company, with whom we had a lot of difficulty over the previous three or four hours, perhaps longer, since dawn, in maintaining the momentum of getting up to Darwin and capturing it, which is why H had gone up there in the first place."[17] Jones did not take his TAC HQ forward in order to assess A Company's situation. He knew, all too well, from Farrar-Hockley, a competent company commander to whom he spoke by radio, that his unit, A Company, had been forced to stop on its own. It is still not publicly known if Jones realized that Farrar-Hockley's attack on Darwin Hill had been made with only two of his three platoons. Jones did know that without A Company's seizure of Darwin Hill and Goose Green itself the whole plan unraveled and that daylight would catch his fighting platoons in the open. Sergeant Barry Norman remembers: "He thought it was a lack of motivation as opposed to firepower. He felt that if it had been handled better A Company would not have been bogged down."[18]

One soldier recalls:

> It was mainly due to the order of march he (Jones) was rear center. Also the lay of the land narrowed at Darwin, he came across Coronation Point and to the foot of the gorse bottom of Darwin Hill. He went up the fold in the ground or gully if you like, it was the most practical route. B Company were on the extreme right, patrols forward. . . . It was probably just starting to get light. . . . He threw a wobbly, wanted to know why we had stopped. Told everyone we must move on. That we could not afford to be bottled up like we were that it would bog down the whole advance. . . . He got a sitrep and bollocked most of the senior officers then disappeared up the gully and into the smoke. . . . Keeble was still moving forward with Batn. Main HQ.[19]

Did Jones have so fine a grasp of A Company's wretched situation that he could devise and execute a resolution that had escaped Farrar-Hockley?[20] An affirmative answer invites the conclusion that Farrar-Hockley had, by that time, failed to meet the challenge posed by the defenders of Darwin Hill. It must be remembered, as a matter of curiosity if nothing else, that Farrar-Hockley had not concentrated his force, but instead dispersed it. Wallis' platoon never attacked up Darwin Hill, but remained out of those troubling four hours of combat. Neither could Wallis support the two platoons that were encapsulated in that hollow, because a tip of Darwin Hill between Wallis and the pinned down platoons prevented accurate aiming of direct fire onto Argentine positions. Yet another example of unknown unknowns, compounded by poor intelligence and questionable tactics on Farrar-Hockley's part, that led to avoidable tribulation.

Or did Jones believe that his presence would galvanize redemptive action by A Company's stalemated Toms? Or did he realize the truth that Farrar-Hockley had failed to maintain the momentum that would have met 2 Para's plan? It was clear then to members of A Company themselves that Argentine defenders had stopped them well before Jones' arrival on Darwin Hill. Sergeant Barry Norman wrote: "We got to A Company—there were dead and injured lying around. The CO went up to the officer commanding A Company [Major Dair Farrar-Hockley] and asked him what the situation was and why they had bogged down; what was he going to do about it?"[21] Until Jones got forward, any residual momentum that A Company's Toms possessed evaporated. For some at least, Jones' presence thenceforth increased the confusion around Darwin Hill rather than reducing it. Worse, his own actions and his stationing of his own HQ under effective Argentine fire isolated him from any action or persons he could not see or hear. The fog of war did not decrease. Jones' verbal jousting with Farrar-Hockley estranged him from the Company OC whom he needed most to break the entropic stalemate. By 0900 or thereabouts, Jones' span of control had collapsed. He no longer managed a battalion in the attack, but limited himself to the fate of several dozen cloistered men and a dozen or so manned enemy trenches. In fairness to Jones, he had implicitly decided that A Company's regained momentum would be the key to the battle. Of course, by then, Jones instead of managing the battle had become the battle.

A new plan of advance might well have centered on Crosland's platoons. Then too, the Milans, now useable in the growing light, had not yet been brought to bear on behalf of any of the British fighting platoons. Major-General Nick Vaux RM, writing about his and 42 Commando's cleverly planned and brilliantly executed attack on Mt. Harriet a few days later, put his own mark on a combat command in crisis: "A Commando HQ that was not embroiled in a crisis would be much better placed to resolve it."[22] Now that Jones seemed consumed by the immediate perils of A Company and unable to understand that his deliverance might be found elsewhere, his actions command our attention and history's too.

When Jones joined the two huddled platoons of A Company and their OC, Major Farrar-Hockley, at about 0900, the Argentineans held Goose Green, its airfield, Darwin Settlement and Hill and Middle Hill. Two platoons each of A and B Company could not maneuver without the certainty of casualties. Wallis' 3 Platoon from A Company remained inert at the causeway connected to Darwin Settlement.[23] A Company was out of the offensive fight. B Company's 5 Platoon, while it was repulsed onto the reverse slope of Middle Hill, could move with minimal possibility of harm.[24] From the reverse slope of Middle Hill, Captain Young 2 i/c of B Company could see the defenders' trenches that bedeviled A Company; he asked Jones that the Milans be brought to his position from which they could take the Argentine positions under fire. The suggestion went unanswered.

C Company's 2 i/c Lt. Kennedy stood on Coronation Ridge, no more than 900 meters from A Company's dilemma. Kennedy offered on the command net to set his 10 or so GPMGs onto the Argentine positions after A Company had identified its own position. Jones replied: "Get off the . . . radio, I'm trying to run a battle."[25] This statement was inaccurate because Jones, at that moment, had turned his full attention to the remnants of A Company's two platoons that were pinned down below the top of Darwin Hill, and not to the battle as a whole. Why Jones answered on A Company's net begs another set of questions. All the while, Farrar-Hockley's third platoon lay unengaged and unopposed on Coronation Point.

Bear in mind that Jenner's Support Company had been left out of the initial attack. Jones had positioned it behind Camilla Creek, several kilometers from the vital ground of Darwin Hill. Their GPMGs and Milans were ineffective in the dark, wherein Jones had posited that all the fighting would occur. Further, C Company could not join the fray without Jones' direct permission. It was only at daylight that Jenner's unit and Main HQ moved to within one kilometer of A Company, the unit most in need of help. Jenner's conversation with Jones is instructive: "did he want us to go forward to assist . . . 'No there are enough people forward here, and we've got problems, and—wait out.'"[26] Thus, Jones refused the possibility of help from the Milans, which proved in the end the most effective weapons against Argentine fixed positions.

No group can function without mutual trust. Yet Jones refused to accept suggestions, even observations, from officers whom he had placed in command of fighting companies and platoons.[27] He, himself, had focused only on A Company's decaying situation, instead of looking elsewhere to resolve 2 Para's problems thru the calculated use of all the assets at his disposal. As mentioned above, the Milans and GPMGs were not brought up in order to fire at Argentine bunkers at first light. Neame's D Company was lightly engaged, but its offer of help was abruptly refused. As Jones became fixated only with what events he could see or hear, the combat energies of 2 Para were dispersed almost into disuse. Jones' failure to see that force and energies other than those around him might turn the tide, was an endogenous conclusion that was not forced on him.

Jones' TAC HQ now mingled with A Company's HQ and the remnants of two platoons, approximately sixty officers, NCOs and men. None could move with safety away from a slight dip or fold in the terrain. Jones' assessment of the immediate tactical situation led him to order Lt. Coe and the mortar officer up to the gorse line in order to find a position suitable for firing on the Argentine trench line. Farrar-Hockley had earlier tried this maneuver without success and, similarly, the two were recalled. Anyway, mortar teams would have faced lethal harm from any position on Darwin Hill, and a meaningful supply of ammunition for the two tubes was not available. There remained no HE and only a few WP rounds. Jones' actions in this incident, his direct order to Coe and the use of his own assessment of the situation rather than Farrar-Hockley's, beg the question of who, then, commanded A Company. At least some present concluded that Jones had taken de facto command of A Company.

After the sun rose, the Argentine defenders enjoyed an unusual confluence of benign inadvertencies. Argentine Lt. Aliaga's unit retreated southwards from positions across the isthmus' neck, stopped at Boca Hill and pinned down Crosland's B Company for four hours. Argentine Lt. Estévez's understrength company of 36 soldiers left Goose Green's schoolhouse and, more or less on its own, occupied the hitherto empty trenches on Darwin Hill, there to maul Farrar-Hockley's A Company. Manresa's ramshackle company had pulled back from the isthmus' neck and also nested into the prepared positions on Darwin Hill. Thus at first light did the Argentineans' tactical confusion and the paras' failure to match the unrealistic demands of Jones' timings make the engagement a real fight.

Yet once nested into their holes, these Argentine units, the majority green conscripts, could not bring it upon themselves to leave those excellent defensive positions in order to counterattack the beleaguered British troops. "If they had counter-attacked at dawn they would have thrown us off the battlefield because we were totally outgunned and wrong-footed."[28] Not all Argentine troops at Goose Green lacked the basic competences of war. For example, Estévez's C Company was, in effect, a reinforced platoon, but it and other drifters who pocketed themselves into prepared but empty positions forced A Company to fight a bloody battle in the open in daylight. Estévez, whose parent unit was Colonel Muhammed Ali Seinelden's well trained and very capable 25th Regiment, was the sole Argentine officer to die on Darwin Hill.[29] It is useful here to repeat that no evidence exists to show that Jones or Farrar-Hockley had precise foreknowledge of their enemies' size, irregular competence or the depth of their positions on Darwin Hill, even after combat began.[30] In fact, the entire Argentine position on Darwin Hill was meant to be held by SubLt. Ernesto Peluffo's understrength company of 76 soldiers. These were later reinforced by dozens of bewildered soldiers, like Estévez's men, who drifted by chance and with no tactical integrity into the prepared dugouts and trenches.

Here it must be said that the steadfast ferocity of A Company's fire should not derogate the many Argentine infantry, and especially artillery men, who fought with valor and competence. An Argentine Master-Sergeant with a good sense of the battle arrived with two 7.62 machine guns that prevented British movement out of the hollow from which Jones tried to sort out the battle. If the total number of Argentine troops that faced A Company on Darwin Hill cannot be measured with precision, it is certain that they numbered at least 110 officers and men, or about twice the number that attacked them.

Next, at about 0930, when he had been with A Company for an hour or less, Jones ordered Farrar-Hockley to seize a well dug-in position sited on a ledge 60 or so feet above their now melded HQs. No artillery or mortar support was available. Mortars still had no HE, but retained a small supply of WP. Anyway, the 105s near Camilla House had run short of ammunition.[31] It was not an organized section or platoon attack directed by Farrar-Hockley, the nominal company commander, but rather a helter-skelter group of officers and men assembled by Jones, in haste, and in no particular order.[32] Jones did not offer any tactical logic for his order, nor is it clear now that any existed. Why Jones forced three captains and a major to make an attack normally assigned to a section or perhaps a platoon of infantrymen, is not known. Enough of them, about 60, lay within the range of his voice. Neither was this singular order the measured and temperate response of one who insisted on fighting a meticulously planned battle. At the moment that Jones ordered this improvident attack, he ceased to be 2 Para's CO and director of its battle and became de facto a platoon leader involved only in what he could see.

Upon ascending the ridge, Captains Wood and Dent and Corp. Hardman were killed straightaway. Farrar-Hockley stepped back into the fray and ordered Jones' attack broken off, and the small disparate group, less its casualties, scrambled back down the hill. The homey good sense of a junior NCO speaking to Farrar-Hockley tells it all: "If you don't f... get out now, sir, you ain't getting out."[33] Jones' tactics and exordium failed. It is not known what effect those deaths had on Jones' subsequent decisions. As the bullets flew that morning, Jones was certainly fulfilling Keegan's counsel that commanding officers be seen to share their men's miseries: "It was shortly after the Adj., Captain Woods, was killed, leading yet another assault, on the enemy trenches, that we saw an Argentinean officer, attempt to throw, one of the grenades, like we had been collecting. It had only traveled, a matter of inches from him, as it arced into the air, when it went off, covering his body, with burning phosphorous. Turning him into a human fire ball. [Sic.]"[34]

As Farrar-Hockley's attack party recovered, Jones, followed at a distance only by his bodyguards, Norman and Beresford, scurried in the opposite direction, left, towards a line of Argentine trenches. Jones had told no one in his chain of command of his intent, and led no organized assault. His unexpected action was not coordinated with any other initiative by 2 Para.[35] Nor was it clear then or later that Jones attacked a crucial part of the Argentine defenses. Neither had Farrar-Hockley's actions proved effective by this time, about 0945. A Company was the point unit for 2 Para's attack and it had, so far, failed. The situation on Darwin Hill had become so confused, and the participants' tactical integrity so compromised just before Jones' death, that, even now, no evidence suggests that Jones had a militarily useful target in sight. Unmindful of a manned trench that he had passed, he was gunned down from the side/rear and died shortly thereafter, about 0945, without regaining consciousness. The soldier who killed Jones probably came from SubLt. Ernesto Orlando Peluffo's platoon of the 25th Regiment of Infantry, yet no one on the British side is certain, even now, who fired the lethal shots. The Argentine soldier who killed Jones was captured shortly after the event and did not realize whom he had shot until he saw the deference being paid to Jones as he was carried out and flown off. While both British and Argentine wounded were being treated, he came to understand that he had killed not merely an officer but the CO.[36] After the war, several Argentine soldiers erroneously laid claim to the lethal shot and one former sergeant with a well-prepared script has made a minor but profitable career out of telling the tale in Argentina, usually in places of low entertainment.

Jones' move was not incident to any other action by A Company or the two thirds of it that lay stopped and prone on Darwin Hill, it was not part of an overall assault; he was exploiting nothing, he led no attack party and doubt must remain of his action's potential efficacy in relieving either A Company or B Company.[37] Jones asked for and got no support from artillery, mortar or machine gun. He ordered no one to follow him except Sergeant Barry Norman, his bodyguard.[38] The reasoning behind a battalion CO's solo attempt at tasks normally assigned to Junior NCOs and private soldiers is difficult to fathom even at this later date. Jones' rush up that hill manifested an engrained military habit: his yearning to shed the harsh light of his fine intellect on any problem before him. Trouble was that, for the first time in Jones' life, real bullets flew around him. But Jones had taken a risk greater than loss of his own life, for history treats its failures harshly. Had 2 Para's defeat followed this great act of courage, he would hardly have remained the figure whom almost all admire.

The manner of Jones' death remains under unneeded dispute. Rumors have abounded that he had been shot by his own men. However much that fevered charge adds to the drama of Goose Green, not a bit of hard evidence has emerged to support the theory. It is true that wildly varying descriptions of his wounds and their placement on his body sustain the notion that the heat of battle prevented anybody's clear retention of the fatal shooting as it occurred.[39] Sergeant Norman, Jones' bodyguard, wrote:

[I] saw the CO take his sub machine gun and start charging up the hill towards the trench that I was firing at. I shouted at him to watch his back because I could see what was going to happen. He ignored me . . . and charged up the hill to neutralize the trench I was firing at. He got to within six or seven feet of that trench and was shot from the trenches behind. You could see the rounds striking the ground behind him, coming gradually towards him and they shot him in the back. The impact of the rounds hitting him pushed him right over the top of the trench he was going for. He lay there and one of the Argentineans tried to lean out to finish him off. He couldn't because I was still firing. . . . He took the whole liter of my drip then I used his.[40]

Sergeant Blackburn stated: "It was a death before dishonor sort of effort: but it wouldn't have passed junior Breton."[41] Blackburn's harsh verdict was, of course, technically correct but missed the point. Jones' act was not rooted in military competence or expectation. The gravamen of the act was moral, not tactical. Jones had the confidence and the timely courage to think and to act outside the box of his own unimaginative plan for the battle and against his best personal interest.

Jim Love, Radio Operator with Forward Observation Officer's Party at Goose Green, described the scene:

> Most of it was already done by the time I got to H's body. He was in the normal position to put somebody in that had been shot in the stomach. The "w" position. He was wearing his puffer jacket but it wasn't zipped up and his trousers had been loosened to administer the drip through/up his rectum. He was wearing Long johns which amazed me as I tend to sweat my Bollocks off and had to keep taking off my water proof trousers, cause I over heated (a problem encountered by bravo 20 a few years later on I believe). I can remember "4" holes that had gone a purple-ly kind of dark red black with bluish rings. He was very ashen and had a bluey grey colour to most of the skin that was exposed. He had the death grimace and in fact a look of amazement on his face or a look of bemusement and quiet disbe-lief. His eyes were still open. One round in the thigh and three from the lower groin up to his abdomen. It must have been a burst. And by the angle he must have been right on top of the trench and they must have been in it crouching and firing up. The trench was empty and we used the wrinkly tin and the frame it had been nailed to as a temporary stretcher, but it was too big and wide and we had it upside down so we could hold the wooden posts to carry it. It couldn't take the weight and split apart. So we used waterproof jackets and FN rifles but that didn't work all that well either. No one had actually said he was dead, but there was no real sense of urgency (nobody said but we all knew he was dead) to get him to the RAP. I don't think I took him all the way down. I stopped quite near Dinger on the way through the position and I think somebody else took over from me. I started to help clear the rest of the trenches with PJ. There wasn't a lot of blood but the cold and shock did have that effect. I don't think there were any exit holes apart from the thigh. but I'm not 100%. [Sic.][42]

Surgeon Captain Rick Jolly, who completed the pre burial examination on Jones, said the high velocity 7.62 round had hit and deflected from the sternum, that bits of bone bounced around the chest cavity and probably were the cause of the numerous blue marks that some saw. Jones was crouching when hit and the shooter almost certainly stood up from his trench.[43]

No one has reported the certain existence of exit wounds nor has any evidence from the post mortem report suggested, let alone confirmed, the existence of any shots from a British weapon. It is entirely possible, but not remotely probable, that Jones was shot by two different persons, one from the back and one from the front. The evidence, as it stands, for a British shot or shots would not deserve an arraignment let alone be sent to trial with any reasonable expectation of a guilty verdict.

When Jones struck out from his TAC HQ just after sunrise, he had to know that his mission order had by then become invalid and that the resulting vacuum created a compelling need for him as CO 2 Para and his unit commanders to reorganize the battalion's efforts towards clearing Darwin Hill, seizing Goose Green and freeing the 130 odd Kelpers incarcerated in their community hall. Whether Jones believed he could break the impasse by his one man attack, or whether he sought to energize A Company's frozen remnants to break the Argentine trench line, or whether he sought redemption for his plan's failure, or whether he craved *keira*, the heroic death, will never be known. Did Jones try to rescue Farrar-Hockley, an admired Company commander, from disaster? If Jones knew it, he did not record the fact that Farrar-Hockley had elected to make his attack with two platoons rather than A Company's three and that perhaps this omission caused Farrar-Hockley's failed push up Darwin Hill. All else aside, it should be noted that Jones decided, at considerable risk to himself and his HQ, to rush to the site of a failed attack by A Company.

Jones had remarked to Major Héctor Gullán: "I am going to die."[44] Perhaps Jones, his privileged life unscorched by the normal hazards that most humanity endures, aspired in his innocence to become the battle himself. The sad possibility remains that Jones may simply have lapsed into a horror that paralyzed his capacity to reason calmly when he realized that A Company's leadership had faltered on that blood soaked hill and that his plan, or what he could see of it unfolding, had shattered. Intellectually gifted and prescient, this excellent man may have glimpsed the awful face of failure. Jones was not a duplicitous man. He was not world-weary. A successful commanding officer must first be honest, warts and all, with himself and then with his men. Jones was both. No taint of ambivalence smudged his integrity or the singleness of his purpose. Imminent war did not subvert or heighten Jones' ego. The prospect of combat and action itself simply gave play to Jones' higher powers. The bird and the plumage remained one and the same. The man who died on Darwin Hill was not a mutant. His behavior there manifested a straight-line continuum of all that he had seen, studied, done and experienced throughout his life. By hard work and extensive practice, he had made himself into what he had wanted to be: a consummate infantry commander. What Jones did on Darwin Hill came from his gut as well as his mind. One cannot envision Jones, had he lived, preening himself before his commander Julian Thompson. Remember the "fucking marine" remark! Jones, gazing into his shaving mirror and congratulating himself for his and his men's splendid victory, is far more likely. He wanted perfection from himself and from his battalion. He and his successor, Keeble, got it from their Toms.

Central to Jones' identity were the notions that his cleverness could overcome all, that he was the complete battalion CO and that his Toms could accomplish any legitimate military task. He was correct in those assumptions. Not to make that charge up Darwin Hill would have destroyed his bond with his Toms and with himself, and that betrayal could not be entertained. The moral imperative, as it almost certainly was, trumped military common sense. All said, fate gave Jones one chance at combat and he failed to live through it. Few have noted that Jones headed the suicide charge himself. He asked no one else to lead it. In his last act, Jones met all too well the ancients' stipulation that heroism requires death.

What remains crystal clear is Jones' descending focus of attention: first, mission orders for the whole battalion; then, joining A Company either to take command of it or merely to spur it on; then, ordering a hasty attack by a heterogeneous party up a troublesome ridge; last, and fatally, a one man attack on the Argentine trench line. The question remains: had A Company fallen apart to the extent that its revival demanded the battalion CO's full attention? Did A Company fail to take the hill because it had already faltered, or did it falter after a failed attack on Darwin Hill? The answer here, if it is ever known, is inconsequential. What is critical is that A Company was stuck before Jones decided to visit A Company's TAC HQ. Was the Argentine defense too resolute for a two-platoon attack to succeed? Did Jones know that an unengaged platoon remained on Coronation Point? Certainly Jones' taste for exquisite plans was not matched by A Company's finesse in battle. On Jones' part, it was a case of less than perfect administration and not a deficit in courage; the military assets to take Darwin Hill were there. Remember that one third of A Company never charged up Darwin Hill and never got pinned down in that hollow. Was it one of fate's dirty tricks or the impossibility of any unit, however well led, of making Jones' timings? If the latter, why did no officer, especially a Company Commander like Crosland who knew that five minutes can mean life or death, suggest to Jones at the O Group that his timings left no chance for delay or error? Most knew, of course, that Jones was seldom averse to controversy, but equally reluctant to grant that privilege to subordinates. Or was it that the skeptical world of professional soldiery simply yawned and determined to win whatever words were flung at them that cold night?

Though only a battalion commander, Jones knew that the first ground battle was utterly critical to the course of the war and that Darwin Hill was the linchpin of that battle. *C'est le premier pas qui coûte,* and Jones knew it. A stalled A Company meant delayed success on every front or a reverse domino effect. Jones' lack of administrative wit that allowed his getting involved in everything led to his involvement in almost nothing. On Darwin Hill, he lacked or more likely put aside *Fingerspritzengefuhl,* that quality of great commanders that permits a sense of the battle beyond conclusions reached from logical analysis of observable data.[45] From the outset, he had demoralized but never dominated his enemy, and in the end, had lost administrative control of 2 Para, its units incoherently scattered over the Isthmus. Of course, that deficit mattered less than it might have because of the Toms' ubiquitous unity of purpose. However distressed, his fighting platoons and sections retained their tactical integrity; they knew what they had to do. They were, after all, Jones' men.

There were few moments when British fire supremacy existed. HMS *Arrow* and its one flawed gun had left at dawn, the mortars were almost silent and the half battery could not fire effectively.[46] For all of Jones' frenetic efforts, A Company and 2 Para were, in a military sense, no better off at his own demise (no later then 0945) than they were when he arrived (no earlier than 0900) at A Company's HQ. Farrar-Hockley had not taken the high ground before first light as he was ordered to do. The Argentine defenders did not surrender and the beleaguered Toms did not rise up to storm the hill.[47] But that is the way of battle since history began. A Company's OC, Major Dair Farrar-Hockley, later commented: "It cannot be said that H's courageous sortie—or whatever he had in mind—inspired the soldiers at the moment, because few if any, were aware of what he was doing."[48] That comment remains open to question.

Unusual for a professional infantry officer such as Farrar-Hockley, recall that A Company's left flank on Darwin Hill had been left open.[49]

That lack of an anchor to the left contributed to the massing of A Company's other two platoons that trickled into their murderous snare on Darwin Hill's side. Here, the lack of an Argentine central commander on Darwin Hill let this omission go unnoticed. Oddly, Wallis' platoon lay within sight of this gap in the attack, but was not ordered to cover the empty ground. The Argentines' oversight here offered a much needed boon to Farrar-Hockley, and it was only later, after Jones' death, that the Toms attended to defenders who, if they had left their holes, might have rolled up A Company's drive. All the while, among the men, heroism flowered. Corp. Abols went over the top twice to rescue Corp. Prior, even though a sniper had a dead accurate bead on the wounded Prior.

As Jones died, A Company was being shredded while one of its platoons and D Company lay idle a few hundred meters away. Its CO dead, one of the world's best shock battalions lay split up and pinned down in the open by an equal number of Argentine infantry who had, until then, never fought a war.[50] It should be emphasized that none of the persons interviewed for this book believed that with Jones' death their defeat lay in the offing. There is no question but that the sight, even to those few who saw him, of their CO risking death alone put steel into their backs. To a man, none present there has ever blamed Jones to the author for A Company's halt or for their own perilous straits. To a man, none ever faulted to the author Jones' courage.[51] To a man, all testified that while the carnage was awful, they saw victory as inevitable.[52] Lord Moran, in his brilliant book *The Anatomy of Courage*, writes: "It is true we have no traffic in heroes, but a good fellow means more than he did. The mask we wear through life drops off leaving men as they really are. It seems almost indecent this exposure of a man in the presence of his fellows, and who for the first time see him in all the nakedness of his natural state." Perhaps the man who charged up that hill was the naked hero.[53]

Darwin Hill saw the most admirable and the most reprehensible that afternoon. Hear a junior NCO:

Re [the British officer] I am not absolutely certain but I think it was after [Jones' death]. It was daylight and the incoming was heavy. I'd spoken to Gerry Gilbert, he'd told me that Chuck [Hardman] was dead, I already knew Chris Dent and Capt. Woods were dead, so it was after. But very close to the actual time [of Jones' death].

It was on Darwin Hill. There were elements of the Mortar Platoon nearby; Sgt. Hall gave me a bollocking for exposing myself, so why was he there? Fire control? If Pip Hall was there, he arrived after Jones was dead, so if you calculate the time it took for Keeble to free things up and Support Company to get forward, it would have been close to then [sic] late afternoon. [The British officer] was groveling on the ground, almost squirming.

It was in a depression—where sheep lie out of the wind. I remember the radio op sitting a few yards away with his back to the wind. [The British officer] was trying to get as deep into that depression as he could, and was using his hands to flick sand away. I just stopped, stared and I got angry. I was beyond caring. That's why I walked across the hill like I did. I remember thinking I can't take any more of this, I wanted it over, I wanted to know if God had it in for me. I did that, walked across the hill to see if the sniper would get me or if the incoming would, and got distracted by [the British officer], that bastard spoiled my moment. It was obvious to me why Pip reacted to save me from myself. He punched me, I remember it. Punched me and dragged me to the ground. I'm scared now, trembling, but it's frustrating. I want to go home, can't. I got up and bolted for the gully. There was a wire splitting a track. 1 Platoon were on one side, 2 Platoon on my side. One of the Toms was running back and forwards with belts of link. Every time he jumped the fence, the sniper popped off at him. That's why he didn't take one at a time. He did this several times, feeding the twins who were harassing a line of trenches ahead of me off to my right. These trenches were about thirty yards in front of [the British officer] so he was just below the brow of the hill. They'd been assaulted by 2 Platoon and were possibly the ones where Chuck, Dent and Woods died, the ones that Jones led an aborted attack? [sic]

Something happened. Was it Dave Abols action? I don't know. He was with Ted Barratt on the other side of the fence. Suddenly I remembered what I should have been doing and legged it down the hill. That's when I saw Steve Adams under the knife in the field. I lit a cigarette. The fighting was over. Clearly A Company had stopped fighting and withdrew. On reflection, did 1 Platoon get split up by the wire fence on both sides of the track? Adams was 1 Platoon, yet the Doc was patching him up below the remnants of 2 Platoon—perhaps some one brought him to the RAP but I am not sure.

Who carried on the fighting B Company coming across the front of A Company? Patrols/C Company? All I can remember is that I started shaking again, astonished at the holes in Steve Adams and the fact that he was still alive.

A Pucara appeared following a Scout, I dropped to the ground, fired a few shots from a Gimpy, but the bandoliers fell from my shoulder and the weight pulled my elbows in and I had to fire with the butt against my sternum. I missed again so let rip at the Pucara til the belt was expended and missed. I saw the rockets hit the Scout and it blew up and crashed and we moved on. Somehow I got forward. Where was Patrols Platoon on the beach? Am I right? All I can remember is C Company's casualties.

There were many, many prisoners appearing from all directions, some walking, others carrying comrades. I saw things that I excused in the heat of battle, forgave the perpetrators for they were reacting to the loss of their friends.

I tended some wounded and after they casevaced I got an urge to move. It felt like some one was yelling at me to move. I did. About ten yards and a shell came in. I hit the deck at this point I'd lost the Gimpy and carried only my issued SMG—that caused me a great deal of pain as I hit the deck. I turned around and saw that the two I had been tending had taken a direct hit. Neither survived that hit. I rudely flushed caution out of my system, felt blessed and knew that I would go home in one piece. I remember then becoming aware of the impending gloom. Night approached and we cleared the area of dead and wounded; the fighting had ebbed and all but died. We re-orged in the gorse and spent the night there.[54]

Battle plans try to translate fugitive abstractions into palpable events. Jones was too smart and too experienced not to know the fragility of the bridge between the two. He knew too that the more stipulations are inserted into a mission order, the more things can go wrong. Yet, no scintilla of risk or mischance had corrupted the pure scholasticism of Jones' plan. It was reheated Staff College gruel that few ingested. Nor did Jones respond to his crisis with subtlety or guile. No evidence exists to suggest that, at the time of his death, he had formulated a scheme to extricate A Company or 2 Para from its ruinous straits. It was as though he had made all his decisions before the battle and saw little need to change his views on the way the battle should run. A sense of order, his order often harshly imposed, permeated his military life and, more gently, his private life. The violation of that order triggered a need immediately to put things right, especially if he were on the scene or could get to it. Jones had no Plan B for his attack before or during the action at Goose Green. That is why no need exists to probe below surface appearances for spurious motivations. What he did was what he intended. There were no false notes on Darwin Hill.

Yet certain innocence colored his intentions, as though their fulfillment in combat were not finally a matter of chance and gore. It seems never to have entered Jones' mind, for example, that usage rates for the 105mm guns would turn out to be four times the army's predicted rate, and that the half battery firing in his support might run out of ammunition before his end of the battle had finished. 2 Para entered combat without its commander's acknowledgment that in war there are knowns, known unknowns and unknown unknowns. He failed to admit that while he could control some actions, others he knew he could not, and that a few terrible incidents would crop up that he could neither foretell nor thwart.[55] Both before and during the battle, he failed to acknowledge that timely and accurate data is as critical to a commander as ammunition, food, morale and training. For Jones, data outside his mindset did not exist. Jones did not admit that mud, blood and dumb luck might thwart the most elegant ratiocinations. True, doubt may not corrode the commander's mind, at least not obviously so. Yet the glistening certainty of Jones' plan masked a certain self-indulgence that seemed out of place in a man so intelligent and self-disciplined.[56]

Of course, this habit of the mind is one side of the extraordinary confidence a battle commander must own if he is to exert any influence over the combat in front of him. John Wilsey has argued in his authoritative biography of Jones that he would have found it difficult, if not impossible, to operate outside the doctrine of the School of Infantry at Warminster. This is a disingenuous argument. Jones was educated, paid and assigned to prevail in battle, not to act according to someone else's script.[57] Anyway, why should a young fire-eater fall back on the hoary, and, as it turned out, inappropriate paradigms of yesteryear? Rommel commented early in the desert war that British plans were fussy and constrained leadership among subordinates to his advantage, and that he [Rommel] had small staffs that left decisions to junior commanders in the field.[58] When Jones died, 2 Para clung by its webbing to its tactical integrity and to the legend of the bridge at Arnhem. But make no mistake, it was Jones' battalion that recovered and did not falter or quit or retreat into a sullen shell of despair. They stayed the course as he expected.[59] Jones' death and the last five minutes of his life have defined him for the public and for history. Unjustly, perhaps, because there was much more to the man and what he gave to his battalion than his bizarre end.

And the Battle Raged On

"Then Hrithgar, the Shieldings' helmet, spoke: 'Rest?
What is rest? Sorrow has returned. . . . Alas for the Danes!
Aeschere is dead . . . and a soulmate to me, a true mentor,
my right hand man when the ranks clashed."[60]

Major Chris Keeble, 2 Para's 2 i/c, had no part in the formulation of
Jones' plan and little to do with its initial execution. Until about 1000, he
had done as Jones ordered and as his plan demanded. After Jones died,
Keeble began the rescue of 2 Para with a blank slate. He had composed
no written plan of his own. War abhors coherence and Keeble knew it full
well from the evidence before him. His notions of combat on Darwin Hill
were simple and pragmatic: "You have got to kill the enemy, you have got
to destroy the machine gun, before he destroys you. Every trench you
attack, you destroy it. You jump in the trench and rake it with fire, and if
you see an Argie, it's either him or you."[61]

Keeble chose not to reinforce A Company's failure—A Company had
by now been stopped for at least three hours—and instead to rely on the
Toms' doggedness and measured success elsewhere on the battlefield.
Neither A Company nor their adversaries were going anywhere. Besides,
untrained peasant infantry nests—it does not counterattack into fire. After
discussion, Keeble delegated command of 2 Para to Major John Crosland,
OC B Company until he, Keeble, could get forward and see the battle for
himself.[62] Crosland retained some ability to move without serious harm;
Neame moved two platoons so that together with Crosland's men they
could bring withering fire down onto Boca House. Its occupants either
fled, died or surrendered, and the position was taken though the event
occurred hours behind Jones' schedule. Argentine soldiers who survived
the engagement at Boca House considered it as far more savage a fight
than the scrap on Darwin Hill. At least 20 Argentine soldiers died there
and probably twice that number were wounded.

Three events now occurred. First, the Toms did not yield to bloody
adversity and continued to wear down their enemy. Second, Keeble
stopped any movement by his fighting units until he could get forward
and assess the battalion's situation with a view to winning the battle, not
merely A Company's part of it.[63] Last, Keeble delegated command to
Crosland, the OC of the only engaged unit, B Company, which had an
immediate chance of breaking the impasse before Keeble arrived at the

fighting platoons. If Jones erred in reposing trust, Keeble did not make the same mistake. To lessen B Company's exposure, Crosland had backed it down the reverse slope of Boca Hill. Crosland has been given far less credit than he deserved for keeping intact B Company, which later provided a backbone for 2 Para's renewed momentum. Several British officers have commented, a few to the author, that Jones might better have gone two hours earlier to Crosland's B Company in order to break the impasse. He chose another route. With his command party, Keeble brought forward resupplies of ammunition and Milan missiles.[64] Jones, in failing to anticipate what his battle winners would be, had kept them in the rear out of the battle. Keeble distributed them to engaged units to be used as each saw fit.[65] Where some see panic and despair, wise commanders know that combat produces unpredictable asymmetries. Victory goes to the commander who first sees their dimensions and acts upon them.[66]

Jones' utter competence shone after his death. So skillful was Jones' immediate successor, Keeble, and so competent were the Toms that they could shift in minutes from Jones' stern control to Keeble's intuitive and decentralized management of the battle. They remained Jones' men as though they wore the letter J on their foreheads. After Jones had died, but not because of it, junior officers and NCOs took a firm grip on events. At about 1000 the scales tipped against the Argentine defenders of Darwin Hill.

Two events did not occur that awful afternoon and gave credit to those involved. Thompson, Keeble's senior as CO 3 Brigade, did not interfere or even come forward. Thompson knew Jones' men too, and let Keeble take actions on the basis of his own assessment.[67] Nor did Keeble cry out for advice. Majors are not normally puissant figures of history. This war proved differently. Major Sheridan RM had saved British operations around South Georgia from disaster; now it was Major Keeble's turn. His task was clear: steady 2 Para, reorganize the attack and then take Goose Green.[68]

Keeble, as much a military intellectual as Jones, was not his doppelganger. He devised no new plan nor did he insist on following a syllabus that had clearly failed. His overarching reaction to the collapse of Jones' plan, to A Company's stalemate and to Jones' death was, first, to do no harm. A certain sense of reality began to infuse the battle's management. Keeble did not break the bonds of Jones' injunct to win, but simply unleashed each fighting unit to fight its own engagements as the company and platoon and, indeed, section leaders saw fit. In Keeble's own words:

I attempted to coordinate the action started by B and D Company with a small fire base of Milan at B Company's rear and complete the turning of the enemy's flank. When the Boca House position was taken I had a quick session of radio orders with B and D Company commanders, endorsed their plans to sweep towards Goose Green and invited A Company Commander to press on to Goose Green since Darwin Hill was unlikely to be retaken. After discussion he declined. [A Company's half sections still had enemy trenches and own wounded to clean up.] I asked Roger Jenner to pass through A Company and maintain the momentum towards Goose Green. He agreed. Thus A Company became the reserve with three fighting units up, each Company Commander reminded about the Mission and able to choose his own path.[69] I then established my own small TAC HQ on the forward edge of Darwin Hill with the BC, [unfortunately the main focus of the 105mm, mortar and AA fire] and sought support from the Harriers to break the enemy's will.[70]

Hear Major Neame, OC of the underused D Company:

> Keeble freed the thing off . . . Suddenly people felt free to use their own initiative and get on with the job . . . Everyone could interpret what was required anyway, but had been inhibited from doing so as long as H was sitting there on Darwin Hill fighting his Darwin Hill battle, and Keeble's contribution was that he freed it off, and then we just got on with it, and used our own initiative and produced the goods.[71]

Neame sought out Crosland with a view to extricating B Company from its frustrations. Not finding him, Neame took it upon himself to go after Boca House. Earlier, Jones had ordered Neame to remain idle, a suggestion taken literally as D Company's stalwarts took their tea and porridge while the battle raged several hundred meters distant on Darwin Hill. After Jones' death, Neame interrupted their al fresco repast, snaked around and south of B Company, his objective Boca House. British fire, and especially Neame's GPMGs and six rounds from Milans, took their toll and white flags began to appear. Neame's men, a hodge-podge from several platoons took a risk—they then marched across 500 meters of open ground to accept the Argentineans' surrender. Inadvertent firing upon the surrendering Argentine infantry by Lt. Hugo Lister's machine gun platoon and a British Milan shot at an Argentine position nearly wrecked the arrangement. A few hotheads normally resist surrendering in such cases, but Neame's adversaries failed to return fire and the engagement ended. Keeble's loose reining of his unit commanders received its first results in that small, but violent and significant victory. It must be remembered that it was Jones' officers and NCOs who reconstituted the battle in spasms of utter violence that their surviving opponents recall as vividly a decade later.

With Jones dead and immediate decisions being made by 2 Para's junior officers and NCOs, the normal inadvertencies of battle were bound to proliferate and they did. One such reverberates to this day. At about 1500, Lt. Jim Barry, OC 12 platoon from Neame's D Company, concluded that the fight was all but over, at least near the schoolhouse, and that the Argentineans were susceptible to an offer of surrender. Quite on his own, against all common sense and probably his company commander's wishes, he raised a white flag and moved forward to confer with Lt. Gómez-Centurión, who turned out to speak fluent English. In his turn, Gómez-Centurión believed that the British officer with whom he spoke was 2 Para's CO and asked him to surrender. The negotiations went nowhere. After a discussion conducted in English, Gómez-Centurión gave Barry two minutes to return safely to his lines. Just then, from several hundred meters distance, a British machine gun fired and the Argentineans reckoned that the truce had been unfairly broken. Straightaway, Argentine fire killed Barry and his accompanying NCOs in front of Lt. Peluffo's position. Two Argentine soldiers, almost certainly unarmed, were also shot and killed. Time and the fog of war continue to mask the many Argentine versions of that sad affair at Goose Green, and bitter but unjustified recriminations continue to burble. Several hours after Jones died, most, if not all, of the still fighting Argentine soldiers believed that he lived and had made the offer of surrender. In his article on the affair,[72] Argentine Lt. Esteban has continued to claim many years later that Gómez-Centurión confronted 2 Para's CO and that his soldiers had killed Jones, not Barry, despite irreproachable evidence presented then and since that Jones had died hours earlier in another part of the battlefield.[73]

From Jones' death, the battle belonged, in a purely administrative sense, to Keeble, the Toms and officers like Crosland, Jenner and Neame who saw opportunities and won their small victories, one by bloody one. Yet it remained very much Jones' fight, still to be won by Jones' men. It is useful to note that by 1330, despite being, in Keeble's tart estimate, "outgunned and wrong-footed," none of 2 Para's fighting elements had suffered an Argentine counterattack. The first British attack had disheartened even the well-entrenched Argentine defenders. Nor had the best Argentine unit, Estévez's motley but oddly competent crew, done anything more than decline Piaggi's order to advance up to the original defense line in support of Manresa. Instead, Estévez took the best course from the standpoint of delaying A Company, and simply hunkered his men down in the lightly manned but well found bunkers and trenches around Darwin Hill. Many of them from the 25th regiment fought well. By this time, about 1100, the tactical chaos surrounding the Argentine defense of Darwin Hill and its environs confused almost everyone on both sides.

Every battle has its own nadir from which the victor emerges. Goose Green was no exception. The Argentineans had no leader on the spot to coordinate the actions of three fighting platoons from different parent units that were commanded by junior officers. Worse, Piaggi lacked instant communications with all his fighting units at Goose Green, though he could see most of them. Yet, willy-nilly, on and around Darwin Hill these 100 or fewer very confused young men assisted by terrain and weather caused Jones' schedule to fall so far behind as to become meaningless, and to force British infantry to fight in daylight, uphill, against artillery that in a few cases could fire over open sights.

Keeble's rightful claim to be outgunned has not received its proper notice. HMS *Arrow* and its single five-inch gun had left just after daybreak. Anyway, the gun had broken down during much of its allotted firing hours and its contribution to the battle proved far less than anticipated or claimed since. That single gun contributed little to the conduct or outcome of the battle. British spotters could rarely distinguish among falling shots. No Argentine officer or NCO has averred that *Arrow*'s fire influenced their actions in any way. Conversely, the Argentine fire that rained down on the Toms after *Arrow*'s departure was not well answered. The half battery of 105s that Thompson's overworked helos had ferried to Camilla Creek House could not display their normal effectiveness because rain and fog cloaked fall of shot and because only direct hits counted in the soft terrain. Oddly, for a scrap that was intended to be fought at night, the half battery had no illumination rounds. 2 Para's Land Rovers that normally transported mortar rounds remained aboard ship for the war's duration. Mortars are the infantry's best friend, but gulp tonnages of ammunition when firing at the usual rate of eight rounds per minute. Each 11 lb. round had, therefore, to be backpacked to the tubes thus diminishing the combat efficiency of the men it was meant to sustain. The tradeoff had a very dysfunctional side, as men needed on the firing line found themselves used as rain soaked sherpas.

Piaggi has claimed that deficits in machine guns and mortars severely crimped his defenses. Partly true, but his principal mistake lay in not coun- terattacking at least one of the pinned down companies and destroying it. Some of Piaggi's troops fought well from their holes; unfortunately for him, those terrified young men would not leave their positions except to surrender or to be carried out. At its most vulnerable, when it could have been broken as a tactical entity, A Company never faced a counterattack. Piaggi had, nonetheless, several Rheinmetal 20mm and Oerlikon 35mm guns that, along with some very competent snipers, kept British heads down more than the Toms liked. Unfortunately for Piaggi, coordination between his infantry and his guns did not exist. Stacks of ammunition for these weapons were found after the battle, along with containers of napalm.

There was never any question of A Company's withdrawal from Dar- win Hill. A junior NCO later stated: "O, no sir, we were going to stay until things got sorted out."[74] In correspondence with survivors from Goose Green, who were very young those gorey days, a certain sureness and competence, devoid of arrogance, resonates. These seem, even now, all of a piece with Jones' character. By 1000, A Company's persevering fire paid off. A British LAW (light anti-tank weapon), fired by Corporal Abols, destroyed an Argentine bunker critical to Darwin Hill's defense and began a piecemeal ending, white flags aflutter, to Argentine resistance there. Peluffo ordered a surrender of his remaining men and 74 Argentine soldiers began fairly disagreeable work under 2 Para's RSM. Battered A Company could not then assume an offensive posture, but by midday it had taken Darwin Hill, and forthwith Piaggi's perimeter shrank into a rough semi-circle around the airfield, the schoolhouse and the settlement of Goose Green itself. Surrender by one unit in plain sight of others begins a virtually unstoppable virus. Argentine POWs, not a few wounded or otherwise suffering from shock, wandered into the British lines from all sides.[75] Did Jones' action invigorate his Toms? All but a few were ignorant of his death until much later. Did Abols stand up, aim and fire from Jones' example? Why did Darwin Hill's defenders slowly, but noticeably, cease fighting at this time rather than at another? This singular action was an inflection point whose causes we shall never know.

About noon, A and B Companies had secured their positions, but at what cost? Farrar-Hockley summed up his situation: "The commander officer's dead, the adjutant's dead, my company second-in-command's dead. What are we going to do?"[76] If Farrar-Hockley's view of the battle was less than confident, others took the opposite stance. Keeble read the battle and took the only prudent risk available. He opted for continued momentum, what little remained, and made the airfield his primary objective while leaving Darwin aside for the moment; after all, A Company and its opponents had pummeled each other into quiet exhaustion. Correctly, Keeble sought momentum at the price of skewed units' boundaries and of marching beyond the range of his direct fire weapons. Worst of all, British troops advancing in the open skirmished into range of every gun that Piaggi's men owned. Control of the battle as taught at the world's staff colleges, let alone Jones' rigid management, went by the boards. C Company, caught in the open, saw more heroism in 60 minutes than in the goriest war film. Capt. Steve Hughes, the battalion doctor, crawled out to retrieve wounded paras; others followed his example and many lives from both sides were saved. Hughes amputated the dangling stump of a corporal's leg while both were under fire.[77]

By mid afternoon, dusk approached and unit boundaries had collapsed. Bowing to the moment, C and D companies put together mixed groups of officers and men in order to take out the schoolhouse and its outlying buildings. Again, no elegant tactical formulation existed for the task. But unity of purpose and superb training carried the day. Junior officers and sergeants rather than the new CO orchestrated the action. C Company's WO2 Greenhalgh, as much as anyone, conducted the attack, kept causalities to a minimum and cleared the structures of their defenders. All this in the face of effective Argentine sniper fire and rounds from the depressed AA guns sited near the community hall.[78] One Tom remembers 20 years later: "The Oerlikons! To this day, I still can't imagine what kind of courage it took to cross that skyline and advance down that slope. Patrols Platoon saw the firepower they faced and decided all for one and one for all, no turning back. It was now or never. If the guns were not taken out, the battle was over for C Company."[79] Among the Argentine defenders Second Lt. Claudio Braghini headed the 3rd section of Battery B 601 Air Defense Artillery. His two Oerlikon 35mm AA guns depressed and fired over open sights against C Company's run up a small rise. Braghini's stream of shots set fire to the schoolhouse out of his belief that British snipers were inside, while at the same time British troopers fired at the structure from outside out of fear that Argentine infantry had taken refuge inside. The schoolhouse caught fire and was destroyed.

Crosland ordered B Company to swing around C and D Companies at the cost of separating himself from the rest of 2 Para. The decision was made in anticipation of a further attack on Goose Green itself, which lay a kilometer away from him. Crosland's sections took out trenches one by one. Momentum and speed took precedence over the niceties of ensuring that each trench was empty of combatants. This particular OC had husbanded his troops in the knowledge that, while others lost men and momentum, he retained the option of maneuver with an intact company. One of his men remarked 20 years later: "Johnny Crosland was a god."[80] While the battle went against them and while units lost communication with each other except by fire, Crosland stands out as one of those commanders, commissioned and non-commissioned, who did nothing reckless or stupid while awaiting what their men did best, breaking their enemy's will to resist.

The battle had become, by early afternoon, an advance to contact as perhaps it should have been from the outset. In the end, the Toms took out trenches one by one. Too tired to attempt frontal attacks, sections and half sections struck the Argentine defenders from the side and carefully killed or captured them. Though insignificant, each by itself, these small ground actions had the effect of shrinking Piaggi's perimeter and of demoralizing his men to the point where some were seen to throw away their weapons. There is an odd condition in war when fear leaves and courage, often alloyed with apathy, floods in. Exhaustion kills fear, too. Perhaps that happened to the young men of 2 Para. On May 28, 1982, from sunrise to sunset, Jones' men did not break or fail to do what needed to be done, but went about the age old business of killing their opponents in order to convince the survivors that they could not win.[81] In correspondence with the author, one soldier recalled a particularly gruesome moment on that day: "Bill Bentley cut off the stump of Chopsie Gray's leg and I placed it on the stretcher."[82]

As light failed, the gods of war offered yet another absurdity to the depleted paras. From its hutch on Mt. Kent, the Argentine 601 Aviation Battalion lifted 125 fresh men (Task Group Solari) led by Captain Edwardo Consigliari, a logistics officer, to a position south of Crosland's B Company and south-east of Goose Green itself.[83] TG Solari carried only personal weapons, except for one 105mm recoilless rifle and an 82mm mortar that lacked a sight. Crosland's B Company, by this time several hundred meters distant from 2 Para's main body (if such could be said to exist after hours of combat), lacked anti-air missiles to strike the helos before they landed. The Toms, almost out of ammunition, looked on with horror as the enemy infantry disgorged from their helos, but fortune chose that day to smile on the wet, the tired and the hungry.

Alma battery's 105s were called and delivered direct hits on the landing troops in very short order. The fire was so timely and accurate that Task Force Solari quickly lost whatever tactical integrity it had. As a consequence, Consigliari's men could not position themselves to attack the gun line, 2 Para's TAC HQ, its very fragile logistics chain or B Company, which lay isolated and well south of 2 Para's other units. Instead, the Argentineans slunk by twos and threes into their shrunken defensive perimeter where they became rag tag sections to deploy, mouths to feed and targets for British guns. Piaggi, who may well not have known that such help approached and certainly did not know when it would arrive, lacked any notion of how to integrate the new arrivals into the shards of his murky tactical plan. Against all military logic, Brigadier-General Parada had ordered his sole mobile reserve into defensive positions to provide more fodder for what had clearly become an Argentine disaster.

Bad weather prevented much air activity over the battlefield by both sides, and it was not until about 1500, just before the winter's early dusk, that two Argentine naval Aeromacchis tried and failed to engage profitable British targets at Goose Green. They returned to Stanley promptly. A further two Aeromacchis attacked D Company as it lay in the open and caused freight, but as fortune had it, no casualties. One plane crashed while avoiding D Company's ground fire. Two Pucarás, one carrying conventional munitions, the other napalm, then flew in to attack British mortar positions. The napalm went wide of C and D Companies and harmed no one. Its deliverer got home with difficulty. A Blowpipe missile fired from Darwin Hill crippled the second plane and it fell, its pilot parachuting safely to ground. As the plane tumbled earthward, it spurted aviation fuel over the very paras who had brought it down. Disaster was averted as the flammable vapors evaporated from the Toms' clothes without kindling.[84]

As night fell, three Harriers jumped to attack the Argentine artillery pieces that had caused so much havoc. Their ordinance failed to inflict much damage, but Keeble and others concluded that the whoosh of jet engines close to the ground and the sheer explosive effect of the planes' bombs devastated what remained of the Argentineans' fighting spirit. Argentine survivors confirmed that this attack was, for many, the last straw. Day's end brought quiet. Ammunition for the Toms, despite their ransacking Argentine dead, wounded and prisoners for rounds to fit captured rifles was low, and the young paras were exhausted, hungry and wet. A Company was not fit for offensive operations. B Company had been marching or fighting without sleep for 36 hours. No ammunition remained for the mortars, and the 105mm guns retained no more than twenty rounds per tube.

An accountant's view of the war must now intrude. Woodward's orders to send his ships eastward at first light conflicted with Clapp's and Thompson's requirements to unload and get supplies correct in kind and quantity to the men who did the fighting. Ships had but six hours of unloading time per day, even after the threats from air, surface and underwater had all but evaporated. The periods devoted to actual unloading never lengthened, despite pleas from the ships' exiguous customers. However hard the men of Lt. Col. Hellberg's Commando Logistics Regiment labored, their lack of practice in such joint operations with double the usual customers and their deficit in ground transport slowed the whole affair. Clapp's ships could unload 80 tons per hour, and that was too much for the ashore logisticians to handle, however hard they strove. They supported, after all, two battalions of army paras in addition to their normal three full-strength Royal Marine commandos, and that without much useable ground transport.

On the afternoon of May 28th, Thompson's concern about sufficient logistical support for major ground operations proved all too prescient. Had Thompson sent two battalions into the attack at Goose Green, as some at Northwood and at 3 Brigade believed necessary, the situation might have stopped not only 3 Brigade's momentum, but all the combat on the battle's second day. Eighty-three rounds for each 105mm gun, two days supply of 10-man ration packs, three days of medical supplies and no spare clothing constituted the Brigade's inventory ashore at the end of that troubling day.[85] One sergeant recalled that, at day's end on Goose Green, he retained one grenade and three rounds for his rifle. Recall that the 105mm guns consumed, in this their first sustained combat, four times the daily rate that had been predicted for a war in Europe.[86]

Mucho Teatro

When asked about the war just as it began, an Argentine taxi driver remarked, "mucho teatro" (too much drama).[87] The Argentine Foreign Ministry's quixotic notions about British responses played well in the streets too. But for the troops, at least, suspensions of disbelief got put aside that wretched night at Goose Green, for darkness gave the men no surcease from the wet and cold. The miseries of the war's first battle lasted well after the initial day's shooting stopped. B Company had, for example, no sleeping bags, let alone tents. The inadequacies of the British combat boots—they let water in but not out—created their own special suffering. Medics kept the wounded alive with their own body heat. The absence of easy helo transport—lacking PNGs for their crews, most helos flew day-time only—left some wounded in the field for over 12 hours, despite the heroic flying of bleary eyed pilots. Ammunition for rifles and general purpose machine guns remained short; Keeble's fighting units faced these same problems, to a greater or lesser degree, everywhere. Then too, Thompson had ordered, at around 1400, that 2 Para was not to leave Goose Green, but was to stay and seize the isthmus. Thus ended the notion of a raid upon which the operation had been predicated.

When darkness fell, not enough food and water, ammunition, some winter clothing and medical supplies came forward, much of it carried in two Snowcat tracked vehicles that appeared out of the gloom, just as mysteriously as had the events of the just ended day. After the Snowcats that Major Rice had organized on the artillery net had deposited ammo forward at Camilla House and at the rear of Darwin Hill for distribution to the infantrymen, they lumbered back to Ajax Bay carrying the dead and a few days work for the weary medics.[88] J Company of 42 Commando was put on standby in case any of Keeble's units needed rescue, but that offer and the presence of 3 Brigade's CO were declined. The remaining six of 2 Para's eight mortars, a half battery of 105mm guns to make 8 Battery (Alma) complete and ammunition for both were brought forward, but few drops of comfort eased the Toms' misery that night. A Company's exhausted soldiers huddled in shell scrapes, put out pickets and scavenged the captured trenches for food, clothing and ammunition. Unusually, it was not the habitual rapacity that victors visit on vanquished. Argentine boots were better than British boots and the Argentineans' 7.62 rifles were better suited to the battle at hand than the sub machine guns that were the Toms' personal weapons. Miserable from the cold, they took turns in putting their backs to the wind so that at least a few would be warm some of the time.[89]

Battle produces: "A derangement of the senses" as Elizabeth Clark said about Rome, but, after sunset, Keeble set about two distinct and rationalized courses of action. Each could proceed in the absence of the other; both could be carried out simultaneously. The first involved the seizure of Goose Green proper through continued military efforts. Piaggi's men were boxed in. They had suffered heavily and no help was available for them, either from the mainland or from Stanley. They had nowhere to go and evacuation by helicopter was impossible.[90] For his part, Thompson stipulated that military victory took priority over the inhabitants' safety and that the community hall could be damaged if the fighting turned that way.[91]

Keeble's second option lay in inducing Piaggi's surrender, a course approved by Thompson, even while he strove to ensure that 2 Para was sufficiently strengthened to win on the morrow if the conflict continued. A civilian farmer was advised to inform Piaggi by radio that a party under white flag would approach his lines with a proposal for his surrender. The war was still on and 2 Para's RSM led a fighting patrol forthwith to ascertain the relative safety of the negotiating site. To convey the terms of surrender to Piaggi (see Figure 5.1), Keeble sent two NCO prisoners under white flag through British lines. Meanwhile, Thompson and Keeble arranged for a massive display of firepower timed to occur the next morning in case Piaggi needed further persuasion that his position was hopeless.

All of a piece with the day's high drama, Keeble decided to negotiate with Argentine officers in a small hut on the edge of Goose Green's airfield. He judged the Argentineans' will to have been broken and that the possibility of harm to himself and his negotiating party was small, yet another example of what a shrewd officer could accomplish when left to his own devices. With tact and deference paid to the defenders' gallantry—Keeble's negotiators went unarmed and TV camera men were forbidden from filming the event—all went well. Early morning on May 29, from Port Stanley, Brigadier-General Parada advised Piaggi and Pedrosa to make their own determinations about continuance of the battle. Unanimously, the Argentine service commanders at Goose Green agreed with Piaggi to yield.

At 1150, May 29, 1982, Piaggi surrendered 500 men from his air force and, much to 3 Brigade's surprise, 1,000 men of the army. Extreme military violence followed by a morally justifiable request (delivered with Keeble's verbal dexterity) to save lives through surrender capped the British victory. Keeble's orchestration of live rounds and calm persuasion had succeeded. His deftness in managing violence only emphasized the dignity and humanity with which he arranged Piaggi's surrender. The Argentineans' capitulation induced Keeble to ask Moore, the just landed commander of British land forces, to press Menéndez for the surrender of

177

Figure 5.1: Text of Major Keeble's Surrender Ultimatum

To: The Commander Argentinean Armed Force (Darwin) (Goose Green)
From: Commander British Armed Forces (Darwin) (Goose Green),

MILITARY OPTIONS

We have sent a PW to you under a white flag of truce to convey the following military options:

1. That you unconditionally surrender your force to us by leaving the township, forming up in a military manner, removing your helmets and laying down your weapons. You will give prior notice of this intention by returning the PW under the white flag with him briefed as to the formalities by no later than 0830 hrs local time.

2. You refuse in the first case to surrender and take the inevitable consequences. You will give prior notice of this intention by returning the PW without his flag (although his neutrality will be respected) no later than 0830 hrs local time.

3. In the event and in accordance with the terms of the Geneva Convention and Laws of War you will be held responsible for the fate of any civilians in Darwin and Goose Green and we in accordance with these terms do give notice of our intention to bombard Darwin and Goose Green.

Signed
C. KEEBLE
Commander of the British Forces*

* Authenticated by Lt. Col. Keeble DSO. The document's rhetorical liberties do not reflect that fine officer's capacity for language, only his lack of sleep for sixty hours during those perilous days.

---

all his forces. Moore failed to act on his own, but pursued the suggestion up the chain of command to Northwood, where the issue died either a bureaucratic or political death. Thatcher and Northwood wanted not only the soup and fish, but the Sunday joint and pudding too.[92]

After Goose Green, "2 Para was like a private army. They would have taken Stanley all by themselves. The new CO had a calming influence on them."[93] Even if the aftermath of such a dramatic battle were plain, 2 Para's weary, rain-soaked infantry could hardly have known what rivers of ink would flow from their bloody toil. So many have hijacked Goose Green for their singular purposes that the battle's reality is barely discernable.[94] Jones' family and friends have had to live with the fact that deification and slander are frequent bedfellows. Worse still, Jones has been defined mostly by his death, and that is a shame, for there was much more to the man than the sad events of May 28, 1982.

The hoopla surrounding Jones and his charge up Darwin Hill has obscured the fact that A Company's failed attack on Darwin Hill and its halt in the open, whatever the causes, brought Jones forward to that stalemate and provided the background and the penultimate cause for his own death. Even though the collapse of his own brittle contrivance and A Company's failure to complete its assignment brought him down, Jones, through his admirers and critics (not a few are both), has come in death rightfully to own the battle, even if Jones' superiors at the Ministry of Defense postulated their own peculiar pantheon.

Farrar-Hockley's lack of success on Darwin Hill got the Military Medal along with Crosland who, with Keeble, many at Goose Green considered the coolest hands on Darwin Hill. Abols, who fired the shot that preceded the Argentine collapse on Darwin Hill, received a not overwhelming decoration reserved for non-commissioned officers. Whatever the nabobs of MOD did, or failed to do, after the war, the close observer can justifiably shake his head and conclude that the existence, conduct and outcome of this battle could have taken place under almost no one else but Jones. It was the genius of Jones, his flaws, his men's training, his assignment of Keeble as though he needed his opposite, his belief in service; his self-centeredness, sometimes benign sometimes harsh; his complete knowledge of his craft; his determination to find his life's peak experience; all that usurped any barren military plan and invested his Battle of Goose Green with a sheen that endures far beyond the awful banalities of an infantry brawl.

Should he have risked a perilous trip through fire to join Farrar-Hockley? Probably not. The reinforcement of failure is taught and rejected at Staff Colleges, as well as at business schools. A Company's gory halt was, fatefully, just the event that a man of Jones' impetuous character did not need to investigate. The wrong man met the wrong event at the wrong time. A more phlegmatic commander might have looked at the broader picture, as Keeble did later, and left Farrar-Hockley to his own devices while using Crosland's B Company to regain momentum and break the ugly stalemate. A few have offered the opinion that, because this battle provided Jones' initiation into live combat, he should be forgiven any errors, and that the awkward thrustings of an ambitious young officer would have turned out right in the end. That judgment remains open to question. What is certain is that Jones would have learned from his mistakes and replaced some officers.

Most battalion-sized battles fought over the centuries for Queen and country fade into lasting insignificance. Thatcher, her war cabinet, Admiral Fieldhouse, Lt. Gen. Trant, Thompson reluctantly and Jones zealously had bet the farm on this one event. All eyes fixed on Goose Green; no other ground combat was in train during those two awful days. In these circumstances, a British loss at Goose Green would, at worst, have stopped the war, given Galtieri a strong negotiating point both domestically and abroad, and led Thatcher's cabinet to arrange a compromised outcome for the war. At best, such a loss would have shifted the moral impetus to the Argentine military forces, severely derogated the British army's professional reputation and resuscitated the ghosts of Suez. America's and Britain's diplomatic initiatives would have stalemated, because diplomacy tainted by military failure itself fails. Haig, Lehman and Weinberger were Jones' silent partner in the dark days of May 1982 when British politicians wanted a sure thing; at Goose Green they got a near disaster. Jones, as the man on the scene, knew precisely what was at stake when he ran up Darwin Hill. It was a battle that Jones had to win because there could be no second chance.

Increase Mather, the 17th Century Boston divine, said of Jones' ancestor, James Bayley, that he was "Discerning of the Times." Jones' blood was clotted with that notion. He had prepared himself to die in battle and it takes little imagination to conclude that he knew he would perish. In a peculiar sense, it was not a sacrifice for him as much as it was for his family. There is no question about that. This half-American wanted to fight and to win the perfect battle for Queen, country and posterity. He had trained and motivated his men to accomplish just that. It was a perfect infantry scrap—if any such can be said to exist—that was won by the perfect British force led for half its hours by the very best of leaders.

Overlooked at Goose Green is what did not happen. Lami-Dozo did not risk his remaining aircraft to beleaguer 2 Para in its worst moments, and Anaya's ships did not close the shore to bombard British guns that could not have answered. No entire units rushed from Fortress Stanley to succor their weary bending platoons. As wretched a victory as it was, Jones and his soldiers laid bare the dishonesty of Argentine leadership, and, incidentally, their own extraordinary competence, for all to see.

Questions about the battle for Darwin Hill and Goose Green linger. G. K. Chesterton's remark that he had seen the truth and that it made no sense comes immediately to mind. Much is to be learnt as the years pass, especially about the sequence of decisions in the UK that led to this militarily profitless endeavor, the reasons behind A Company's halt, the relations between Jones and Farrar-Hockley, the probability of Jones taking de facto command of A Company, the reasons behind his quirky immolation and, most telling of all, what went through this officer's fine mind as he ran up the hill to his death. Like many before and after him, Jones strove for heroism and got felled by tragedy, doomed to fail at what he most loved. He was his own muse and it is certain that he did not mind dying at what he did best.

The bodies had scarcely been placed in that obscene trench alongside statesmen's blunders, but that politicians and others recruited the living and the dead for their own often shabby causes.[95] "You were certainly right about this one," one can almost hear Whitehall's faceless whisperers. Hagiographers have turned Goose Green and Jones' death into a myth whose dimensions have grown while its content has blurred.[96] Major Hugh McManners, in his review of John Wilsey's book on Jones, wrote: "Then something incredible happened, as if a hand had reached deep into the sewage and cleared the blockage. The blue Chinagraph arrows started moving south, the Para machine chewing through the Argentine positions. Our land war was up and running. The enemy was broken. And all because of one man's extraordinary heroism."[97] Aside from the inappropriate metaphor, this comment is inaccurate in its entirety. Few Toms knew right away that the CO was dead. Argentine resistance on Darwin Hill simply petered out in the daylight hours after Abols' shots, although desultory artillery and machine gun fire continued most of the afternoon. The tattered remnants of A Company could not and did not resume the offensive and became part of the battalion reserve. The other platoons continued their own gutter fighting. In any case, their fighting stopped only at sundown, about 1600.

Hear Major John Crosland, OC B Company, "When the news came over the net that H had been killed, I said to Corporal Russell, my signalman, 'That doesn't go any further. We've got enough problems without letting that out.' I was very close to H.—We thought along the same lines. His death certainly stiffened my resolve. I mean I was always determined that we were going to win, but his death added a little more ommpf."[98] Perhaps the moral ascendancy that Moore stipulated is, in fact, gained only through hard combat in which one side convinces the other that it is the better fighting unit. Perhaps too, the British victory at Goose Green offered the exception that proves the rule, for the Argentine commanders on Falklands did not lessen their efforts, let alone sue for peace. While his soldiers skulked in Goose Green's trenches or moped in their POW cages, Galtieri, in mock splendor, hid behind the sycophancy of his immediate circle and the bluster of false hope. The war would go on.

Notes

1. Farrar-Hockley, quoted in Spencer Fitzgibbon, *Not Mentioned in the Despatches* (Cambridge: Lutterworth, 1995), p. 57. John Frost, *2 Para in the Falklands* (London: Buchan and Enright, 1983), advances this version, pp. 66–67, which has become the semi-official rendition of the event.

2. Sergeant Barry Norman, Jones' bodyguard, quoted in John Wilsey, *H. Jones VC: The Life and Death of an Unusual Hero* (London: Hutchinson, 2002), pp. 274–275.

3. See Fitzgibbon, *Not Mentioned in the Despatches*, pp. 62–63, for quoted testimony. None of the many interviewed for this book replied that Jones had ordered a stop to A Company's advance.

4. "The CO got on the radio and told them to get a grip, speed up and continue the movement which they couldn't. So he said; 'I'm not having any of this' and decided to go up and join A Company." Sgt. Barry Norman in Michael Bilton and Peter Kosminsky, *Speaking Out: Untold Stories From the Falklands War* (London: Andre Deutsch, 1989), p. 133.

5. Fitzgibbon, *Not Mentioned in the Despatches*, p. 62.

6. Fitzgibbon, ibid.

7. A Company NCO present in the reentrant during the confrontation between Farrar-Hockley and Jones, letter to the author, February 2002.

8. If alive, Jones might have found rational and balanced critics. In death, he has found a treacly hagiographer in Major-General John Frost, whose *2 Para in the Falklands* omits by way of example but not of limitation critical discussion of: Jones' plan; the limited reconnaissance of Goose Green and Darwin Hill; the difference between raid and capture; Jones' relationship with Farrar-Hockley when the latter got stuck; Jones' de facto assumption of command of A Company; Jones' positioning of Support Company out of the battle; and Jones' refusal to listen to his own unit commanders.

9. Frost, *2 Para in the Falklands*, p. 67.

10. Major John Crosland, OC B Company, quoted in Fitzgibbon, *Not Mentioned in the Despatches*, p. 75.

11. Fitzgibbon, ibid., p. 79.

12. Julian Thompson writes in *No Picnic: 3 Commando Brigade in the South Atlantic, 1982* (London: Cooper, 1985), pp. 87–88, that A Company occupied Coronation Point. It had early on. Only one platoon—Wallis'—stayed, and by Jones' direct order it remained out of the worst of the fight for Darwin Hill. Earlier conjecture by Jones had assumed an Argentine position of company size on Coronation Point. In fact there was none.

13. Jones owned a unique confidence in himself that, not surprisingly, he lacked in his subordinates. The extremely competent Keeble, who had in fact commanded 2 Para for four weeks on the trip south, seems from the available literature and conduct in battle the only officer who met Jones' standards.

14. Perhaps in keeping with Sir Walter Raleigh's remark that dogs bark only at what they do not know, British and American ground officers have asked the author, a former naval officer with a background in amphibious operations, what his solution would have been. The questions were posed in a demotic language not normally used in historical writing. Jones had not read the battle correctly, but he was incapable of passivity. The answer was to stay away from A Company. Failure is a catching disease and should never be reinforced. Send Keeble to A Company with orders to straighten it out by whatever means necessary. The command attention should then have focused on Crosland's B Company who retained tactical integrity and space to maneuver, and should have advanced to contact. The Milans, war winners in the daylight, should have been brought forward straightaway for distribution at daybreak to those in need.

15. Wilsey quoting Sir John Keegan, in *H. Jones VC*, p. 269.

16. Rear Admiral E. A. Cruise, USN, to author, March 1957.

17. Keeble, quoted in Fitzgibbon, *Not Mentioned in the Despatches*, p. 136.

18. Norman conversation, December 6, 2000, with Wilsey, quoted in Wilsey, *H. Jones VC*, p. 273.

19. Jim Love, Radio Operator with Forward Observation Officer's Party at Goose Green. He assisted in carrying Jones' body to the helo LZ. Communication to author, December 2001.

20. After Jones had directed A Company's actions, after he had ordered Farrar-Hockley up the ridge and after his own fatal foray, A Company's situation remained no better than when he arrived. Jones' act was a moral one and had no military content.

21. Sergeant Barry Norman in Bilton and Kosminsky, *Speaking Out*, p. 133.

22. Nick Vaux, *Take That Hill* (McLean: Brasseys, 1986), p. 161.

23. Wallis' platoon was intended to give fire support to the rest of A Company.

24. Piaggi had finally ordered Lieutenant Aliaga's platoon from its useless position on Salinas Beach to Middle Hill where, probably by chance, they found and pinned down Crosland's two platoons.

25. Kennedy, 2 i/c C Company, quoted in Fitzgibbon, *Not Mentioned in the Despatches*, p. 92.

26. Major Hugh Jenner, OC 2 Para Support Company, quoted in Fitzgibbon, ibid., p. 93.

27. A Company was commanded by Dair Farrar-Hockley, the son of a serving general and a hero of the Korean war; B Company's OC was John Crosland,

a distinguished veteran of the SAS; C Company was led by Major Roger Jenner, a very skilled and experienced officer; and D Company was headed by Phil Neame, whose father, a retired general, had won a Victoria Cross. These men's backgrounds, professional competence and zeal could scarcely be questioned. Of course, once having assigned them, the political repercussions of their dismissal in the jungle of informal relationships that infest the British army would have to be finely calculated.

28. Major Chris Keeble, 2 i/c 2 Para, quoted in Bilton and Kosminsky, *Speaking Out*, p. 145.

29. Juan Pozzi, letter to author, December 2000.

30. "The SAS had not gone and looked properly." Thompson interview with author, November 1997. Keep in mind that Jones' plan was not intended to lure his troops into disaster, but was rather a learned reaction to the problem before him. He was almost certainly incapable of beginning the battle in any other way. Jones, by sheer intelligence, energy and will had shaped 2 Para into a splendid military instrument whose excellence was diluted by the sere formulaics of a rusty system that had not been tried in war since Suez in 1956. It was when the battle started and became an impasse that Jones relied on his best side, the moral or spiritual one that has been known over the years to win much more than it lost.

31. Frost, *2 Para in the Falklands*, p. 71.

32. Why the attack was made by 15 or so officers and NCOs, and not by the remaining members of the two pinned-down platoons testifies to the disorder, haste and urgency with which Jones issued his order.

33. Junior NCO who participated in the attack, quoted in Fitzgibbon, *Not Mentioned in the Despatches*, p. 100.

34. Jim Love, *2 Para in Darwin Hill,* Britain's Small Wars Web site, www.britains-smallwars.com.

35. Frost claims that "H intended to take the Argentines in the flank while they were still distracted by the attack on the ledge." Frost, *2 Para in the Falklands*, pp. 76–77. This conclusion is entirely erroneous. The Argentines on the ledge had, before Jones set off, repulsed Farrar-Hockley's makeshift bound-to-fail attack. If anyone was distracted, it was Farrar-Hockley, not the Argentines. Moreover, Jones was not seen by many of his own or of the enemy to go off.

36. Communication from a distinguished Argentine citizen, December 9, 2002. The soldier in question has declined to identify himself to the author and that wish has been respected.

37. See statement by 2nd Lieutenant Coe, in Mark Adkin, *Goose Green* (London: Orion Books, 1992), p. 241. In Farrar-Hockley's presence, Jones also gave direct orders to Coe about resiting mortars, thus raising again the question of who commanded A Company in its moments of peril.

38. Corp. Abols, Sergeant Blackburn and 2nd Lieutenant Coe agree that Jones' rush was sudden and unannounced. See Adkin, *Goose Green*, p. 121.

39. In his very fine biography of Jones, John Wilsey puts Jones' time of death at 0930. This time may be early, because Jones made for A Company's TAC HQ in the light and needed cover from smoke. He remained there alive but not sentient for about 45 minutes. Sunrise on May 28, 1982, occurred at 0746, accord-

ing to the U.S. Naval Observatory, Washington, D.C. Jones died probably at 1000 local time. Frost says 1345; Benest says 1330. Fitzgibbon, *Not Mentioned in the Despatches*, p. 121. The 3 Brigade log reported CO down at 1331. These times are difficult to accept because Jones arrived at A Company no later than 0830 and remained there not more than ninety minutes before his death.

40. Bilton and Kosminsky, *Speaking Out*, pp. 135–136.

41. Quoted in Adkin, *Goose Green*, p. 247.

42. Written communication to author, March 2002. Published with permission.

43. Interview, author to Jolly, March 13, 2002.

44. Wilsey, *H. Jones VC*, p. 264.

45. Had he lived, Jones would have enjoyed the epiphany of knowing that his men, almost to a man, were as competent and as steadfast as he himself. He would also recall what he had seen in battle, that a few had failed and that others showed themselves as splendid combat leaders. From all this comes the property of knowing how the battle "runs".

46. Gunfire support by a single gun from one ship does not satisfy the requirements of any distressed body of infantry.

47. Then Major Tony Rice RA, Jones' battery commander and present with Jones at the bottom of Darwin Hill, has contended that Jones' death provided the adrenalin that restarted the attack on Darwin Hill. (Conversation with author, April 13, 2002.) It is certain that Jones' presence, aside from the petty annoyance of having the CO watch the carnage, heartened the men, but it is far more likely that Abols' successful shot into an Argentine bunker and the paras' sustained fire broke the defenders' will. Rice's belief invites the speculation that, had Jones waited 15 minutes for Abols and others to take out the bunkered positions, the battle might have ended without Jones' death.

48. Adkin, *Goose Green*, p. 253.

49. Ibid., p. 167.

50. Frost's statement in *2 Para in the Falklands*, p. 95: "He [Jones] had shown that 2 Para was just not stoppable" is wholly erroneous. At the hour of Jones' death, 2 Para was stopped and being mauled to boot. The battle's culmination supports Frost's view in a manner possible very different from that general officer's intent.

51. The most uncomplimentary comment that this author heard from one of his men about those tragic minutes came from a 2 Para veteran of Goose Green who was not in A Company: "I heard the CO got himself killed. He was a daft man, but warrie."

52. Farrar-Hockley claimed to Adkin, *Goose Green*, p. 188: "I do not agree that a particular piece of ground was taken on his account." To Fitzgibbon he claimed: "within fifteen minutes of his carrying out his action, we were able to bring the thing to a conclusion." Fitzgibbon, *Not Mentioned in the Despatches*, p. 120.

53. Lord Moran, *Anatomy of Courage* (Boston: Houghton Mifflin, 1967), p. 127.

54. 2 Para junior NCO present at Goose Green. March 2002 correspondence to author. The letter has been edited only to omit personal references to the let-

ter's author and to the author of this book. The British officer's name and function are known to the author and have been omitted deliberately.

55. For example, gusts of wind changed artillery shells' flight and made accurate call of shot extremely difficult. Soggy ground greatly reduced the shattering effect of what rounds did land near their intended targets. Several participants in the battle have remarked to the author that the naval gunfire did little tactical good because fall of shot could not be determined. One officer claimed that so many rounds were fired, neither he nor his NCO's could discern the shots' origins, friend or foe. The shelling, finished at dawn, may have lessened the defenders' will to fight at that time.

56. Jones' plan has raised detailed and sober reflections on his actions at Goose Green. In the Army Quarterly, July 1995, pp. 263–265, by way of admitting his own mistakes at Goose Green, Major-General Julian Thompson, Jones' immediate senior, objected to the tone (wiseacre) and substance (Jones isn't here to defend himself) of Spencer Fitzgibbon's book. However salutary it is to admit to one's own mistakes, Thompson raised the wrong ones. The near disaster at Goose Green in no way rests on his shoulders, yet he should have had the Scimitars and Scorpions tested to discover if they could safely traverse Falklands' bogs, and he should have insured, through his liaison at 2 Para, Major Héctor Gullán, that Jones planned a raid, not a seize and hold operation. As for Jones' inability to defend himself, no history could ever be written, by definition, if criticism of the dead were omitted. Anyway, no historian may sneer with the ghosts of the dead looking over his shoulder. See, also, Ian Cobain, "General Takes Blame for Death of Colonel 'H'," *Telegraph*, March 26, 2000, electronic news, p. 1.

57. There is a conundrum here. Surely, any leader must have a plan and the men must have confidence in it and in their leader. However, the fact that a plan has worked one hundred times does not mean, in pure logic, that the same plan, when applied to a new set of circumstances, will succeed similarly.

58. See David Frazer, *Knight's Cross, A Life of Field Marshall Erwin Rommel* (London: Harper, 1993), p. 270 etseq.

59. Jones' refusal to ingest the pertinent facts of battle, as they appeared, is almost incomprehensible. Field-Marshall Montgomery, the prickly autocrat of World War II's combat, spent thousands of hours pouring over intelligence reports and his own dispositions down to the battalion level. He organized a corps of liaison officers, all young and keen, who had access to allied head quarters and command posts with a view to giving Montgomery a timely and honest view of affairs, not always available through official channels. Their reports proved invaluable, especially in times of crisis such as the Battle of the Bulge. At least two of this group were killed, several were wounded and one became, after the war, a very famous Master of Foxhounds. For many examples of this very useful administrative tool of war, see Nigel Hamilton, *Monty The Battles of Field Marshall Bernard Montgomery* (New York: Random House, 1994).

60. Seamus Heaney trans., *Beowulf* (New York: Norton, 2000), p. 93.

61. Mullen and Leuer, in *Close Combat: Light Infantry In Action*, Part 11, Newsletter No. 2–88.

62. British Army's practice dictates that in the event of the CO's inability to complete the mission, the Battery Commander (BC) takes command until the 2 i/c comes forward. Rice's reluctance was justified. He was pinned down with A Company and knew less about the battle than had Jones. "That is why I admire Keeble. He knew where to put his trust." Trooper A, written correspondence to author, January 2002.

63. Postwar comments and letters by Argentine infantrymen stationed on Darwin Hill that day frequently mention "La ferocidad de la lucha." However stuck A Company was, in the end its firepower bent its enemy's fighting spirit. At Jones' death, CSM Price had already collected 58 prisoners. Robert Fox, *Eyewitness Falklands* (London: Methuen, 1982), p. 180.

64. Milans are direct fire, line of sight weapons that lack night sights. Jones had presumed that the battle would be won by first light.

65. In judging that they had survived with little fire support, many if not most of the Toms were unaware that the Milans had been left out of the battle until Keeble brought them up. It is almost inconceivable that a light infantry unit lacking heavy weapons in the attack should have left its Milans behind.

66. Very early one morning in 1959, in Saigon, a successful and soon-to-retire colonel of infantry roared to a very young naval officer that a commanding officer had to know "weather, terrain and the enemy." With prescience, he claimed knowledge of the first two (in SE Asia) but not the last.

67. Frost (*2 Para in the Falklands*, p. 94) criticized Thompson at length for not coming forward after Jones' death in order to confer with Keeble. Frost showed the same lack of confidence in the 2 i/c that Jones manifested in a few of his officers. Quite properly, Thompson gave Keeble full sway to conduct the battle as a competent professional officer on the spot. Frost seems unaware that the last vexation a battle commander wants, under such circumstances, is a visit from the boss. Major Héctor Gullán, 3 Brigade's liaison with 2 Para, stayed by Keeble's side and kept Thompson fully informed.

68. T. S. Elliott wrote a splendid phrase: "Seeing God through the ashes." Keeble had to bring victory through the rain and smoke from the burning gorse.

69. Author's note: The well battered A Company could hardly be said by then to constitute by itself a useful reserve.

70. Keeble, letter to author, September 14, 2001.

71. Fitzgibbon, *Not Mentioned in the Despatches*, p. 150.

72. See Britain's Small Wars website, www.britains-smallwars.com.

73. See Gómez-Centurión, "Yo creí que usted venía a rendirse!" in Britain's Small Wars website, www.britains-smallwars.com.

74. Junior NCO present at Darwin Hill, to author in conversation, February 2001.

75. Argentine prisoners received the same excellent medical care from Captain Steve Hughes, Surgeon Commander Jolly and his team as did British causalities. Care and evacuation were given according to the wounds' seriousness and not by the color of the uniform. Initial difficulties in finding the wounded and evacuating them were resolved by the intrepid airmanship of Greenhalgh and Walker in their Scout helicopters.

76. Farrar-Hockley, OC A Company, speaking to OC C Company after Darwin Hill was taken. Quoted in Adkin, *Goose Green*, p. 296.

77. Surgeon Captain Rick Jolly RN (ret) later commented on June 13, 1998, at the Drumhead Service, Aldershot: "It's all down to their basic fitness, plus the wonderful work done by the RMO of 2 Para, Captain Steve Hughes and his battlefield medic teams."

78. There is no question that Piaggi stationed guns close to the community hall and its captured Kelpers in order to prevent British attacks from land and air. Keeble has been faulted unfairly for using C Company here, because putting it into the attack was overkill and left him bereft of an effective reserve element. Keeble needed momentum. Roger Jenner's two platoons had some of 2 Para's best soldiers and Jenner himself was, in Keeble's words, "brave, clever and unflappable." Keeble retained HQ Company in reserve and his own party with Milans, MMGs and snipers as fire base/reserve.

79. Trooper A, not a member of C Company, eye witness, written communication to author, February 2002.

80. Trooper B, no longer in the British Army, quoted to author in written correspondence, February 2002. A senior British officer and student of the battle has stated to the author that Crosland has gotten far less credit than he deserves for the success of the battle. A senior NCO, present at Goose Green but not in Crosland's company, agreed vehemently.

81. Jones' death did not affect the men very much, they had to stay alive and fight the battle, whereas some officers were seen to be very moved. Trooper A in written answers to author's questions, February 2002.

82. Trooper A in written correspondence to author, February 2002. Bentley received the Military Medal (MM) for his continuous bravery under fire.

83. The nominal commander of TF Solari declined to transport himself to Goose Green with his men.

84. Again, the Argentine staffs made for the least profitable target. Its size and emission of signals would have identified 3 Brigade's HQ to the bleariest eye. A napalm drop on those huddled worthies might have changed the war.

85. R. E. Bell, *Logistical Support of British Land Forces in the Falkland Islands Campaign 1982*. Unpublished.

86. See W. J. Tustin, "Logistics of the Falklands War," *The Army and Defense Quarterly* 114, no. 4 (October 1984).

87. James Markham from Buenos Aires, *New York Times*, April 13, 1982.

88. Twenty years later, all the participants in the battle who were interviewed for this book still praise not only the treatment afforded by Surgeon Commander Jolly and his team, but also the training that the platoons underwent on the trip south.

89. Battle's mental and physical intimacies surpass those of school and work and often those of bed and family.

90. Post war interrogations revealed that Argentine ground troops had little confidence in the ability or resourcefulness of their helicopter pilots, who could not, in any case, fly safely at night.

91. Thompson's statement to Keeble, reiterated publicly since then, shows an unusual twist. It is permitted to kill or wound civilians in order to save them.

92. Clausewitz believed that nations, especially those in conflict, try to surpass each other in spheres other than combat. It was unlikely that General Galtieri, leader and product of a nation known for its addiction to fast cars, polo and a pseudo European café life, would have acquiesced to cold military logic.

93. Eyewitness NCO, not from 2 Para.

94. Certainly, Jones sought professional renown for a grand victory, yet no member of 2 Para who was present at Goose Green and to whom the author has spoken or written has stated, suggested or implied that Jones sought his own glory at the expense of his subordinates. The paras were all dogs in the same hunt; Jones made no bones about who was the lead hound.

95. *The Falklands Campaign: The Lessons* is a storehouse of misinformation. Inter alia it stated: "2 Para began by attacking Darwin"—not so, Burntside House was the first objective; "the settlement was secured by mid-afternoon"—not true, it fell the next day, the 29th of May.

96. Field Marshall Bramall, then Chief of the General Staff, wrote to 2 Para: "the battalion has executed a feat of arms probably unsurpassed in the glorious history of the British Army." Frost, *2 Para in the Falklands*, pp. 178–179. Giddiness of the moment probably explains this mawkish hyperbole. Brammal's judgment does not stand close examination. Slim's Burma veterans might well protest. This admirer gives pride of place to the action at Kohima.

97. Major Hugh McManners, in the Sunday Times Book Review, March 17, 2002.

98. Max Arthur, *Above All Courage* (London: Sphere Books, 1986), p. 206.

6

Conclusion:
Cui Bono?

Myths are widely accepted stories of what happened or what is believed to have happened. They are meant to sustain, to encourage and often to excuse. They build trust. They are the psychological ganglia of armies. The British army desperately needed a victorious encounter in which it could clearly show that it retained the ability to field a CO who could win critical battles under the worst circumstances. Once committed, the British army could not fail in the Falklands. Haig, Lehman and Weinberger knew that too, even if Nott and others saw only gloom and defeat. That hopeful view applied to the Parachute Regiment and to the British army as a whole. It wanted a continuation of Arnhem and the battles of North Africa, and not of Suez. Jones and 2 Para were the self-elected point men. Yet, throughout the war, British commanders at Northwood, who had never commanded major combat assets under fire, behaved as though this were not an overarching purpose of the war. In setting the British Army back aright, Thompson, the professional infantry officer who had performed brilliantly in getting his troops ashore, had a far more difficult time with his seniors at MOD, Nott and Trant than Montgomery ever had with Bradley, Eisenhower and Patton or that his fighting platoons had with their Argentine enemy.[1] But that is another story.

Before Jones' men had fought and won the battle of Goose Green, the junta had circulated its diplomatic death rattles through Costa-Méndez, its foreign minister. This initiative, conveyed through the Peruvian foreign office, gained the most attention—though, like Haig's negotiations, it lacked sufficient substance to stop the fighting. Each member of the junta, and several others, could and did veto any Argentine diplomatic move. The junta stipulated that all agreements apply to South Georgia as well as to the Falklands; that all military forces return, within a 30 day period, to their home bases; that the UN provide the functions of government; and that Argentina and its citizens have full access to the islands.[2] These terms were clearly unacceptable to Margaret Thatcher, yet they remained the essence of the junta's proposals even after the Argentine defeat at Goose Green. Despite substantial losses in men and materiel, Argentine resistance stiffened after Goose Green, as the bloody battles of Wireless Ridge and Tumbledown Mountain were to show.

One thing was, is and always will be clear: No one with an ounce of military sense could claim that the gore of Goose Green had advanced, in a purely military sense, the British recapture of Port Stanley by one jot or tittle. In fact, final victory was delayed. The mere occurrence of the battle constituted a failure of direction by meddlers 8,000 miles away. Politicians manipulate voters and their money. Some do it well. Almost none has contrived successful battles. There is a mordant connection to this practice and habit of mind that seems almost an ingrained property of constitutional government. It seems never to change that wars are politicians' nearly unbreakable toys in need of expensive mending by individuals such as Jones and the men in 2 Para.

Jones and Keeble in the Battle for Darwin Hill and Goose Green

"There is a gap between the literary legend, the paper description of politics, and the reality. It is a gap which begins with the description given by journalists, who are describing it from the outside and then confirmed by the academics who read the journalists' articles and regard them as accounts of what really happened."[3]

Keeble has proposed that battles are lost, not won. This may be so, and Goose Green offers good evidence for his argument. Had Argentine artillery fired VT fuses that explode shells in the air rather than HE rounds that plopped into the wet earth, 2 Para's casualties would have risen geometrically. Combat is, after all, one of man's most entropic endeavors. From the first shot, both sides get diminished toward nothingness. Surely, combat drains will power and fighting spirit more readily from some than from others, and weather and ground, for example, play a lesser role than the *philosophes militaires*, the logical positivists, believe. Certainly, those who acted as though elegant technologies put into play by heavy battalions would prevail in Vietnam were wrong, but huge forests have been slaughtered to provide paper for that unfinished discussion.

2 Para won at Darwin Hill and Goose Green because of Jones and despite him. His plan had not so much failed, as Goose Green was not the kind of engagement suited for the military thinking behind the plan. Darwin Hill was not Kursk. The *langue* of Camberly Staff College did not fit an infantry brawl where each side knew little about the other. A Company's failure to take Darwin Hill anywhere close to Jones' timings and its heavy casualties made the plan appear worse than it was. But 2 Para's unity of purpose, its cohesion, its resolute NCOs, its hard training, its basic military competence, its failure to crack even as the ground was littered with its bodies—all that was Jones' doing and it carried the day. Of course, Jones had accepted and retained Keeble as his 2 i/c and quite obviously his equal as a professional military officer. That was one of Jones' better choices.

A leader's first task is to transfer his values to his subordinates and to convince them to act on these values. Jones' were the primal military virtues capped by the absolute need to win. Courage is the flip side of fear. Jones feared failure, as a moral man must, and that is why he performed the ultimate act of courage. After 18 months, the Toms understood Jones' message. When all share the same values, everything else falls into place. It is clear to this admirer of the Toms that, once having given them their assignment, Jones might well have remained considerably back, allocated fire support and let the fighting platoons win the battle. It is not too much of an exaggeration that after the shooting started they had little need of him. The men's combat skills and their loyalty to each other and to their immediate leaders surpassed any dry instruction. Even now, the British survivors of Goose Green remain reluctant to discuss the event, except in terms of their mates' bravery and accomplishments under fire.[4]

Jones is widely if rather grudgingly admired, but he is not widely discussed. The Toms insist ardently that they won the battle on their own, without help from air, sea or artillery support. Perhaps in the doing, few realized that they accomplished precisely what Jones had in mind and in a manner of which he would have approved.[5] While all those interviewed for this book admitted that Jones did not fit the mold of a beloved commanding officer, all did strongly aver that it was Jones' regime, writ large that got them through a very nasty two days. That fact can never be too well remembered. What must also be graven in stone is that so well trained was 2 Para, that, in the worst of times, it could switch from Jones' self-centered and iron-strict method of fighting a battle to Keeble's delegation of his combat assets to where bullets flew.[6]

Few second-in-commands dare not mimic their immediate seniors or their plans. Keeble was cut from a different mold. Using Jones-trained soldiers, he administered his battle as differently from Jones as was possible.[7] Of course, he drew victory from the men that Jones had molded. What Keeble accomplished was as important as what he did not attempt, because his non-invasive administration, to borrow a civilian term, triumphed. His common sense, his confidence in his subordinates and the ethical sense to work for a surrender of the Argentine garrison rescued 2 Para from stalemate and saved lives, too. Few combat officers face imminent disaster such as beset Keeble and go on to win.

Keeble has stated: "The victory, however, was H's. The inspiration of 2 Para came from him, and my role was merely to act on his behalf in his absence."[8] Hardly ever has a significant historical judgment been more modest or less accurate. True, Jones was a larger than life presence on Darwin Hill. His conduct there—imagined and real—and his bizarre death have made him the cynosure of politicians' and historians' eyes. The sad fact remains that his plan for taking Goose Green was too complex and his execution of it fell well behind his impossible timings (his enemies have made that more evident than was necessary), though surely little of A Company's collapsed attack on Darwin Hill can be placed at Jones' door. It was Keeble's acuity in seeing how the battle ran[9] and his astute tactics that saved the day.[10] Not enough have noted that Keeble's tactics succeeded because he employed Jones' men to finish his work. Those interviewed for this book, an unscientific sample, believe that, aside from Abols, Crosland and the paras' medic, Steve Hughes, Keeble stood out above the others. The Ministry of Defense was not in full accord with the common opinion.

Yet as Great Nations in crisis must proffer, Britain and Thatcher needed a single hero upon whom all could focus. Argentine bullets chose Jones. A close family lost a devoted husband and father.[11] British life lost a very good but ill-omened man. Upon reflection, one does not crave to emulate Jones in battle; he gave himself up when, as military commander, he need not have done so; his men would have won the battle for Goose Green with Jones dead or alive. The canny and humane Keeble or the bluff "Four miles west of the moon" Crosland or the "Tea and Porridge" Neame seem the more admirable exemplars of calm leadership under fire. After all, they had rescued Thatcher's war cabinet and 2 Para from the disaster that befell an ill-advised plan that was based on fundamental misconceptions, not of Jones' doing, about how the war should run.

Some historians have written that the allies' superiority in materiel, and not their soldierly skills, won World War II. The reverse held true in Goose Green.[12] Lord Moran, Churchill's physician and a veteran of trench warfare in World War I, claims that each man has an impalpable and fixed stock of courage that, once exhausted, is forever gone. Training, hard work and a certain spirit fill that store. Jones saw to it that his men, and he, entered battle with their courage account filled to the top. As Neame stated, "I just don't think that the Battle of Goose Green as we know it could have happened without him."[13] Outnumbered and outgunned, it is the Jones-trained Toms, their discipline and self-discipline, their guts and steadfastness that most demand our admiration.[14] Jones was posthumously recognized with the Victoria Cross (see Figure 6.1).

The victory at Goose Green did not end the war, but it did derogate the smug and patronizing manner in which Argentine military and political society moved. Remember that after Galtieri's men had occupied the Falklands, he stepped onto the world's stage or at least on the front pages of major newspapers. This armchair general, who idolized George Patton and habitually watched his movies, had his very brief day in the sun. There was a sensuous, almost erotic, aura about him and his audience when, just after Stanley fell, he spoke to insensate throngs from the balcony of the Casa Rosada, the Argentine White House. Both he and his audience expected the country—and the world, for that matter—to accept, even to applaud, his lunatic and bloody schemes. After all, Argentina was the fantasized Europe of South America with cafes and psychiatrists' offices that would provide fodder of any satirist if he cared to look. Galtieri behaved as though the world had suspended its powers of observation, set aside its capacity for outrage, and rejected its unspoken conclusion that Argentina could not manage its own affairs. His was an age-old delusion. He offered seduction rather than reasoned conviction. Dictatorships, and Galtieri's was no exception, hide their sins beneath a veneer of veiled force and saccharine cajolery. A little bread and some circus do no harm either. After Goose Green, Galtieri's skills at dissimulation wore thin and his regime's ugliness popped to the surface for all to see.[15]

Figure 6.1: Lt. Col. H. Jones Posthumous Victoria Cross Award

MONDAY, 11th OCTOBER 1982
MINISTRY OF DEFENSE

HONOURS AND AWARDS
ARMY DEPARTMENT

The QUEEN has been graciously pleased to approve the Posthumous award of the VICTORIA CROSS to the under mentioned in recognition of gallant and distinguished service during the operations in the South Atlantic:

Lieutenant Colonel Herbert JONES O.B.E. (465788), The Parachute Regiment

On May 28th, 1982, Lieutenant Colonel Jones was commanding 2nd Battalion, The Parachute Regiment, in operations on the Falkland Islands. The Battalion was ordered to attack enemy positions in and around the settlements of Darwin and Goose Green. During the attack against an enemy who was well dug-in with mutually supporting positions sited in depth, the Battalion was held up just South of Darwin by a particularly well-prepared and resilient enemy position of at least 11 trenches on an important ridge. A number of casualties were received. In order to read the battle fully and to ensure that the momentum of his attack was not lost, Colonel Jones took forward his reconnaissance party to the foot of a re-entrant, which a section of his Battalion had just secured. Despite persistent, heavy and accurate fire, the reconnaissance party gained the top of the re-entrant, at approximately the same height as the enemy positions. From here, Colonel Jones encouraged the direction of his Battalion mortar fire, in an effort to neutralize the enemy positions. However, these had been well prepared and continued to pour effective fire onto the Battalion advance, which, by now held-up for over an hour and under increasingly heavy artillery fire, was in danger of faltering.

However many mistakes Northwood committed, and they bumbled often, it was clear to the outside world that the war was all but over, however long it lasted, once Jones and his like appeared on the scene. Liberal democracies seem to cough up such individuals as Jones and his men in the nick of time. Jones and the Toms had also shown the junta, in the most blatant way possible, that another kind of leadership existed. Though Galtieri was a son of the people, he had no lasting connection to them. No electricity carried his moral authority—it did not exist—to the troops in the field or to his electorate. Both wanted to hear something redemptive that was not in his power to say. Galtieri's ability to govern never grew. His will to fight never existed. His power to do evil never lapsed. Even now,

In his effort to gain a good viewpoint, Colonel Jones was now at the very front of his Battalion. It was clear to him that desperate measures were needed in order to overcome the enemy position and rekindle the attack, and that, unless these measures were taken promptly, the Battalion would sustain increasing casualties and the attack would perhaps even fail. It was time for personal leadership and action. Colonel Jones immediately seized a sub-machine gun, and, calling on those around him and with total disregard for his own safety, charged the nearest enemy position. This action exposed him to fire from a number of trenches. As he charged up a short slope at the enemy position, he was seen to fall and roll backward downhill. He immediately picked himself up, and again charged the enemy trench, firing his sub-machine gun and seemingly oblivious to the intense fire directed at him. He was hit by fire from another trench, which he outflanked, and fell dying only a few feet from the enemy he had assaulted. A short time later, A Company of the Battalion attacked the enemy who quickly surrendered. The devastating display of courage by Colonel Jones had completely undermined their will to fight further.

Thereafter, the momentum of the attack was rapidly regained, Darwin and Goose Green were liberated, and the Battalion released the local inhabitants unharmed and forced the surrender of some 1,200 of the enemy.

The achievements of 2nd Battalion, The Parachute Regiment, at Darwin and Goose Green set the tone for the subsequent land victory on the Falklands. They achieved such a moral superiority over the enemy in this first battle that, despite advantages of numbers and selection of battle-ground, they never thereafter doubted either the superior fighting qualities of the British troops, or their own inevitable defeat. This was an action of the utmost gallantry by a commanding officer whose dashing leadership and courage throughout the battle were an inspiration to all about him.

Source: Supplement, London Gazette, published by authority October 8, 1982 (Issue 49134).

not a few Argentine military and politicians marvel at "Ganso Verde y Jones." They had not been warned that war could end that way.

A Post-War Assessment

"Trust Not In Princes" [16]

Despite the euphoria of victory, many British, especially those who had lost members of their family, demanded to know the reasons for the war and the dead and the mutilated.[17] Some confused Thatcher, the Warrior

Queen, with Thatcher, the clever administrator who stood astride city and shire alike in June 1982 as had few before her. Few troubled to investigate and to note the difference between the two. In truth, she had told her military to get on with it and they had. She was not that "great she-elephant from Finchley" as Denis Healey cruelly called her, but rather a lucky politician who had superb infantry at her disposal. But the victor's crown lay uneasily on her well-groomed head until she could offer good and sufficient reason as to why the war had been let start and why the hospitals had so many new patients. Had the butcher's bill been necessary after all? In summer 1982, Thatcher retreated into a familiar guise, the successful politician who did her daily best for a proud and not too curious electorate. Victory is a one-dose opiate that sedates all, and she knew it.

On July 6, 1982, Thatcher appointed a six man panel, headed by Lord Franks, to investigate the causes of the war and the reasons for the Falklands' temporary, if humiliating, loss. The Franks Report, as it was known, was to "review the way in which the responsibilities of Government in relation to the Falkland Islands and their Dependencies were discharged in the period leading up to the Argentine invasion of the Falkland Islands on 2 April, taking into account all such factors in previous years as are relevant and to report."[18]

The panel's birth and first days of life were difficult. Thatcher's predecessor as head of the conservative party, Edward Heath, said: "those of us who have experienced the treatment of previous administrations by herself and her advisors . . . [had] . . . no confidence whatever in her plans for the Falkland inquiry."[19] James Callaghan, a former labor Prime Minister, questioned whether Mrs. Thatcher had: "acted prudently and with foresight in the early months of [1982]."[20] He also wanted control over access to his cabinet papers, which are normally reserved from public scrutiny for thirty years. Neither party favored careful inquiries into the messy Falklands business, because no one really knew what blunders might come to light. Yet hundreds of needless deaths and the expenditure of millions of ill afforded pounds demanded some explanation, especially when victory's glow might camouflage cruel truths that could later emerge in unsympathetic hands.

That the Franks committee of Lords Barber, Lever, Watkinson, Sir Patrick Nairne and Merlyn Rees, in fact Thatcher's counsel for her defense, should be called in their mandarinate splendor to judge the performance of their fellow members of the political establishment suggested a literary tea of the blandest blanc mange. And so it turned out. The committee and its minions interviewed fewer than 60 persons, received written depositions from many others and never released any verbatim and unexpurgated testimony. Thus, we must take these witnesses' paraphrased language at its reported value.

The Franks Report

The Franks Report titillated a public starved by the Official Secrets' Act for glimmerings into the workings of government. Franks took that narrow road in order to disguise the paucity of relevant and true facts and to cover the Thatcher government's failure to foresee the war. Franks' elegant prose beguiles and finally numbs, even if, after all these years, its causidical felonies still astound and affront. Righteous tedium was its realized purpose and the report itself was all but forgotten a year after its presentation to Margaret Thatcher on December 31, 1982, and its publication on January 18, 1983.

After reading a few pages, Franks' linguistic excellence conjures up the suspicion in readers' minds that something perhaps too clever is afoot. Still, the knowledgeable reader pauses and admits to himself that bureaucracies must practice elfish but acceptable duplicity in order to survive. A few more pages and he realizes that the authors of the Franks Report fulfilled their duty to excess. According to Franks, no one could be held culpable for the war's sudden arrival. The buck stopped, in fact, nowhere.

First, by way of example, but not of limitation, Franks' errors of commission:

- Par. 12, line 2. Jack Solis was not, as written, the only RN representative on Falklands. Several naval members of HMS *Endurance*'s crew were conducting surveys away from Stanley.
- Par. 12, line 2. HMS *Endurance* was not a converted Ice Breaker.
- Par. 65, line 4. Most persons at King Edward Point did in fact know details of Davidoff's contract.
- Par. 70, line 5. "Impossible terrain"? How could they then "scramble" over it?
- Par. 145, line 3. No ice cap exists at the extreme NE point of Stromness Bay or anywhere else in the vicinity.
- Par. 169, line 7. The defaced notice said nothing about unlawful landings. In fact, it stated: "British Antarctic Survey, Leith Harbor Depot, Unauthorized entry prohibited" with the last line in Spanish, Russian, Polish and French.

- Par. 169 line 9. Captain Briatore of the *Bahía Buen Suceso* claimed his permission to enter Leith Harbor came from the British Foreign and Commonwealth Office, not the British Embassy in Buenos Aires.
- Par. 170. The observation party was not at Leith, as stated in paragraph 171, but near Jason Point on the Busen Peninsula, about 7 km away across Stromness Bay. It occupied a high pass with a good view of all the whaling stations in Stromness Bay. Activities at Leith were observed through powerful binoculars, and Argentine VHF communications were monitored on March 21st by a British survey officer who understood Spanish. The report of the lowering of the Argentine flag was made by the field party at Leith who photographed it at approximately 0800 on March 20th as they withdrew from the area. The British Observation Post was established about noon on March 21st.
- Par. 171. "No sign of shore party." The observation post reported that there were at least six to ten Argentineans at Leith after the *Bahía Buen Suceso* had departed and that they had heavy plant, two boats and other items. It was also reported that one of the two boats had blown across Stromness Bay. Shortly afterwards, the reception in Leith of the yacht *Cinq Gars Pour* was described.
- Par. 263. "The actual order to invade was probably not given until at least 31 March." The adverb "probably" robs the statement of any evidentiary use. It can safely be said that the participants had been mobilized, that the necessary forces were at sea and that the invasion was in train many days before March 31st, and that the order to go over the beaches, pushed up after Britain threatened to retake South Georgia, was given on March 26, 1982.
- Par. 266. "The invasion of the Falkland Islands on 2 April could not have been foreseen." The use of the exact date forecloses an affirmative answer that the invasion might have been foreseen on the 4th or 5th of April or at any time other than the 2nd. That statement is probably the report's sleaziest in a mare's nest of verbal muck.
- Par. 277. "Argentina always had the capability successfully to mount a sudden operation against the Islands." The adjective "sudden" voids this statement as true fact. Contrary to Franks' assessment, any invasion took weeks to mount after months of planning. Any Argentine invasion fleet would need, and did in the event need, at least three days and probably five from the time it

left port to put troops ashore onto the Falklands from the Argentine mainland. All this assumes the most favorable weather.

One wag commented to the effect that: "The intelligence business is a Sargosso Sea of bits and pieces." Possibly true for those British intelligence persons who dealt with Argentina. Most raw intelligence and the conclusions drawn therefrom are blatantly and often horrifyingly clear upon first reading. It is unknown whether the Sargosso Sea, known for its soggy and virtually impenetrable mats of seaweed, has more bits and pieces of anything else in it than any other sea.

There are several questions and issues not clearly discussed in the Franks Report for which a reasonable man might have sought explication:

- Par. 208. Press Reports of Argentine/Uruguayan naval exercises. In fact, these reports were without substance and were used by the junta to cover ships' departure from home ports. A phone call to Uruguay could have confirmed that the exercise did not exist. The notion of two nominally Christian countries putting fleets to sea in an unprecedented and unannounced exercise close to Easter seems not to have bothered Protestant Northern Europe.
- Par. 264 and General. In March 1982, 17,000 British citizens lived in Argentina where many administered banks, social clubs, polo teams, schools, a newspaper and businesses. Is it possible that none of these could not have noticed the administrative and materiel preparations for war? Ships loading, marines' barracks and bars empty, frigate *Guerrico* prematurely pulled from overhaul? The submarine base and its ships at Mar del Plata are visible from a civilian road.
- General. Why did the Franks committee fail to ask Margaret Thatcher why she had not sent an ultimatum to the junta that invasion of the Falklands would precipitate war?
- General. Why did Franks neglect to ask Nott, Carrington or Thatcher why the Falklands had not been declared to the junta as a vital interest?
- General. In 1977, during a perceived threat to the Falklands, the British government sent a small flotilla, including a nuclear submarine, to stand off South America and to be noticed. The Argentine threat evaporated. Why was this incident and the lesson that might have been drawn therefrom not explored in Franks?

- General. Why did the Franks committee fail to ask Thatcher how the Falklands was not an item for Cabinet in March but became a vital issue on April 3rd and was worth 255 lives later on?
- General. Chilean Naval Intelligence meetings focused during March 1982 on the possible invasion of the Falklands and concluded that such was possible in late March/April. If Chile masticated this possibility, why could not the British have known?[21]
- General. British Ambassador to Chile Heath telephoned Ambassador Williams to say, "War tomorrow." Williams replied, "What war?" Why was this conversation not investigated and the results not published?
- General. Why did Franks not discuss the dispatch of HMS *Endeavor* to South Georgia and the failure to send a nuclear submarine earlier when such a move had earlier succeeded in frightening Argentina away from invasion? Lombardo has stated for public consumption that the *Endeavor*'s southward movement in late March 1982 triggered Anaya's signal to invade because he could not bear the humiliation of British recapture of the island.[22]
- General. Why were no Spanish speakers assigned to the Franks staff in order to read Argentine documents pertinent to the report's preparation?
- General. British Intelligence performed poorly in warning of the invasion. Or did it? Why not investigate the actions of the Cabinet and its interaction with British Intelligence that led to downplaying the worsening drama?
- General. British diplomacy ante April 1, 1982, has been omitted by intention because its utter failure needs a book by itself. The sure diplomatic hand—or was it laziness—did not, in the end, save lives, safeguard property or preserve liberty. Diplomats' idleness ruined bodies and lives long after their boneless efforts ended. Yet it is reasonable to ask why years of negotiations failed to reach a settlement and, not having done so, why Argentina would not then fail to seek a military solution.
- General. Every Argentinean in either political or military service to whom the author has spoken or written in preparation of this book, has stated unequivocally that the withdrawal from its South Atlantic station of HMS *Endurance* signaled to them the end of Britain's interest in and protection of the Falklands and South Georgia. Several Argentine naval persons have accused (to the

author) HMG of perfidy in violating what was to them a clear diplomatic signal that the Falklands were being let go. Why did Franks not take up this issue?

- General. During March and February 1982, the Argentine 2nd Marine Regiment left its barracks in Puerto Belgrano in plain sight and conducted over the beach exercises on Valdés in Patagonia. No reason existed for these very expensive, obvious and realistic evolutions except as preparation for a real invasion. The only target for any amphibious invasion by Argentine forces was the Falklands. Why this sizeable military evolution that involved troops, ships and helicopters was not noticed and remarked upon is difficult to entertain.
- General. Why were no public hearings held? After all, 255 men died public deaths.

The Franks Report also includes statements that a reasonable man might dismiss out of hand or find impossible to credit:

- Par. 312. "The military attaché in Buenos Aires had neither the remit nor the capacity to cover Argentine preparations of this kind." That person, charged with selling arms to his host country, would be in the best position to notice the weapons, parts and technology bought for war, whose preparations then could hardly have been missed. Any intelligence person serving abroad has, by definition, the remit to report assiduously on potential harm to his country. Colonel Love did so in an exemplary fashion (see Appendix A), yet his evidence and other data that showed a hotting up in Buenos Aires were not discussed in the Franks Report.
- Par. 296. "The FCO judgment was reasonable in light of the circumstances; it proved to be a misjudgment and no one individual could be blamed." There is precious little tar here and a very small brush. The head of the government and the person(s) charged with providing or not forwarding an assessment on the Falklands were responsible.
- Par. 261. "Our account demonstrates conclusively that the government had no reason to believe before March 31, 1982, that an invasion of the Falkland Islands would take place at the beginning of April." In its disingenuous defense of the British intelligence services' and the Joint Intelligence Committee's mistakes, Franks indicts the entire premise on which any country's intelligence ser-

vice is based. By definition, intelligence services stand guard against the bizarre, the unexpected, the unusual, and the untimely. The adjective "no" indicts and convicts, but did not sentence. Franks might have gotten away with "little," but many indications (see above) screamed war.[23] The Argentine invasion fleet had put to sea under orders on March 26, 1982. Prior to that day the air force's pilots were recalled, mechanized troops had clanked aboard their assigned ships, fuel was loaded, camps emptied and docks were strained to fulfill military requirements, all that under the eye of any and all who cared to watch.

- Par. 312. "If as we believe the decision to invade was taken by the Junta at a very late stage, the intelligence agencies could not have been expected to provide earlier warning of the actual invasion on 2 April." The decision to plan an invasion was made on December 15, 1981. The staff work and planning was completed no later than February 22, 1982. The Argentine marine units who performed the landing were fully trained by March 1st. To admit that one of these events went unnoticed is fair; to dismiss all three as unknowable tests readers' credulity. The decision to load out and to put Argentine troops over the beach was made on March 26, 1982.[24]

The Franks Report and Goose Green: A Final Thought

On whether Martinelli should continue his History of
England to the present day, [Dr.] Johnson stated:
"No, Sir; he would give great offense.
He would have to tell all the living great
what they do not wish told." [25]

Goose Green, its deaths and its maimings, would not have taken place if the events and lapses mentioned or suggested in the Franks Report had not occurred. The battle was fought and the soldiers died because Thatcher's Foreign Office failed to tell the junta that the Falklands were a vital issue and because Nott as Minister of Defense had not bothered to inquire if Thatcher would fight in the event that the junta took military action.[26] So much for the collegiality widely bruited to exist among cabinet ministers of the same government. Except for soldiers' courage, the resources needed for victory 8,000 miles from London did not exist on

April 1, 1982. They had been slashed from the defense budget by Nott on Thatcher's order to cut spending.

The Franks Report had an unwritten premise: the victory at Goose Green showed what a heretofore failed government could accomplish to recoup itself in the face of mean adversity. Thatcher was in the dock and needed cover for a failed defense policy and her carefully selected liege men, who scribbled the Franks Report, gave her just that. Make no mistake, it was not the government, but rather Jones and his men and the others who fought and bled who saved Thatcher's bacon. If the Roll of Honor from Goose Green had hung on a wall overlooking the Franks Report's composers, it would have dripped tears of anger and shame.

If deceit succeeds, the cause usually lies in readers' slackened attention to the text. So slick that it bored, the Franks Report discouraged all but the most attentive from completing the read. Yet the Franks Report was a work of art in that it completed a circle begun in the parliamentary debate held Saturday after the Argentine invasion, when Nott and Carrington were savaged and Thatcher faced a revolt from her own side of the House. At least 30 backbenchers would not have answered the government whip on that perilous Saturday. Sundry others simply wanted her scalp for what they considered a national humiliation. Just as Margaret Thatcher needed, or thought she needed, Goose Green to keep parliament and the people with her, so she needed Franks afterwards to validate that artful maneuver and its succeeding bloodshed for history; and incidentally to clear the way for her continued leadership. To paraphrase Burke: Thatcher knew nothing of war but she mastered the passions that it had created. Even in her memoirs she wrote erroneously about the war.[27] Not to worry, Franks' airy logic held that the war was unforeseen, that Thatcher could not be held culpable, that the ensuing bloodshed could not have been prevented either and that, by inference, Thatcher had rescued the country from humiliation.

Franks makes a show of divulging the inner work of state in a time of crisis. Yet it is clear that Franks' trove of incomplete fact, self-serving conjecture and spurious conclusions did unwittingly portray the humdrum donkey-work of a not very efficient administration that bumbled along in a state of what British Ambassador Williams called "General Micawberism." However glib and slick, Franks fails, upon close reading, to exonerate Thatcher, Carrington, Nott and the Joint Intelligence Committee. Franks uses words in profusion that qualify and dilute: "reasonable, moderately, probably and at least." Absent ice clear conclusions, culpability never landed on any single committee, department, office or person.

For all its ersatz elegance, Franks never stated that the British Intelligence Service failed in its principal mission: To tell the truth to power, to shout it from the rooftops if necessary.[28] For all its frequently used term "reasonable," Franks never asks and answers fully one question: "Was it reasonable to assume that the dispatch of a nuclear submarine in winter 1982 or the shooting down of an Argentine reconnaissance plane in April 1982 would have ended the affair there and then and left the Junta to topple from its own economic and political ineptness?" The Franks Report has one grace: it does not deny that, under Nott as Minister of Defense, British territory was lost to military force for the first time since World War II.

Thatcher's placemen, cleverer than she, gave her more than she sought or knew. First of all, they were protecting their colleagues' and their role in British life, and only after that task was completed did their rich prose obfuscate Thatcher's blunder and gild her, perfectly coiffed, onto history's shiny pages. They bleached failure's stain from her civil service, they thought, and gave their patroness a needed exercise in euphemism. So what if legalistic duplicity dusted their rounded sentences. So what if the blood, the pain, the vanished three billion pounds, and the plastic surgeons' full employment were too hard to take for a just-rescued government.

Jones fell into the apologists' paradigm very nicely: He was a hero from "Boys Own," rather too sparkling for the gray British military society where he worked, but brave in his way and almost mystically a man who died abroad in high drama for his country. Whispered was the premise that governments trip up from time to time, but roared was the axiom that Jones and his like quickly appear at the head of young and undereducated celts and saxons from British industrial slums in order to repair the damage. Any notion that Britain had lost among the 255 dead a potentially great man, and that a family had lost its head, and that his own men rescued Thatcher from the history's darker pages, and that a gigantic misjudgment in governance had been pasted over, got left out. Franks' authors preened while Jones moldered.

There can be little doubt that the Franks Report triumphed, at least for the moment. Its pervasive deception confounded many and jaded most. A sure proof of its success is that few remember it with all the acuity with which they recall the battles and bloodshed it was meant to justify. Franks seduced the public mind, but whether it forever corrupted a factual and pragmatic assessment of the war remains to be seen. What is clear is that Franks became a sump for all seasons; all manner of bad things got pitched into it, never to appear again. Thatcher retained the glow of victory and was propelled into lifelong employment. The plastic surgeons' ongoing work, the suicides, the broken families were quietly passed over. No person was made to assume guilt in public and, consequently, mud slinging was kept to an acceptable minimum. Systems, vaguely defined, were indicted, but not people. Contrived and fuzzy prose kept the debate about the war's cause away from the popular press and inside the political and governmental establishment. The Franks Report's chilling effrontery that no single person or entity had dropped the ball ensured that any debate about the British government's negligence would center on the report itself and not on lapses that led to the war.

Beyond its sophistic ability to deceive, language possesses the power to redeem, to renew, to solace. Here, Franks' graceful mutterings failed. There is one saving grace, however: Franks' tawdriness has almost been forgotten, but Jones' and 2 Para's integrity and selflessness live.

Notes

1. Montgomery's problems were solved locally; Thompson's vexations germinated at Northwood, 8,000 miles away, and had to be solved there. It must be noted here that Montgomery was not so much a tactician as a trainer. His extraordinary feat of returning to active service the 50,000 or so deserters and malingerers who hung about Cairo and Alexandria after and as a result of Rommel's splendid victories, and of restoring high morale to defeated divisions, are too little understood and praised (for more on this, see note 36 in Chapter 4). He was a modest and conservative tactician whose skills had worn thin by a needless rivalry with Patton and by such failures as Goodwood. Another layer of meaning that concerns the myth of Goose Green's outcome remains in play. Goose Green was a continuation of Arnhem and of the battles of North Africa, as much as it was a part of the Falklands War. Victory there and ubiquitous American aid expunged the bitter taste of Suez.

2. Thomas A. Sancton, in "Falklands," *Time Magazine*, May 31, 1982, p. 37. The Peruvian initiative may have occurred as a matter of comity rather than as a sincere attempt to further negotiations. The Peruvian minister of defense graduated from the Argentine Military Academy and was a personal friend of the Argentine foreign minister Costa-Méndez. The Peruvian Prime Minister had spent time in exile in Buenos Aires.

3. Richard S. Crossman, *The Myths of Cabinet Government* (Cambridge: Harvard University Press, 1972), p. 9.

4. During interviews and correspondences for this book, the author had to plough through references to "my mates" and "Alf and Sid." It soon dawned that "Alf and Sid" were what the battle was all about, at least to its participants.

5. The author served for three years of intense and very sensitive work under a famous U.S. Navy Admiral. All knew his values and therefore what he wanted to accomplish. Such was his brilliance and integrity that he gave only one order to us during that time.

6. Several soldiers interviewed for this book showed disdain for Jones' run. They claimed that they intended to win and that, even to those few who knew of his death, his heroic charge was superfluous to their efforts.

7. Nonetheless, Keeble has stated: "He was one of the few men in my Army career with whom I felt in immediate harmony." Max Arthur, *Above All Courage* (London: Sphere, 1965), p. 186.

8. Arthur, *Above all Courage*, p. 194.

9. The use of this verb is intentional. One of Montgomery's most stinging comments on a subordinate was that he, the subordinate, lacked the capacity to understand how the battle ran. See Max Hastings, *Overlord: D-Day & The Battle for Normandy* (New York: Simon & Schuster, 1985), for several examples of this habit of Montgomery's mind.

10. Keeble has also credited the Argentine defeat to a breakdown in the relationships between officers and their men. Many Argentine soldiers were recalled conscripts from the North, whose first language was an Indian dialect and not Spanish. Some mothers hid their sons from the call up.

11. Self-serving discussion of Jones' acts during the battle for Darwin Hill has brought distress to Sarah Jones, his widow, and to his family. Neither she nor her children were present that dreaded day when their family's head died. They bore no responsibility for Jones' acts. None has sought glory from the fact that it was Jones' men who finally triumphed. They are very comfortable in their own skins and Sarah Jones and her family have, if anything, fled notoriety. From the text above, it may be discerned that in the author's judgment, Jones erred perhaps in his plan or perhaps because he placed reliance on one or another who could not shoulder the burden of combat. Others will judge differently. In a very familiar British way, there have appeared only two sides to this issue: one is either for Jones or against him. The discussions are either hagiographic or cruelly mischievous. John Wilsey's fine book, *H. Jones VC: The Life and Death of an Unusual Hero* (London: Hutchinson, 2002), has partially rescued Jones from both hero-worship and vilification. It seems to have escaped the collective that Jones was a very good man who made mistakes that were retrieved by persons whom he had trained to his own very high standards and who fought the battle with an intensity and an intelligence similar to his. Haphazardly, Jones, the man, has not been separated from Jones' acts. Jones was not cowardly, disloyal, foolish, inattentive, lazy or stupid. Quite the opposite! Many of those whose actions or lack thereof led to the battle of Darwin Hill cannot claim this. The hubris that Jones' detractors attribute to him has found a ready home among some who have never enjoyed the bliss of a spent round passing safely by. On this subject, see Amelia Hill's essay "Falklands Widow," *The Guardian*, March 31, 2002, p. 1.

12. See especially Hastings, *Overlord*.

13. Phil Neame, OC D Company, in Arthur, *Above All Courage*, p. 265.

14. General Martín Balza, Argentine Army (ret), who was a Lt. Col. of artillery on the Falklands and a British POW, has claimed that the victor in the Falklands War needed supremacy in the air and at sea. Perhaps this was true. Neither protocol was relevant to 2 Para's victory. There, it was the men alone who were responsible. See Balza's statement in *The Guardian*, February 25, 2002.

15. The approaching end of the war failed to stay the Argentine Air Force's zeal for combat. An Argentine C-130 cargo plane, patrolling far north of the Falklands, came upon a large oil tanker sailing north in ballast. The plane's crew opened the plane's rear ramp, rolled out several 500 lb. bombs and holed the tanker. A surprised Italian crew took to their boats and watched as their innocent ship gurgled to the bottom. Predictably, lawyers on three continents took up the case. Their fees and expenses from 1982–1989 would have supplied 2 Para with beer and bullets for several wars. In 1989, the case ended up in the U.S. Court of Admiralty, where it was held that the Foreign Sovereignty Immunity Act barred Amerada Hess, the lesser of the now rusting tanker, from seeking remedies against the Argentine government. Argentine Republic vs. Amerada Hess Shipping, 488 (1989).

16. Psalm 146.

17. Not all had blindly supported the war. After the war, the Church of England held a commemorative religious service conducted in St. Paul's by the Archbishop of Canterbury at which Margaret Thatcher was made to sit behind a massive pillar, little seen and seeing less.

18. "Cmnd. 8787," *Falkland Islands Review* (London: HMSO, 1983), known as the "Franks Report." The Report's charge was incomplete, as it did not mention the invasion of South Georgia. That was a dependency of Great Britain administered from Port Stanley and not a dependency of the Falklands, as the charge implies.

19. R.W. Apple, Jr., "Falkland Inquiry: Mrs. Thatcher's Stake is High," *New York Times*, July 7, 1982, A2.

20. Peter Riddell, "Callaghan Joins Row Over Cabinet Papers," *Financial Times*, July 3, 1982, p. 3.

21. See Nigel West, *The Secret War for the Falklands: The SAS, MI6, & the War Whitehall Nearly Lost* (London: Little, Brown, 1997), p. 119.

22. Lombardo, written answers to author's questions, December 2001.

23. Countries have their own logic for action and almost always indicate when they are about to war or to effect a destabilizing move. Terrorists' actions are very difficult but not impossible to predict.

24. The source of this information is a distinguished Argentine former naval person who worked within the junta's command element and who chooses to remain anonymous.

25. James Boswell, *Life of Johnson* (Oxford: Oxford University Press, 1953, unabridged), p. 516.

26. Richard Crossman, in his Godkin Lectures, Harvard, 1970, stated a Minister need know nothing to get the job. Crossman did not say that the Minister should learn nothing after he was installed.

27. Thatcher identified Woodward as: "Operational commander of the surface ships in the force." Margaret Thatcher, *Downing Street Years* (New York:

Harper Collins, 1995), p. 189. Woodward commanded only the battle force. Commodore Clapp commanded the amphibious ships. "The truth is that the invasion could not have been foreseen or prevented," *Downing Street Years*, p. 177. That is an unusually disingenuous statement from a pragmatic politician. The British Intelligence Service was chartered and funded to forewarn about invasions of British territory. "The Argentines subsequently left and the Argentine government claimed to know nothing about it," *Downing Street Years*, p. 177. According to British Antarctic Reports, 8–10 Argentineans, almost certainly marines, remained on South Georgia after their ship departed. Argentine marines were certainly members of the landing party which unloaded far more stores and equipment than was judged necessary by the observing party from the British Antarctic Survey.

28. The head of the Joint Intelligence Committee, which should have done the shouting prior to war's outbreak, was Sir Antony Acland, once British Ambassador to the U.S. and a graduate of Eton College some years before Jones.

Afterword

In their first glory days, dictators enjoy one characteristic in common: they consider their powers to be absolute and ubiquitous. Later their survival demands that they cloak themselves in the false if giddy approval of electorates that are brutalized and humiliated into the silent acceptance of their misery. Theirs is the only show in town, their newspapers, radios, television and sycophants proclaim. A single exception must be made for those Argentineans who formulated and executed foreign economic policy. Their financial community was given vast leeway to do whatever necessary in order to keep open lines of credit in London and New York. That thin coating of legitimacy gains the Galtieris of this world a kind of shameful acceptance by the outside world. But the junta was wrong about all this too, because the central figure who changed all that at Goose Green—the junta's first and disabling battle—was a rather junior officer, a battalion commander, Lt. Col. H. Jones VC.

In great dramas, players of the second rank, not Presidents or Prime Ministers, often emerge from the muddle as the most puissant and memorable figures. Jones did not manage the war or even command his brigade, but he will always be the most celebrated figure of the war. On the Argentine side, and true to the mores of tyrants, the cynosure of all eyes was not Piaggi, Estévez or that reluctant dragon and Goose Green's nominal commander Wilson Pedrosa. It was the near buffoon, Galtieri. On May 27 and 28, 1982, Jones' men pierced the cocoon of his fantasy. After all, how fearsome is a *soi-disant* omnipotent general who cannot defeat a few hundred

211

exhausted soldiers fighting uphill against prepared positions? In fact, 2 Para's victory and Jones' death created new and painful asymmetries for the junta and its successors; some have never been resolved.

When Galtieri changed the negotiating site from the UN's faux elegance to the freezing mud of Goose Green he risked his country's destiny in ways not understood then or much later. Earlier, Galtieri behaved as though the world had suspended its powers of observation, its capacity for repugnance and its unspoken conclusion that Argentina could not manage its own affairs. Goose Green changed all that. Jones, Keeble and their men brought ugly truths to light. Suddenly, the hypocrisy, the cruelty and the incompetence were exposed for all to see. Defeat on Darwin Hill ejected, in the end, a corrupt and useless junta. Latin American *caudillismo* got a crippling if not lethal stroke. Great Britain's victories at Goose Green and later at Stanley did not, on the other hand, change its society, but only proved its validity.

At Goose Green, and later too, Galtieri seemed almost to glory in the abasement of his troops. He offered them no hope, no new plan, nothing except humiliation and death or surrender. Torturing wretched civilians at the Naval Mechanics School proved different, he discovered, from confronting Jones and the Parachute Regiment's young toughs. Galtieri alerted his country neither to the efforts necessary for victory nor to the possibility of defeat. He seemed not to realize that men such as Jones and those of 2 Para existed to thwart men such as he. Neither Galtieri nor the junta ever squeezed meaning from the most obvious and powerful fact: that Margaret Thatcher, who daily faced the danger and humiliation of losing her job, was their opponent and that she had deputed roughnecks from the Parachute Regiment and the Royal Marines to travel 8,000 miles in order to force that reality upon him.

Galtieri, Anaya and Lami-Dozo never learned that successful leaders, even though they led from splendid isolation, knew and got along with what we identify as common people. The junta's members failed this critical test. Jones, the Etonian of wealth, passed it with flying colors. There was an almost magical connection here, for Thatcher, the grocer's High Tory daughter as different from Jones as any two humans could be, knew the British middle classes and how to get their blood boiling. Galtieri did not know that common men led by professional elites fight and win modern wars. Though a man from the people, in fact from the lower classes, he did not understand that his electorate's sullen passivity could quickly turn to rage and that Argentina did not own a bellicist elite.

Like a man in a darkened room unable to find the light switches, Galtieri led from stumbling isolation. He could not fathom what his electorate wanted or what they would tolerate; he did not know what professional British infantrymen like Jones' 2 Para could accomplish. Twenty years later, some Argentine military men still refuse to believe that Jones' 500 men defeated them at Goose Green, so shattered were they by 2 Para's intrusion into their master scheme.[1] The junta and its toadies failed to understand the relationship between political survival and brute military strength skillfully applied. If Galtieri understood that his story could have a nasty end, he never showed it. If Jones and 2 Para even suspected they could lose, they never showed it. Still unanswered is the question: did Galtieri believe himself? His roseate oratory could only feign closeness with the people's aspirations; and these were indeterminate, skin deep and probably misconstrued at that. So much so, that the first signs of Argentine military ineptitude at Goose Green pushed a flighty electorate into not so sullen desperation.

Argentina was not a great nation. Competition with a strong neighboring power had never pricked it into modernity nor had an industrial elite propelled it to parity even with the sluggish economies of Western Europe. It was not that the people's energies were not harnessed and properly directed; they did not exist. Argentina never had armed forces strong enough to subdue a neighbor nor never a neighbor strong enough to conquer it. In the recent decade, Argentina had been content with patty cake border wars and papal good offices to settle problems that were puerile compared to that of facing the Warsaw Pact. Professionally, Al Haig went slumming when he tried to talk sense with Galtieri.

The junta first erred when it shifted to the politics of the sword from maintenance of the balance of power through negotiation. The reasons for this fatal adventure were the usual ones. Unable to govern comfortably at home, the junta sought to conquer and to administer without let or hindrance distant islands whose language, governance, customs and way of life varied almost grotesquely from its own. The Argentine political elite took the FCO's diffidence and slackness as the telling part of Thatcher's government. They mistook the world's capricious ignorance of the Falklands for lack of concern about the defenseless inhabitants of those islands.

Argentina's initiation of war and its hope for victory hung on transient conditions: weather, surprise, the remoteness of its quest from the United Kingdom and the United States and from their foreign military endeavors, the assumption that Latin American nations would rally against Great Britain, the imminent withdrawal of HMS *Endurance* and the absence of a UK garrison. All these led the junta to believe that it could rule the sea and air space around and above the Falklands. A torpid and feckless British foreign office, a defense establishment busy staring down the Russian bear and an apparent lack of harmony between Haig and Kirkpatrick on America's position in Latin America offered a comforting backdrop to the junta's adventurism. Still, *le tout* Buenos Aires, the city that prided itself as a curator of European elegance, showed its autistic side when it misjudged both would-be allies and real enemies. Neither the junta nor its sycophants knew one clear fact: great powers that are also liberal democracies do not normally lose the last battle.

Once the flimsy possibilities inherent in these accidents of fortune were exhausted, the probability of a triumphant Argentine end game vanished. As soon as the permanent elements of the conflict—like U.S. support for the United Kingdom, a splendidly fungible UK military machine, cold wet weather, a betrayed Argentine electorate, poor military leadership and glaring logistical deficits—came into play, the junta's and Argentina's doom was certified. Fifteen years later, several Latin American diplomats predisposed toward neutrality at war's outbreak suggested that the long train of British ships heading south, bannered daily on the world's press, signaled the junta's defeat however long the garrison at Port Stanley took to raise the white flag.

Galtieri knew less about the Northern world's political axioms than perhaps any other contemporary leader of a major state. Al Haig was, first and foremost, not the person to put moldy, almost indecipherable texts and the mob's caterwauling ahead of common sense. Besides, anyone professionally interested in Argentina knew that the real sticking point with the North lay in others' disgust at Argentina's terrorist state and at the amount of debt that it had run up with London's and New York's banks. At war's outset, Argentina's domestic problems compromised its capacity to behave as a nation state, for no war was ever declared, the country was not put on war footing and the electorate never actively assented to the bloodletting that combat inevitably brings. In fact, not a few of Argentina's peasant infantry shivering and dying in their East Falkland holes never knew the islands' location, only that it was cold there.

By invading the Falklands, Galtieri resorted to a bleak *raison d'état*, the fulfillment of a scatty national myth at the expense of a defenseless, free people. In this he erred because the invasion did not advance the condition of the state and of its people, including the Kelpers. Galtieri's efforts did not strengthen the world's order, redress a skewed balance of power or thwart the United Kingdom's desire to increase its share of that impalpable property of nations. Very simply, no geopolitical reason existed for Argentina's invasion of the Falklands. The junta's policy remained, in the eyes of the Great Powers, irrational, unpredictable and therefore unacceptable because unreasonable acts bring justice or worth to no one. North and South all agreed that fracturing arrangements for doing business among great nations could not be stomached and that therefore a return to *status quo ante bellum* demanded military attention. That showed the difference between Galtieri and Jones. Galtieri was irrational and acted without perduring moral purpose. Jones was over-zealous and his charge up the hill moral. It is a paradox that when one acts against all logic and common sense, and surrenders his life while doing so, he is at his most human.

After May 29th, Galtieri resorted in vain to a national honor that had existed only in his and very few others' fantasy. His political and diplomatic vaporings only embarrassed. The Argentine defeat at Goose Green could not be recouped because 2 Para's victory was too blatant; Jones' death too dramatic, too much out of classical history. The United Kingdom had a new hero, while in Buenos Aires vulgar introspection festered as their champion became *hijo de puta*. The only collective that Argentina and Galtieri could muster was the one that wanted his neck. Judged by their pallid reaction to his entreaties, neither he nor his audience ever knew which Argentina claimed paternity of his failed policies: the Argentina of the disappeared, the Argentina of the impoverished, the Argentina of the Indian provinces, the Argentina of the salons or the Argentina that didn't care.

Galtieri never sought to conduct his negotiations abroad in concert with the enduring premises of American foreign policy. He remains perhaps the only chief of state in recent times to refuse a telephone call from an American president. He never understood the impalpable but real ganglia that bound the United States to the United Kingdom. He dreamt that an attack against a world power would be countenanced by its principal partner. In the end, Galtieri bore the catastrophic consequences of an American view of the world of which he was unaware or, even more stupidly, chose to ignore. It was not a matter of a relationship with America grown rusty. Galtieri never accepted that the United States would act from the central themes of its own interests: friendship with nations of the

North Atlantic and the containment of the Soviet Bloc. He never understood that a Jones, by whatever name, would arrive in the Falklands to stifle his insolence, and that those who toil in labyrinths of American foreign policy knew that too.

Few knew or cared that Jones was half-American. If Argentina had a foreign intelligence service, it either failed to understand the English-speaking world or failed to convince its masters of the manner by which matters are decided in the Northern Hemisphere. The junta did not know that American mechanics based on Ascension Island, and quite far from Washington's *haute politique*, willingly lent their own wrenches to RAF maintainers. Such was the junta's and Galtieri's near autism that they had not replicated the Northern Hemisphere's technology and thus forewent from the first engagement any chance of defeating British forces. They did not know that mastery of military technology had become the *sine qua non* of political success. They did not understand that contumacious democracies, however groggy they seem to outsiders, gestate men like Jones and his lads from 2 Para.

Galtieri saw the Falklands' capture as an opportunity to retake land that a hokey myth had made part of Argentina. He failed to admit that adherents of liberal democracy, unlike Tony Benn who considered political freedom a matter of numbers, long ago made morally autonomous Falklanders preeminently responsible for deciding who should govern them, however shamefully members of the Foreign Office and the budgeteers at MOD clung to contrary notions.

Galtieri and Anaya misjudged the non–English speaking world too. Galtieri's invasion never asked and answered the age-old question: "Cui bono?" The silence of Argentina's neighbors made it clear. There were no nations on earth whose fortunes or prestige would be enhanced by political or military support of Galtieri's regime. The junta's belief that the community of nations would either avoid mentioning the invasion or applaud it confirmed a failure of the regime's diplomats to inform their masters of the truth, or, most likely, the junta's blindness, to the outside world's habits of mind. Galtieri's sour and murderous vision of Argentina's future, well understood abroad, not only meant repression of a free people, but also his country's isolation from modern democracies' most intense beliefs about diversity and choice. In their own blunt way, Jones' 2 Para and the other British battalions at the Falklands purged the Argentine political system of much that was nasty, self-destructive and plain wrong. Perhaps even Thatcher failed to realize that the subtle and fragile balance that keeps the world aright demands the existence and use of such as Jones' band of very unusual men.

As long as Argentina continued to negotiate the Falklands' ownership, it retained a moral and legal stance on that matter more or less equal to its adversary's. Nor were 3 Commando Brigade and 2 Para then needed. Once the junta took up arms against a non-belligerent people who had given no offense, it lay open to charges of militant imperialism and colonization. Galtieri and his colleagues failed to grasp that diversity and self-determination remained the overarching system of beliefs which the free world promoted at blood cost. As far as its Latin neighbors were concerned, Argentina's invasion proved the notion that, in the junta's mind, a turn to war could resolve diplomatic entanglements and supercede the wishes of indigenous peoples. Henceforth, according to Argentine practice, all the wretched problems of contested borders and self-determination that dot the South American landscape, and that seemed so petty when viewed in the context of a possible nuclear war, might be washed away with the blood of peasant infantry.

Galtieri and his junta had no inkling of their neighbors' intuitive opposition to such intrusions. That felt belief was the fundamental cause for Argentina's neighbors' failure to assist, even at the margins, in the war and in Argentina's quest for a settlement. Jones' and 2 Para's victory at Goose Green confirmed the correctness of their decision. Many from the Southern Hemisphere who were interviewed for this book augured that even while the task forces sailed southward, 2 Para or its like and Jones or his equal would somehow appear on the scene to settle the affair in favor of Great Britain and against Argentina. These beliefs seldom appeared in official statements, but came from the gut and were all the more efficacious and true for being so impalpable. After the victory at Goose Green, formal diplomatic pronouncements may have leaned towards nebulous neutrality, but the world's chanceries knew and applauded the fact that Jones and his muddy Toms had won and that Galtieri would lose. Even so, few could have predicted the wretched collapse of dispirited and angry troops that began on Goose Green and ended in front of Port Stanley.

The Argentine government and its military—which in April 1982 were one and the same—showed a special ignorance of the relationship between political goals and military means when they sent conscripts from the Indian provinces against the hard cases of 3 Commando Brigade. Argentine units in the field proved incapable of imposing their will on a numerically inferior force that operated far from home. Jones' 2 Para

217

began an offense that never stopped until Stanley fell, mostly because light infantry, brilliantly led by officer and NCO alike, proved its worth again. The Toms, that brazen and humorous collective of late adolescents, seldom faltered. No Argentine leader ever fixed the site, date, circumstances or tempo of battle despite an advantage in time, numbers and short logistics lines. It was Brigadier Thompson who accomplished all that, and Jones was his advance man.

No Argentine officer or soldier had ever been subjected to continuous pounding from perhaps the best light artillery in the world. Galtieri and his juniors did not know that the tempo of battle and thus the outcome of a war can be changed through the disruption of a major force by a minor one: 2 Para at Goose Green. Argentine military historians had forgotten or neglected to teach that U.S. Admiral Sprague's destroyers took on Japanese Admiral Kurita's battleship fleet off Samar Island and covered Halsey's mistake in leaving San Bernardino straits open and in deploying Admiral Lee's battleships so that that they left the Japanese surface force uncovered. No such instinctive cooperation existed among the Argentine commanders anywhere, at any time, during the entire conflict. Its army, navy and air force may just as well have been fighting different wars. When ideology and the vagaries of domestic intrigue substitute for military professionalism, disaster is certain.

Galtieri did not understand that democratic practices like negotiation and patience could achieve his purpose in the face of a tottery British government whose resolve did not harden until after Jones' and 2 Para's victory. Instead, he left the decision about his government's future up to his derided enemies, 3 Commando Brigade and Jones' 2 Para. In a different but ironical way, a majority of Thatcher's government also wanted shut of the islands.[2] Even the casual observer cannot help but feel that a British defeat on the beaches or soon thereafter would not have been unwelcome in the darker corners of Whitehall and parliament. Jones and Keeble, military intellectuals of vastly different inclinations, turned that moral deficit on its heels.

Successful politicians know in their bones what must be done or avoided in order for them to survive. Simply put, they define their constituencies and calculate each one's response to political acts and their consequences. For example, Stalin knew he could cause death for millions during the Great Terror and, except for history's posthumous judgments, get away with it. His domestic and international constituencies were then gulled, petrified and weak. By contrast, Galtieri knew so little of his own country that he failed to predict Argentina's and the world's response both to his political debility and to military defeat. Though he was a son of the people, he retained no connection with them. Despite his visit to Goose Green a few days before the battle, no impalpable energy carried his moral authority to the troops in the field, either because his moral side did not exist or because his army knew that he had deceived them. By contrast, the moral component of Jones' leadership led to his death and his men's victory.

Galtieri's ignorance of a world beyond the South Atlantic astounds even today. Despite study and life in America, he could not grasp the notion that in matters of war, whatever the pundits blurt, the United States and the United Kingdom were virtually of one mind, and that each would axiomatically take up arms against aggression and would almost certainly ally if one or the other were attacked. As Argentina stood on March 31, 1982, anyone who thought that it could effect major change in the world's order and in the Anglo-American view of it, was insensate.

Democracy often appears through the thicket of the oppositions' hard words as governance that will shilly-shally and stumble away from painful decisions. Absolutist rulers see disorder, vilification and restraint in parliament and in Congress as weaknesses when, in fact, they prove their strength. Galtieri concluded that Mrs. Thatcher could not or would not act. He was wrong. Knowing little of democracy and of the graces it affords its troubled leaders, he could not predict that, from the depths of her political failure, she might rally a nation to fight a war whose drain on her country's financial capital was enormous and whose inconclusive end would surely finish her career. Like Owen Glendower, who could call spirits from the "Vasty deep", Thatcher, Jones and Keeble, each in her or his own way, drew on something impalpable that cannot be measured but only admired.

The Falklands War was not at its heart about ownership of the islands. It was a dispute about the purpose of nations contended by two disparate cultures and settled by the fruits of both combatants' ethos and traditions. Free men, mostly undereducated, who could have bought their way out of their military obligations for a pittance and who labored under a prickly and wealthy half-American from the upper classes, employed organized violence that accomplished in a few days what diplomacy failed to gain in dozens of years. Wars are paradoxical—they maintain nations' status quo but they also shift societies into new directions. In the case of Argentina, as one general put it, "The Falklands forced us to change. . . . The army is now completely subordinate to civilian power."[3] The junta fled, and on the road to stability its country plunged down to new levels of despair and dysfunction. The junta's unanswered cries to its neighbors for help ended the folly of considering Latin America a homogenous bloc that would act in unison especially against intrusions from the North.

By contrast, Prime Minister Thatcher, buoyed by the pervasive enthusiasm of her electorate, had sent a professional army on a licit enterprise and incidentally gained life-long employment. She could not be said to have glutted on the victory. But almost! At blood cost, the British Army resumed its proud place in the world's stock of power for the good. Willy-nilly, Thatcher had sent the right people to war for the right reasons, and out of that act Jones came to be forever her and the war's *vert gallant*. He personified the confidence in his society that its defenders must always show if that society is to survive. He exemplified a bellicist spirit, encouraged in democracies that the world forgets at its peril. The junta trusted in flabby legal claims, in smarmy diplomacy, in the cheap shot, in Potemkin coups, in the use of force against defenseless civilians, in a malleable electorate uninformed to the point of numbness, in armed forces maintained to guard the transfer of power from one corrupt and ineffectual regime to the next, in death squads formed to kidnap nuns rather than to fight a modern war, in diaphanous help from Latin American allies and in the neutrality of the Northern World and of the United States. This went wrong at Goose Green for all the world to see and to remember. Jones and his colleagues saw to that. Seldom have continental politics and a small battle's outcome been so closely intertwined.

Galtieri fought the wrong war against the wrong opponent with the wrong persons. Quite legitimately, Jones lusted to cap his career with a great military victory. Few have noted that he strove inside the political system that he protected. In death, his plan failed, but in death, his men, his own men, gave him a rough edged win. In the watches of the night, Jones VC and Goose Green will conjure up the same notions of valor—foolish valor, perhaps, but selfless bravery always. Rightly, his men's triumph inscribed his name with all that it conjures up on history's pages. Rear Admiral Woodward's statement that the war was a close-run thing may have touched a rhetorical nerve, but it did not approach the truth. After 2 Para's victory at Goose Green, the Argentine junta could not win. Its rickety popular approval dissipated, its air force tattered, its fleet cowering inshore, its putative allies silent, British victory was in the air and all knew it in Buenos Aires, London and Washington. Dead under the Falklands' mud, vivant and feted forever in history and myth, Jones VC had won more than a battle.

Notes

1. A senior Argentine official claimed to the author that British forces at Goose Green comprised 2,000 men. He would not be dissuaded.

2. See Rex Hunt, *My Falkland Days* (London: David and Charles, 1992), for British efforts, John Ure's and Nicholas Ridley's especially, to convince the Falklands' inhabitants to surrender their independence. It is painful and sad reading.

3. General Martín Balza, Argentine Army's one time Chief of Staff and a former POW on the Falklands, *The Guardian*, February 25, 2002.

Glossary

2 Para: One of the 3 battalions that comprise The Parachute Regiment.

7.62: The very useful rifle used by the Argentine Army.

29 Logistics Regiment: The regiment tasked to provide logistical support to 3 Commando Brigade. It performed superbly during the war.

105mm gun: The artillery weapon used by the Royal Marines' Commando Brigade, but attached to 2 Para for the Battle of Goose Green.

AIM-9L: Air-to-Air missile.

Alma Battery: A six 105mm gun sub unit of 29 Artillery Regiment. Three of Alma's guns supported 2 Para's attack on Goose Green.

Casa Rosada: The Argentine White House.

Chinook: A heavy lift helicopter that carried five times the weight of its next largest vehicle. Invaluable during the war.

CINC: Commander in Chief, Admiral Fieldhouse.

CO: The individual appointed by his service to command a major unit.

FCO: The Foreign and Commonwealth Office.

HMS: Standard abbreviation for Her Majesty's Ship.

Kelper: An inhabitant of the Falkland Islands, beside which are substantial beds of kelp.

Lt. Col. Italo Piaggi: The Argentine CO in charge of Goose Green's defense.

Milan Missile: A wire-guided, very accurate missile used to support infantry. It destroyed many Argentine fixed positions..

MOD: British Ministry of Defense.

Northwood: The British command center near London.

OC: An individual appointed by his CO to command a minor unit.

SAS: The Special Air Service, the British Army's Special Warfare Group whose regiment is 22 SAS.

SBS: The Special Boat Service, the Royal Marines' special warfare unit that works close to or on hostile shores.

Sea King Helicopter: The mainstay of British logistics.

SecDef: The American Secretary of Defense.

SecNav: The American Secretary of The Navy.

SecState: The American Secretary of State.

Stirling: The rapid-fire sub machine gun carried by 2 Para.

STUFT: Civilian cargo ships taken up from trade by government order to support the military operation around the Falklands.

Task Force: Just that, a group of persons and military assets formed to complete a discreet military task.

The Parachute Regiment: The administrative home of the 3 Para battalions that comprise it.

Appendix A

Colonel Stephen Love's Report, March 2, 1982

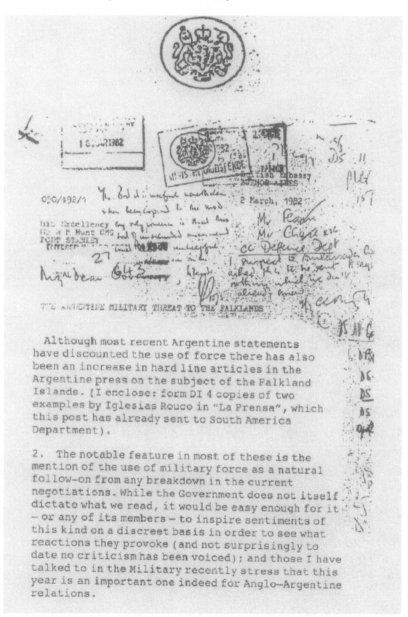

THE ARGENTINE MILITARY THREAT TO THE FALKLANDS

Although most recent Argentine statements
have discounted the use of force there has also
been an increase in hard line articles in the
Argentine press on the subject of the Falkland
Islands. (I enclose: form DI 4 copies of two
examples by Iglesias Rouco in "La Prensa", which
this post has already sent to South America
Department).

2. The notable feature in most of these is the
mention of the use of military force as a natural
follow-on from any breakdown in the current
negotiations. While the Government does not itself
dictate what we read, it would be easy enough for it
– or any of its members – to inspire sentiments of
this kind on a discreet basis in order to see what
reactions they provoke (and not surprisingly to
date no criticism has been voiced); and those I have
talked to in the Military recently stress that this
year is an important one indeed for Anglo–Argentine
relations.

3. Putting the worst possible interpretation on
things this could mean an Army President, who has
already demonstrated his lack of patience when
frustrated over such issues (Chilean frontier closure
April 1981) giving orders to the military to solve the
Malvinas problem once and for all in the latter half
of this year, and in so doing aiming to secure at least
one invitingly easy looking point at a time when it
may quite possibly seem most attractive to him to do
something popular.

4. Following my recent private visit to the Islands,
we have been giving this problem some thought here
and feel it would be useful to record what the
military options might be, and to look briefly at the
intelligence problems they pose. This paper does not
address itself to non-aggressive measures.

"Shots across the bows"

5. Until and unless the talks break down the most
likely threat is posed by *the Navy*. Possibilities
for action by them are legion, but might include for
example,
    i.   the establishment of a Naval "research
           station" on an outlying island,
    ii. the helicopter landing of marines on one of
           the islands for a 24-hour exercise coupled
           perhaps with low level overflights of Port
           Stanley, or
    iii. the denial of access to supply ships.

Such measures would be designed to demonstrate to
the Islanders how the Argentine claim to sovereignty
could be backed by strength whilst our own forces
could guarantee no effective protection. Successfully
carried out they would not result in bloodshed, would
therefore be unlikely to be condemned too harshly by

others and would help to convince the United Kingdom of both the seriousness and the urgency of the problem. The Navy moreover would be politically keen to flex their muscles in an area they regard as their own and these sort of pranks would not need the support of either of the other Services – an attractive feature when the practice of joint operations is not the norm. They would not moreover be overly dependent on good weather.

"Invasion"

6.   The new danger is perhaps that the Argentines might in days to come no longer believe a negotiated settlement of any sort to be possible, and therefore a military plan designed to prod Britain into talking more seriously (in however changed an atmosphere) might at that point seem to them outdated. A straight seizure of the Islands is an obvious alternative.

7.   Although Navy and Marines could of course still be used in any number of ways to land a force and take Port Stanley, surprise could not be assured and the possibility would exist of quite numerous casualties being suffered by both sides. This consideration might be overriding and cause them to think instead (or additionally) of airborne delivery of a smaller specialist force at Port Stanley followed by air or sea landing of marines. One has to remember that the military coup is a fairly well practised art here in Argentina and it is also a fact that the Army study and admire *coup de main* operations of all sorts. Of course such a plan would carry high risks but the follow-on force would be available for early committal if things went wrong.

8.   The obvious first task in such an assault would be the neutralisation of NP 8901's capability to react

(destruction of arms, telephones, vehicles?), the
capture of government, communications facilities,
seizure of the FIDF armoury; next would come the
securing of air field and jetties. The capture of
Governor and key personnel would follow and Argentine
military replacements would move in.

9.   Our ally in this scenario is the Falkland Island
weather with its capability for rapid and unforecast
changes particularly in cloud base and wind speed.
Although parachute operations should not be ruled
out, once the decision was taken, troops would have
to be prepared to spend several days waiting for good
conditions, preferably as close to the Islands as
possible to reduce the possibility of still having to
abort on account of changed conditions after launch.
Of course accurate and timely intelligence from Port
Stanley itself to the mainland presents no problem to
the Argentines; our own ability to give early warning
would depend upon any coverage of airfield activity
in Córdoba, home of the airborne brigade, and possibly
Rio Gallegos, nearest field to the Islands. With
present arrangements we could not realistically hope
to get any information at all. Otherwise any warning
would depend on NP 8901's ability to watch the western
approaches to the Islands particularly during first
light on days when conditions were judged good.

10.   A further conclusion which the Argentines might
have drawn is that the clandestine delivery of an
assault party, possibly in plain clothes and with
weapons concealed on their persons, could be a simpler
(and cheaper) alternative. The easiest way for the
group to arrive would be piecemeal week by week by
the scheduled LADE F 28 under the guise of tourists or
technical personnel or by special flight made under
different cover (eg in one of the Argentine Air Force
C130s which occasionally make freight deliveries).

Their approach to the primary objectives (paragraph 8 above) could then be made at their convenience any time after arrival. The only intelligence which could be gained that such an attempt was being undertaken would be through the Port Stanley airport Immigration authorities' records of Argentines arriving in the Colony.

Conclusions

11.   From a Buenos Aires perspective then the following conclusions can be drawn:

    a.   it would be difficult to see any operation mounted at the present stage or in the future which did not involve the Navy – and very probably the Marines;

    b.   an airborne or clandestinely-mounted *coup de main* attempt against Port Stanley would have definite appeal to a force planning the seizure of the Islands;

    c.   special arrangements could enhance our chance of providing early warning from Argentina, but at present we could not realistically expect to be able to detect any moves;

    d.   important dividends can be gained by constant vigilance in the Colony itself and over its surrounding waters, as the knowledge that surprise would be hard to obtain is in itself a deterrent to a potential enemy aiming for an easy and clean win.

12.   I apologise if on the basis of an all too short private visit I might have worked with incomplete knowledge on territory which is theoretically outside my area of concern (and possibly arriving at conclusions contrary to official views to which I am not privy). However, I am sure that as the diplomatic

exchanges reach the crunch point, we, the intelligence
machine, should be clearing our minds as far as is
possible on what realistically the military threat
comprises (at the same time considering how we could
keep ourselves better informed upon it) — and the
forces which pose this threat are very definitely of
my concern.

13. We should be glad to hear any comments which you
might have on all of this.

cc: DI 4   Stephen Love (Colonel)
        Ministry of Defence   Defence Attaché
        Dept

Source: British Defense Attaché's telegram of March 24, 1982, taken from Nigel
West, *The Secret War for the Falklands* (London: Little Brown, 1997), pp.
238–243.

Appendix B

American Aid to the United Kingdom During
The Falklands War

"It was the right thing to do."[1]

When asked why, in his opinion, America rushed to Britain's side at war's inception and provided millions of pounds of aid a retired Royal Navy officer answered: "Blood is thicker than water."[2] During the first few days of the war, two U.S. tankers were diverted to Ascension Island in order to provide fuel for the task forces steaming south "without which the Task Force could not have made it to the Falklands."[3] A system already existed by which navy-to-navy communications, operating practices, weapons transfers, etc., had been accomplished regularly farther back than anyone then serving could remember. Such things were simply done with a wink, a blink and a nod.

Very early in the war, three hundred AIM 9 L Sidewinder missiles were shipped to British forces. Close friendships between the special forces of both countries resulted in Stinger ground-to-air missiles and bits and pieces of that community's military oddments being handed over immediately. The paperwork for that elegant military administration caught up much later, if at all. The transfers accumulated to such substantial amounts that an as-yet-unidentified monitor of such things in the Pentagon cried out for at least a truncated accounting. As Lehman remembers: "the requests were handled routinely, without reference to higher authority."[4] It surprised many here that some abroad might think this practice excessively casual. It is nonsense that America and Great Britain speak different languages. At their peril, a few abroad had dismissed the idea "it is a truth universally accepted" that the Special Relationship meant much to both.[5]

Secretary Weinberger, a man of very precise habits, ordered the transfers made with a "pay later" proviso and put in place a short administrative chain. The military supermarket remained open twenty-four hours per day, seven days a week for the war's duration. Still, when Lehman visited London on May 31st, he suffered resentment from MOD over the United States' lack of enthusiasm for supporting Great Britain, all this after U.S. fuel had kept the task forces steaming. Thompson was not the only person to suffer from MOD's and Nott's ignorance about what was happening where it counted.

Sir Nicholas Henderson claimed that Secretary Weinberger: "had undertaken to give us anything we wanted militarily. I'm sure Haig did not know of this."[6] On this matter, Sir Nicholas was incorrect. Haig knew. Henderson also gives credence to the notion widely bruited in the U.S. Navy at the time that Weinberger could and would provide a carrier if asked. What was not widely known is that the RN was given its choice of two such. Henderson's summation says it best, although it omits the willingness and good cheer of those bidden to the feast: "The Americans provided us with equipment and intelligence facilities from their satellites. . . . The Prime Minister has conceded that, without the new Sidewinder missiles that the Americans provided, we would not have won the war. We have a lot to be grateful for, even if there were difficulties along the way."[7]

Nott's statement that: "In so many ways the French were our greatest allies"[8] is not only wholly untrue and defamatory, but also testament to the poor judgment that got Great Britain into a war that cost 255 British lives and kept the plastic surgeons of that country busy for their professional lives.[9] It is not difficult to conclude that Nott knew less about his friends than he did about his enemies.

The following list of items sent or given to British forces by and from America is incomplete:

- Use of Wideawake Airbase on Ascension Island
- 12.5 million gallons of aviation fuel
- 300 Sidewinder AIM 9 L air-to-air missiles
- Shrike radar seeking missiles
- Stinger shoulder fired AA missiles
- Long Range Patrol Packs (many)
- Mortar rounds (copious)
- Data on countermeasures and disarming of U.S. made bombs
- Intelligence information
- Use of U.S. communication satellites[10]
- Matting for Harrier landings
- Medical supplies and equipment (Copious)
- All USAF equipment at Wideawake, from screwdrivers to electronic parts, was made available to British forces
- Twelve F-4 Phantom jets were sold to the British post hostilities at inconsequential prices for Stanley's protection.

Notes

1. Caspar Weinberger. Conversations with the author.

2. Retired British Naval Officer and veteran of the Falklands War. This expression is credited to Commodore Josiah Tattnall USN, who during the second China War pulled British boats out of danger and gave this expression to Sir John Hope, the British commander, as his justification for this benign interference. See Peter Kemp, editor, *The Oxford Companion to Ships and the Sea* (London: Oxford University Press, 1976), p. 89.

3. Secretary of the Navy John Lehman, Letter, *Daily Telegraph*, March 30, 2002, p. v.

4. Ibid. Many who served under Secretary Lehman remain amused at his working definition of the words: "routine or routinely."

5. Any sailor worth his salt knows that helping a British service man, especially a sailor, to get his bed and board and perhaps more is part of naval life. The practice is well reciprocated.

6. Ibid.

7. Ibid.

8. John Nott, *Here Today, Gone Tomorrow* (London: Politico's, 1992), p. 305.

9. "The British operation to recapture the Falklands in 1982 could not have been mounted, let alone won, without American help." Goose Green and the entire Falklands war were the first such to be won by British forces fighting alone. *The Economist*, March 7, 1984. Not a few asked during and after the Falklands War if Nott had known the Falklands' location.

10. *The Economist*, March 7, 1984.

Appendix C

Argentine Plan for the Defense of Goose Green/Darwin Hill

The following is a summarized explanation of why it was decided that Darwin-Goose Green should be defended.

When studying the Falklands War, one must understand that the Argentine authorities of the time decided to occupy the islands—an operation that was executed very efficiently—without having drawn any plans for their defense, because it was thought that the British would accept the fact without a military reaction, only a diplomatic one.

One must also bear in mind that the recovery plans were initially set for the month of July, then May. And later, due to the heightening of the Georgias' issue and to the announcement by Great Britain of a reinforcement of its forces in the Falklands, the decision was made on March 26th and the plan was executed on April 2nd.

After concluding that Great Britain would not mount a military campaign, the idea was to take the islands and leave behind a reduced garrison to support a newly-established government.

On April 5th, in light of Resolution 502 and of the military measures being taken by Great Britain, the military junta, at the suggestion of Gen. García, commander of the Falklands Theater of Operations, ordered the transfer of reinforcement troops whose numbers were then gradually increased as military tensions rose to a point of no return.

These troops were eight Panhard vehicles from the 181st Armored Cavalry Reconnaissance Detachment, two Panhard vehicles from the 9th Armored Cavalry Reconnaissance Squadron, the 8th Infantry Regiment and the 3rd Artillery Group. As a consequence, the lack of foresight led to hasty decisions that would take too long to enumerate.

Regarding the defense of Darwin-Goose Green, the second most important area in the Falklands in terms of population, it should also be understood that this location was considered by the successive commands of the land forces (there were three different commands during the month of April) as one of the strong points of the archipelago. As a result, actions taken were based on this resolution and on events as they unfolded in that location.

Briefly, the following can be stipulated:

Mission Orders 1/82 (Defense) from Brigadier General Américo Daher (Commander of Land Forces of the Theater of Operations), dated April 7th at 2400, stated:

3. Execution
a. Operational concept
1) Maneuvers (Annex 2)
A system of strong points will be developed to defend key posts (Port Stanley and environs, Fox Bay, Darwin-Goose Green)...

This is the first reference to the establishment of defense forces at Goose Green, assigning this mission to C Company of the 25th Infantry Regiment, which had been in place since April 3rd. Goose Green was also considered the main connecting point between Gran Malvina Island [West Falkland] and Puerto Argentino [Port Stanley].

On April 9th, the 10th Mechanized Infantry Brigade was assigned to the South Atlantic Theater of Operations and was to be employed in the Falkland Islands.

Mission Orders No. 1/82 (Defense) by Brigadier General Oscar Luis Jofré (Commander of the Falklands Army Group), dated April 15th at 1200 (first given verbally, the written version of these orders was produced the following day at 0810), read as follows:

2. Mission
The Falklands Army Group will defend once the enemy initiates operations, the port sectors of the Falkland Islands, Darwin-Goose Green and Fox Bay, to contain, dislodge, repel and annihilate any form of land attack, with the objective of preventing the recovery of the islands by Great Britain and of supporting the actions of the Military Government.

3. Execution
b. Operational concept
2) Maneuvers
The operation will consist of a zone defense executed by forces of the army, navy infantry and air force, conceived on the basis of mutually supporting strong points with local reserves to counterattack. Two mobile air subunits, prepared to engage successively in support of the sectors of Stanley, Darwin; and two sections of

VCE-Panhard in support of sector Stanley will act as a reserve for the Group.

On April 14th, Condor Military Air Base, administered by the Argentine Air Force, began operations at Goose Green, the precarious spot used as an airport. This settlement's mission was to bring the Pucará squadron to a state of readiness to launch and sustain combat air operations.

The reason for putting this base in operation lay in the anticipated arrival of materiel and military personnel through the Falklands Military Air Base (in the Falklands capital). The latter would be extremely congested and would hamper the Pucará operations; furthermore, with the imminent onset of hostilities it was clear that it would be the principal target of the British forces.

Goose Green did not offer the most ideal conditions for combat aircraft operations but, after analyzing various alternatives, it was deemed the best one available. A maximum of twelve Pucará aircraft conducted their activities in this base; in addition, two helicopters CH-47 Chinook and two Bell 212, all from the Argentine Air Force, were assigned to the base.

On April 17th, the commander of the Falklands Air Component required support from an infantry company and air defense artillery for the protection of Condor Base. The next day, it was decided that a section of 35mm Oerlikon guns from the 601st Air Defense Artillery Group would be sent and, for ground forces, a gunnery section from the 8th Infantry Regiment, which was stationed at the city of Comodoro Rivadavia. This section arrived at Goose Green on April 22nd.

On April 21st, Gen. Cristino Nicolaides, Commander of the 1st Army Corps, arrived in the Falkland Islands, followed on April 22nd by the Commander-in-Chief of the army, Gen. Leopoldo Fortunato Galtieri. After these visits it was decided that the islands would be reinforced with the 3rd Infantry Brigade, whose members began arriving on April 25th.

The 12th Infantry Regiment, a member of this brigade, received orders to go to Darwin-Goose Green and take charge of the defense of the post and the landing strip, accompanied by C Company of the 25th Infantry Regiment and an artillery battery from the 4th Airborne Artillery Group. However, it had to spin off one company (B Company, "Solari" Combat Team), which remained as a reserve force at the Puerto Argentino [Stanley] position.

The arrival of the 12th Infantry Regiment at Darwin-Goose Green started on April 30th and culminated on May 21st, and it was conducted in an irregular fashion due to various factors there and to the availability of helicopters. Once established, it was assigned an additional mission: to set up as a reserve land force, for which, if employed, it would be granted helicopters.

The artillery battery of the 4th Airborne Artillery Group arrived at Goose Green as follows: two howitzers on board *Río Iguazú* (which had to be retrieved from the ship after an attack by two Sea Harriers on May 22nd disabled it; the guns arrived at their destination on the 24th), and two other howitzers, transported by helicopter on May 26th. This was, in sum, the build up to the defense of Darwin-Goose Green.

It would be well to comment on the extremely precarious conditions in which the 12th Infantry Regiment had to confront the British troops. It lacked its organic support weapons, it had not reached its effective strength and it had recently incorporated personnel at the officer, subofficer and soldier levels.

Original Text in Spanish

En forma resumida trataré de explicarle porqué se decidió defender la zona de Darwin-Goose Green.

Lo que usted debe tener muy en claro al estudiar la campaña de las Malvinas es que las autoridades argentinas de aquel entonces decidieron ocupar las islas, operación que se ejecutó en forma muy eficiente, sin haber realizado planes para su defensa porque se consideró que los británicos aceptarían ese hecho sin reaccionar en forma militar, sólo diplomáticamente.

También hay que tener en cuenta que los planes de recuperación estaban previstos en principio para el mes de julio, luego para mayo y más tarde, debido a la escalada del asunto Georgias y al refuerzo anunciado por Gran Bretaña de las fuerzas en Malvinas, el hecho se decidió el 26 de marzo y se ejecutó el 2 de abril.

En realidad, y pensando que no se montaría una campaña militar por parte del Reino Unido, la idea era tomar las islas y dejar una guarnición reducida para el sostenimiento del gobierno que sería instaurado.

El día 5 de abril, a la luz de la Resolución 502 y a las medidas militares que tomaba el Reino Unido, la Junta Militar, a proposición del general García, comandante del Teatro de Operaciones Malvinas, ordenó trasladar a las islas algunas tropas de refuerzo las que luego se irían incrementando en forma paulatina en una escalada que no tuvo retorno.

Estas tropas eran 8 vehículos Panhard del Destacamento de Exploración de Caballería Blindada 181, 2 vehículos Panhard del Escuadrón de

Exploración de Caballería Blindada 9, el Regimiento de Infantería 8 y el Grupo de Artillería 3.

Consecuentemente, la falta de previsiones hizo que se tomaran medidas en forma apresurada, que serían largas de enumerar.

En lo que se refiere a la defensa de Darwin-Goose Green, el segundo sitio en importancia poblacional de Malvinas, también debe entenderse que este sitio fue considerado por los sucesivos comandos de las fuerzas terrestres (hubo tres relaciones de comando distintas a lo largo del mes de abril) como uno de los punto fuertes (*strong point*) del archipiélago. En consecuencia, se fue obrando en base a esta resolución y a los hechos que se fueron produciendo en aquel sitio.

Resumidamente, se puede decir lo siguiente:

La Orden de Operaciones 1/82 (Defensa) del general de brigada Américo Daher (Comandante de las Fuerzas Terrestres del Teatro de Operaciones), fechada el 7 de abril a las 24.00 horas, establecía:

3. Ejecución
a. Concepto de la operación
1) Maniobra (Anexo 2)
Se organizará un sistema de puntos fuertes para defender los terrenos claves (Puerto Stanley y alrededores, Bahía Fox, Darwin-Ganso Verde)...

Esta es la primera referencia al establecimiento de fuerzas de defensa en Goose Green asignándose esta misión a la Compañía C del Regimiento de Infantería 25, la cual se encontraba en el lugar desde el día 3 de abril. Además, Goose Green era considerado el punto de enlace entre la Isla Gran Malvina y Puerto Argentino.

El día 9 de abril el Comando de la Brigada de Infantería Mecanizada X recibió la orden de quedar asignado al Teatro de Operaciones Atlántico Sur para su empleo en las Islas Malvinas.

En la Orden de Operaciones Nº 1/82 (Defensa) del general de brigada Oscar Luis Jofré (Comandante de la Agrupación Ejército Malvinas), fechada el 15 de abril a las 12.00 horas (aunque fue impartida verbalmente y por escrito el día siguiente a las 8.10 horas), se lee:

2. Misión
La Agr Ej Malvinas defenderá a partir que el enemigo inicie las operaciones, los sectores de Puerto de las Islas Malvinas, Darwin-

Goose Green y Bahía Fox, para contener, desarticular, rechazar y aniquilar cualquier forma de ataque terrestre, a fin de impedir la recuperación de las Islas por parte de Gran Bretaña y apoyar las acciones del Gobierno Militar.

3. Ejecución

b. Concepto de la operación

2) Maniobra

La operación consistirá en una defensa de zona ejecutada por fuerzas de Ejército, Infantería de Marina y de la Fuerza Aérea, concebida sobre la base de puntos fuertes apoyados entre sí con reservas locales para contraatacar y como reserva de la Agrupación, dos subunidades aeromóviles en condiciones de ser empeñadas sucesivamente en apoyo de los sectores Stanley, Darwin y dos secciones de VCE-Panhard en apoyo del sector Stanley.

El día 14 de abril, comenzó a funcionar en Goose Green, en el precario terreno utilizado como aeródromo, la Base Aérea Militar Cóndor, a cargo de la Fuerza Aérea Argentina. La misión de este asentamiento era la de estar en condiciones de realizar y sostener operaciones aéreas de combate del escuadrón Pucará.

La razón de la puesta en operaciones de esta base era que, previendo la llegada de material bélico y de personal militar a través de la Base Aérea Militar Malvinas (en la capital malvinense), esta iba a estar sumamente congestionada dificultando las operaciones de los Pucará y, además, sería el principal blanco de las fuerzas británicas ante el inminente comienzo de las hostilidades.

No reunía el campo de Goose Green las mejores condiciones para la operación de aviones de combate pero, luego de analizarse varias alternativas, se decidió que era la mejor de ellas. Un máximo de 12 aviones Pucará estuvieron desarrollando sus actividades en esta base; además, fueron asignados a la misma 2 helicópteros CH-47 Chinook y 2 Bell 212, todos de la Fuerza Aérea Argentina.

El día 17 de abril el comandante del Componente Aéreo de Malvinas requirió efectivos de una compañía de infantería y de artillería de defensa aérea para la protección de la Base Cóndor. Al día siguiente se decidió el envío de una sección de cañones de 35mm Oerlikon del Grupo de Artillería de Defensa Aérea 601 y, como tropa terrestre, una sección de tiradores del Regimiento de Infantería 8, el que se encontraba en la ciudad de Comodoro Rivadavia. Esta sección llegó a Goose Green el 22 de abril.

El 21 de abril estuvo en las Islas Malvinas el Comandante del I Cuerpo de Ejército, general Cristino Nicolaides y el día 22 las visitó el Comandante en Jefe del Ejército, teniente General Leopoldo Fortunato Galtieri. A partir de estas concurrencias se decidió reforzar las islas con la Brigada de Infantería III, los elementos de la cual comenzaron a llegar a partir del día 25.

El Regimiento de Infantería 12, integrante de esta Brigada, recibió la orden de trasladarse a Darwin-Goose Green para hacerse cargo de la defensa de la localidad y de la pista de aterrizaje, agregándosele la Compañía C del Regimiento de Infantería 25 y una batería de artillería del Grupo de Artillería Aerotransportado 4. Sin embargo, debió segregar una compañía (Compañía B, Equipo de Combate "Solari") la que quedó como reserva de la posición Puerto Argentino.

La llegada del Regimiento de Infantería 12 a Darwin-Goose Green comenzó el 30 de abril y culminó el 21 de mayo, realizándose en forma irregular debido a las variantes de la situación y a la disponibilidad de helicópteros. Una vez establecido se le asignó la misión adicional de constituirse como reserva de las Fuerzas terrestres para lo cual, en caso de empleo, le serían asignados helicópteros.

La batería de artillería del Grupo de Artillería Aerotransportado 4 llegó a Goose Green de la siguiente manera: dos piezas a bordo de la patrullera *Río Iguazú* (debieron ser rescatadas de debajo del agua luego de que la nave fuera atacada por dos aviones Sea Harrier el 22 de mayo, quedando una fuera de servicio; el 24 llegaron a su destino), y otras dos piezas, transportadas por helicópteros, el 26 de mayo. Este fue, en pocas palabras, el montaje de la defensa de Darwin-Goose Green.

Quedarían para comentar las precarísimas condiciones en las que el Regimiento de Infantería 12 debió enfrentar a las tropas británicas que lo atacaron, sin tener sus armas de apoyo orgánicas, disminuido en su fuerza efectiva y contando, además, con personal incorporado recientemente a esa unidad, ya sean oficiales, suboficiales y soldados.

Source: This appendix is the kind contribution of a distinguished Argentine historian who wishes to remain anonymous.

Appendix D

Mission Orders for Goose Green Received at Camilla Creek House
May 27, 1982

GROUND

a. Isthmus dominated by a spine running NNE-SSW

b. Prominent hedge 633593 649581

c. Prominent tracks

d. Dead ground approaches

e. DARWIN
(1) 6X Houses in Darwin
(2) Large empty house 653585 for accommodation near stone corral
(3) Manager's house 652586
(4) Outhouses in area En trench posns
(5) Settlement is in a bowl dominated by hill 649585 and hill 652583 with flag pole on top, covered in gorse. Likely en posn
(6) Footbridge in disrepair
(7) Large pond 650586 not marked on map
(8) Track via re-entrant 650582
(9) Good approaches from CAMILLA CREEK to 634593—hedgerow to track above stone corral. Re-entrant 646589 then coastline to settlement

f. GOOSE GREEN
(1) Population 125+
(2) Dominant building—Black woolshed 641563
(3) Bunk house (80 men) 644561 (long bungalow)
(4) 15 civvy houses and outhouses
(5) Veh Garage 639565
(6) Generator in settlement 639565
(7) Dominated by airstrip to N. Airstrip has hut & flagpole and Red/ White painted drums and line of pens to NNE

g. School 645570

(1) Large wooden building

(2) Re-enterant to E

(3) Can fire on Goose Green from school

h. Dairy 642575 in dead ground. Large gate on track. But approaches from N or SW.

SITUATION

a. Enemy

(1) Elements 12 Regt in area with minimum of 3X companies

(2) En at Darwin 653587 on peninsula but now depleted. Minefields on beach from peninsula to sea. Minor Guard

(3) Goose Green Old deployment?

(4) Roads not mined

(5) Company (-) moved N to stop us getting in

(6) Airfield 636569 has 3X AA guns on Sedge

(7) Helicopters roost in settlement

(8) Stores area 643570 N of airfield and at 633550 but probably destroyed

(9) Company dug in with 2X SF's covering E and NW at 653617

(10) Platoon 645607

(11) 16 trenches no overhead cover. Possible platoon position with tents 643592

(12) 5 trenches in platoon position S of BOCA HOUSE 634588

(13) Dug in position? 643590

(14) Company position Coronation Point 659595

(15) En have withdrawn from old positions to defensive positions facing N. Platoon positions BURNSIDE HOUSE. Scoff point?

(16) 3X Minefields:

    (a) DARWIN—along coastline

    (b) N of school bridge

    (c) S of school

    (d) But more minefields possible

(17) En dress—cam jackets—green trousers, U.S. style helmets

(18) Wpns: FN's, poor condition

(19) Artillery: 3 guns 638592, 653595, 643564

b. Friendly Forces

2 PARA supported by HAS ARROW, Harriers, Tp 8 Battery, 2X Blow-pipe sections

MISSION

2 PARA is to capture DARWIN and GOOSE GREEN

EXECUTION

a. General outline. 6 phase night/day, silent noisy attack, each En posn taken in turn
(1) phase One. C Coy Recce routes find and prepare/protect start line
(2) Phase Two. A & B Coy's attack first posns, A first then B
(3) Phase Three. A & D Coys go for second line posns
(4) Phase Four. B Coy pass through D Coy to Attack reserve posns (BOCA HOUSE). If necessary B Coy halts at HEDGE ROW and D Coy overtake
(5) Phase Five. Exploitation up to DARWIN/GOOSE GREEN. C Coy clear airfield
(6) Phase six. Take DARWIN/GOOSE GREEN

b. Grouping
(1) A Coy; MFC, FOO, RE Sect.
(2) B Coy: MFC, FOO, RE Sect.
(3) C Coy: MFC, RE Sect.
(4) D Coy: MFC, FOO, RE Sect.
(5) Sp Coy: MFC, Anti-tanks, MMGs, Snipers, NGFO to set up fire base to support western (B & D) Coys fwd.
(6) Mortars independent
(7) Defense/Assault Engineers Platoons ammo carriers, P. W. 's, Assault Engineers then to C Coy

c. A Coy
(1) Phase One. Reserve
(2) Phase Two a. Capture BURNSIDE HOUSE
(3) Phase Three. Destroy En CORONATION PT.
(4) Phase Four. Reserve
(5) Phase Five. Exploit to edge of DARWIN
(6) Phase Six. Take DARWIN

d. B Coy

(1) Phase One. Reserve

(2) Phase Two B. Destroy En 650615

(3) Phase Three. Reserve

(4) Phase Four. Defeat En 640590

(5) Phase Five. Reserve

(6) Phase Six. Reserve. Be prep to attack schoolhouse

e. C Coy

Phase One. Clear Fwd and mark and protect start lines for A & B CoYs. Clear gun posn 660626

(2) Phase Two. As above

(3) Phase Three/Four. Reserve

(4) Phase Five. Clear Airfield. Destroy Tripi As

(5) Phase Six. Exploit to BODIE CREEK BRIDGE

f. D Coy

Phase One. Reserve

Phase Two. Reserve

Phase Three. Destroy En posn 645605

Phase Four. Reserve. BOCA HOUSE if necessary

Phase Five. Exploit behind C Coy to GOOSE GREEN

Phase Six. Take G

g. Sp Coy

Phase One. Fire base 640615

Phase Two. Support B Coy

Phase Three. Support D Coy

Move to join the Battalion

Phase five/Six. In Reserve

h. ARTY.

Phase One. HMS ARROW on priority call to C Coy during fly in of guns of 8 Bty.

(2) Phase Two.

Arrow pri call to B Coy

Guns pri call to A coy

Mortars in reserve

(3) Phase Three.

Arrow to D Coy
Guns to A Coy
Mortars reserve

(4) Phase Four. Arrow/guns to B Coy then D Coy if passed through. Mortars reserve

(5) Phase Five/Six. Mortars pri call to A Coy. Guns to D Coy. Milan/MMGs to B Coy

i. MORTARS. Base plate area 6462. Not in action Phase One and 2

j. Defence Platoon. Available to Sp Coy for Ammo (MMG+Milan) One officer from Bn HQ with OC Sp Coy to bring Def Platoon back

k. RAP. 83A to 660626 then on track (overiding DARWIN) as Bn centre line. Bn main to leave someone on junction near DARWIN

l. Order of march. C Coy, Sp Coy, A Coy, TAC one, B Coy, Main HQ, D Coy, (RAP with main)

m. START LINE
(1) Phase Two Agreed between Coy comds & C Coy
(2) Subsequently each Coy holding ground then forms the start line

n. ROUTE. Track (A Coy divert to bridge on track)

o. TIMINGS
(1) C Coy move after last light
Sp Coy move after C Coy
A Coy depart 0300 or at Coy Comd's discretion
Phase 2 H hr 0600
Phase 3 H hr 0700
Phase 4 H hr 0800
Phase 5 H hr 0900
Phase 6 H hr 1030

p. Blowpipe. 4X RA. Blowpipe to remain at Camilla Creek House. 2X Royal Marine Blowpipe with main HQ

q. FAC NGFO to travel with main or CO to delegate to Coys

r. Guns. At Camilla Creek House C/Sgts to use CCH for AMMO re-sup

s. Casualties. ON centre line, the to RAP

t. Ammunition. Csgt VALE to organise (to use captured landrover after mortars for MMG re-sup) 84mm MAW to be avail as required

u. Scout/Gazelle. On call after first light (SS? 11)

v. Harriers. To attack on point targets

w. Prisoners. To main HQ (RSM) guarded by defense platoon, then to rear

COMMAND & SIGNAL

a. TAC (CO) on track behind coys

b. Main On track 660626

c. Rear Camilla Creek House

d. Password. II until 1200Z, then 7 until 291200Z, then 5, then 9. e. Codes. Moving now – ZULU

Source: Benest's transcription of Jones' plan. Benest Papers in Fitzgibbon, *Not Mentioned in the Despatches.*

Appendix E

British and Argentine Goose Green Casualties

British Dead From Goose Green

Lt. Col. H. Jones VC	Commanding Officer, 2 Para
Captain C. Dent	A Company
Captain D. A. Wood	Adjutant
Lt. J. A. Barry	D Company
Cpl. D. Hardman	A Company
Cpl. S. R. Prior	A Company
Cpl. P. S. Sullivan	D Company
L. Cpl. G. D. Bingley MM	D Company
L. Cpl. A. Cork	D Company
L. Cpl. N. R. Smith	D Company
Pte. S. J. Dixon	D Company
Pte. M. W. Fletcher	D Company
Pte. M. Holman-Smith	HQ Company
Pte. S. Illingsworth DCM	B Company
Pte. T. Mechan	D Company
Lt. R. J. Nunn	Royal Marines
Corp. D. Melia	Royal Engineers

Argentine Dead From Goose Green

Lt. Roberto Néstor Estévez	25th Infantry Regiment (Estévez)
Lt. Miguel Angel Giménez	Air Force
Lt. Daniel Enrique Miguel	Navy
Sgt. Sergio Ismael García	25th Infantry Regiment (Centurión)
Tech. Sgt. Francisco Tomás Luna	Air Force
Pte. (I) Miguel Angel Avila	25th Infantry Regiment (Centurión)
Pte. (I) Mario Rodolfo Castro	25th Infantry Regiment (Estévez)
Pte. (I) Raúl Adrián Gómez	12th Infantry Regiment
Pte. (I) Edmundo Federico Marcial	12th Infantry Regiment

Pte. (I) Héctor Rubén Oviedo	25th Infantry Regiment (Centurión)
Pte. (I) José Luis Ríos	12th Infantry Regiment
Pte. Celso Alegre	12th Infantry Regiment
Pte. José Luis Allende	25th Infantry Regiment (Centurión)
Pte. Ricardo Andrés Austin	25th Infantry Regiment (Centurión)
Pte. Ofelio Víctor Avalos	12th Infantry Regiment
Pte. Omar Alberto Avalos	12th Infantry Regiment
Pte. Rafael Barrios	12th Infantry Regiment
Pte. Ramón Cirilo Blanco	12th Infantry Regiment
Pte. Ramón Angel Cabrera	25th Infantry Regiment (Centurión)
Pte. Fabricio Edgar Carrascull	25th Infantry Regiment (Estévez)
Pte. Carlos Agustín Díaz	12th Infantry Regiment
Pte. Vladimiro Dworak	12th Infantry Regiment
Pte. José Alberto Encina	12th Infantry Regiment
Pte. Carmelo Fernández	12th Infantry Regiment
Pte. José Ramón Ferrau	12th Infantry Regiment
Pte. Carlos Alberto Frías	12th Infantry Regiment
Pte. Ramón García	12th Infantry Regiment
Pte. Horacio Lorenzo Giraudo	25th Infantry Regiment (Estévez)
Pte. Rubén Horacio Gómez	12th Infantry Regiment
Pte. Fernando Jesús Lugo	12th Infantry Regiment
Pte. Daniel Omar Luque	12th Infantry Regiment
Pte. Ireneo Osvaldo Maciel	12th Infantry Regiment
Pte. Ireneo Mendoza	12th Infantry Regiment
Pte. Luis Miño	12th Infantry Regiment
Pte. Juan Carlos Monzón	12th Infantry Regiment
Pte. Alberto José Moschen	12th Infantry Regiment
Pte. Guillermo Núñez	12th Infantry Regiment
Pte. José Honorio Ortega	25th Infantry Regiment (Centurión)
Pte. Carlos Omar Osyguss	12th Infantry Regiment
Pte. Néstor Oscar Avelino Pegoraro	12th Infantry Regiment
Pte. Juan Anselmo Peralta	12th Infantry Regiment
Pte. Vicente Ramón Pérez	12th Infantry Regiment
Pte. Rubén Norberto Ramírez	12th Infantry Regiment

Pte. Segundino Antonio Riquelme	12th Infantry Regiment
Pte. Víctor Rodríguez	12th Infantry Regiment
Pte. Julio Romero	12th Infantry Regiment
Pte. Gabino Ruiz Díaz	12th Infantry Regiment
Pte. Roque Evaristo Sánchez	12th Infantry Regiment
Pte. Higinio Segovia	12th Infantry Regiment
Pte. Arnaldo Enrique Zabala	25th Infantry Regiment (Estévez)
Recruit Héctor Walter Aguirre	Air Force
Recruit Luis Guillermo Sevilla	Air Force

Selected Bibliography

Adams, James. *Secret Armies*. Berkeley, CA: Atlantic Monthly Press, 1988.

Adams, John Quincy. "Account of the Cabinet Meeting of November 7, 1832." Documents relating to American Foreign Policy before 1898. Mt. Holyoke College, courtesy of Prof. Vincent Ferraro.

Adkin, Mark. *Goose Green*. London: Orion Books, 1992.

Allan, Phillip. *British Foreign Policy Under Thatcher*. New York: St. Martin's Press, 1988.

Amnesty International. *Military Juntas and Human Rights*. London: Amnesty International, 1987.

Andersen, Martin Edwin. *Dossier Secreto: Argentina's Desaparecidos and the Myth of the Dirty War*. Boulder, CO: Westview Press, 1993.

Andrews, Kenneth R. *The Last Voyage of Drake and Hawkins*. Cambridge Press for The Hakluyt Society, 1972.

———. *Trade, Plunder and Settlement, 1480–1630*. Cambridge University Press, 1984.

Arce, José. *The Malvinas (Our Snatched Little Isles)*. Madrid: Núñez de Balboa, 1951.

Ardent du Picq, Charles. *Etudes sur le combat*. New York, 1921.

Arendt, Hannah. *On Violence*. New York: Harvest Books, 1970.

Arthur, Max. *Above All Courage*. London: Sphere Books, 1986.

Bagehot, Walter. "The Bovine Stupidity of the Average MP," in *Godkin Lectures at Harvard 1970*, by Richard Crossman. Cambridge: Harvard University Press, 1972.

Bamford, James. *Body of Secrets*. New York: Anchor, 2002.

Barker, Nick. *Beyond Endurance*. London: Cooper, 1997.

Barnett, Anthony. *Iron Britannia*. London, New York: Allison and Busby, 1982.

Barrie and Lovell. In *Britain's Small Wars*, www.britains-smallwars.com.

Basílico, Ernesto. *La armada del Obispo de Placencia*. Buenos Aires: Instituto de Publicaciones Navales, Centro Naval, 1967.

Bates, D.B. *Incidents on Land and Water*, 5th edition. Boston: E.G. Libby, 1858.

Bauer, John. "The Welsh In Patagonia." *Hispanic American Review,* vol. 34, no. 4, 1954.

Beaufre, André. *An Introduction to Strategy.* London: Faber and Faber, 1966.

———. *Strategy of Action.* London: Faber and Faber, 1967.

Beck, Peter. *The Falkland Islands as an International Problem.* London: Routledge, 1988.

Bell, R. E., *Logistical Support of British Land Forces in the Falkland Islands Campaign 1982.* Unpublished.

Benn, Tony. *The Benn Diaries.* London: Arrow, 1996.

———. *On The Falklands War.* NEC Resolution, April 28, 1982.

Bethune, C.R. Drinkwater, ed. *The Observations of Sir Richard Hawkins, Knt., in his Voyage into the South Sea in the Year 1593.* London: Hakluyt Society, no. 1, 1847 (reprinted from the edition of 1622).

Bilton, Michael, and Peter Kosminsky. *Speaking Out: Untold Stories From the Falklands War.* London: Andre Deutsch, 1989.

Bishop, Patrick and John Witherow. *The Winter War: The Falklands.* New York: Quartet Books, 1982.

Blackman, Raymond. *Ships of the Royal Navy.* London: MacDonald and Jane's, 1973.

Blakeway, Denys. *The Falklands War.* London: Sedgwick and Jackson, 1992.

Bloch, Marc. *The Historian's Craft.* New York: Knopf, 1953.

Booth, Ken. *Strategy and Ethnocentrism.* London: Croom Helm, 1980.

Boswell, James. *Life of Johnson.* Oxford: Oxford University Press, 1953, unabridged.

Bourne, William. *A Regimen for the Sea and Other Writings on Navigation.* Ed. E.G.R. Taylor. London: Hakluyt Society, 1963.

Boyson, V.F. *The Falkland Islands.* Oxford: Clarendon Press, 1924.

Briasco, Jesús Romero and Salvador Huertas. *Falklands: Witness of Battles.* Valencia: Federico Domenech, 1984.

British Foreign and State Papers, vol. 20.

Brown, Cynthia, ed. *With Friends Like These.* New York: Pantheon, 1985.

Brown, David. *The Falklands War.* Annapolis: U.S. Naval Institute Press, 1987; and London: Cooper, 1987.

Burden, Rodney A. *Falklands: The Air War.* London: Arms and Armour Press, 1986. Also published as *Falklands: The Air War,* Burden, Draper, Rough, Smith and Wilton, British Aviation Research Group, Twickenham, Sussex.

Burns, Jimmy. *The Land That Lost Its Heroes*. London: Bloomsbury, 1986.

Byron, John. *Byron's Journal of his Circumnavigation, 1764–1766*. Edited by Robert E. Gallagher. London: Hakluyt Society, 1964.

Calvert, Peter. *The Falklands Crisis: The Rights and the Wrongs*. London: Continuum International Publishers' Group, 1982.

Cardoso, Oscar Raúl, Ricardo Kirschbaum and Eduardo van der Kooy. *Malvinas: La Trama Secreta*. Buenos Aires: Sudamericana-Planeta, 1983; and Surrey, UK: Preston Editions, 1983.

Carlyle, Thomas. *The French Revolution: A History*. Oxford University Press, 1989.

Carrington, Charles Edmonds. *A Subaltern's War*. London: Peter Davies, 1929.

Carrington, Lord Peter. *Reflections on Things Past*. London: Collins and Sons, 1988.

Cavalini, Enrique H.J. "The Malvinas Falkland Affair: A New Look." *International Journal of Intelligence and Counterintelligence* 2, no. 2.

Cawkell, Mary B.R. *The Falkland Islands*. London: St. Martin's Press, 1960.

Chamorro, Edgar. *Packaging the Contras: A Case of CIA Disinformation*. New York: Institute for Media Analysis, 1987.

Chapman, Guy. *A Passionate Prodigality: Fragments of Autobiography*. London: Ivor Nicholson and Watson, 1933.

Charlton, Michael. *The Little Platoon*. London: Basil Blackwell, 1989.

Chase Manhattan Bank. "Latin American Business Highlights," New York, January 1978–December 1984.

Clapp, Michael, and Ewen Southby-Tailyour. *Amphibious Assault Falklands*. London: Cooper, 1996.

Clark, Alan. *Diaries*. London: Weidenfeld and Nicolson, 1993.

Clark, John G. *La Rochelle and the Atlantic Economy During the 18th Century*. Baltimore: Johns Hopkins University Press, 1981.

Clarridge, Duane R. *A Spy For All Seasons*. New York: Scribner's, January 1997.

Clowes, William Laird. *The Royal Navy: A History from the Earliest Times to the Present*. London: Chatham, 1901, vol. 6.

Coll, Alberto and Anthony Arend, eds. *The Falklands War: Lesson for Strategy, Diplomacy and International Law*. Boston: Allen & Unwin, 1985.

Comisión Nacional sobre la Desaparición de Personas. *Nunca Más*. New York: Farrar, Straus, Giroux, 1986.

Connell-Smith, Gordon. "Latin America and the Falklands Conflict." *Year Book of World Affairs,* 1984.

Cooke, Edward. *A Voyage to the South Sea, and Around the World, Perform'd in the Years 1708–1711.* London: B. Lintot and R. Gosling, 1712. Reprinted 1971.

Cordesman, Anthony H. and Abraham R. Wagner. *The Lessons of Modern War: The Afghan and Falklands Conflicts.* Boulder, CO: Westview Press, 1990.

Coronelli, P. *Planisfero del Mondo Nuovo, descrito dal P. Coronelli Cosmografico Pubblico.* On exhibition, Museo Storico Navale, Venice, 2004. Published 1592.

Corradi, Juan E. "The Culture of Fear in Civil Society." In *From Military Rule to Liberal Democracy in Argentina.* London: Westview Press, 1987.

Craddock, Percy. *In Pursuit of British Interests.* London: John Murray, 1997.

Craig, Chris. *Call For Fire.* London: John Murray, 1995.

Crossman, Richard. *Godkin Lectures at Harvard 1970.* Cambridge: Harvard University Press, 1972.

Dalyell, Tom. *Misrule.* London: Hamilton, 1987.

Dampier, William. *A New Voyage Around the World.* London: Argonaut Press, 1927.

Defense and Foreign Affairs, Ltd. Conference on "The Lessons of the South Atlantic War," Washington, DC, 1982. Department of State Bulletin, March 1982–August 1982.

Delbrück, Hans. *History of the Art of War within the Framework of Political History,* vols. 3 & 4. Westport, CT: Greenwood Press, 1985.

Dickey, Christopher. *With the Contras: A Reporter in the Wilds of Nicaragua.* New York: Simon and Schuster, 1987.

Dickie, John. *Inside the Foreign Office.* London: Chapmans, 1992.

Dillon, Sam. *The Commandos.* New York: Holt, 1991.

Dixon, Norman F. *On the Psychology of Military Incompetence.* London: Cape, 1976.

Dobson, Christopher, John Miller and Ronald Payne. *The Falklands Conflict.* London: Coronet Books, 1982.

Drake, Sir Francis. *The World Encompassed.* London, 1971.

Dupuy, Trevor Nevitt. *The Evolution of Weapons and Warfare.* Indianapolis: Bobbs-Merrill, 1980.

———. *A Genius for War.* London: MacDonald and Jane's, 1977.

English, Adrian. *Battle for the Falklands: Two Naval Forces.* London: Osprey, 1987.

Ethell, Jeffrey, and Alfred Price. *Air War South Atlantic.* New York: Jove Books, 1986.

"Exercise Welsh Falcon." *Honor Regained,* in *Britain's Small Wars,* www.britains-smallwars.com.

Falkland Islands' Company (FIC). *The Falkland Islands' Company Ltd., 1851–1951.* London: FIC, 1951.

Falkland Islands Gazette. Port Stanley, January 1, 1891–present.

Falkland Islands Review. Franks Report. London: HMSO, 1983.

Ferns, Henry Stanley. *Britain and Argentina in the Nineteenth Century.* Oxford: Clarendon Press, 1960.

Fischer, David Hackett. *Historians' Fallacies.* New York: Harper and Row, 1970.

Fitzgibbon, Spencer. *Not Mentioned in the Despatches.* Cambridge: Lutterworth, 1995.

Fitzroy, Robert. *Narrative of the Surveying Voyages of His Majesty's Ships Adventure and Beagle Between the Years 1826 and 1836, 1839.*

Foreign Affairs Committee, Session 1984–1984. Third Report. Events of the 1st and 2nd of May 1982. London: HMSO, 1985.

Foster, Nigel. *The Making of a Royal Marine Commando.* Novato, CA: Presidio Press, 1988.

Foster, Sir William, ed. *The Voyage of Sir Henry Middleton to the Moluccas, 1604–1606.* London: Hakluyt Society, 1943.

Fox, Robert. *Eyewitness Falklands.* London: Methuen, 1982.

Frazer, David. *Knight's Cross, A Life of Field Marshall Erwin Rommel.* London: Harper, 1993.

Freedman, Lawrence. "The War of the Falklands, 1982." *Foreign Affairs,* Fall 1982, vol. 61, no. 1.

———. *Signals of War: The Falklands Conflict of 1982.* London and Boston: Faber and Faber, 1991.

———. *Britain and the Falklands War.* Oxford and New York: B. Blackwell, 1988.

Frezier, Amadee François. *A Voyage to the South Sea.* London: Jonah Bowyer, 1717.

Frost, John. *2 Para in the Falklands.* London: Buchan and Enright, 1983.

Fundamentos de la acusión a las militares para Malvinas. Buenos Aires: Ediciones El Centro Dos de Abril, 1986.

Fussell, Paul. *The Great War and Modern Memory*. Oxford University Press, 1975.

Gavshon, Arthur L. and Desmond Rice. *The Sinking of the Belgrano*. London: Secker and Warburg, 1984.

George, Bruce and Michael Coughlin. "British Defence Policy After the Falklands." *Survival (IIS)*, September–October 1982.

Gillespie, Richard. *Armed Struggle in Argentina*. Washington, DC: Organization of American States Report on Human Rights and Oxford, 1982.

Globe and Laurel. RM Secretariat. July/August 1982.

Goebel, Julius. *Struggle For The Falklands*. New Haven, CT: Yale University Press, 1927.

Gómez-Centurión. "Yo creí que usted venía a rendirse!" In *Britain's Small Wars*, www.britains-smallwars.com.

Goncharov, N. *The Malvinas Crisis*. Moscow: Editorial Board of the Academy of Social Sciences, 1984.

Graves, Robert. *Goodbye to All That*. New York: J. Cape and H. Smith, 1930.

Green, Leslie C. "The Falklands, the Law and the War." *Year Book of World Affairs*, 1984.

Gustafson, Lowell Steven. *Sovereignty Dispute over (The Malvinas) Falkland Islands*. Ann Arbor, MI: University of Microfilms, 1984.

Haig, Alexander. *Caveat*. New York: McMillan, 1984.

Halperin, Morton. *Bureaucratic Politics and Foreign Policy*. Washington, DC: Brookings Institution Press, 1974.

Hamilton, Nigel. *Monty The Battles of Field Marshall Bernard Montgomery*. New York: Random House, 1994.

Hart, Liddell, ed. *Rommel Letters*. New York: Harcourt Brace, 1953.

Hastings, Max. *Overlord: D-Day & The Battle for Normandy*. New York: Simon & Schuster, 1985.

———, and Simon Jenkins. *The Battle for the Falklands*. New York: Norton, 1983.

Hawkins, Sir Richard. *Observations of Sir Richard Hawkins*. London: Hakluyt Society, no. 1, 1845.

Healey, Denis. *The Time of My Life*. New York: Norton, 1990.

Heaney, Seamus, trans. *Beowulf*. New York: Norton, 2000.

Henderson, Sir Nicholas. *Mandarin*. London: Weidenfeld and Nicolson, 1994.

Her Majesty's Stationary Office (HMSO). *Battle Report, Falklands War, 3 Commando Brigade*. London: HMSO, 1983.

———. *Battle Report, Falklands War, 5 Infantry Brigade*. London: HMSO, 1983.

———. *Battle Report, Falklands War, British Army*. London: HMSO, 1983.

———. *Battle Report, Falklands War, Royal Air Force*. London: HMSO, 1983.

———. *Battle Report, Falklands War, Royal Marines*. London: HMSO, 1983.

———. *Battle Report, Falklands War, Royal Navy*. London: HMSO, 1983.

———. "Cmnd. 8787." In *Falkland Islands Review*. London: HMSO, 1983.

———. *Economic Survey of the Falklands*. London: HMSO, 1976.

———. *Falkland Islands: Negotiations for a Peaceful Settlement*. London: HMSO, May 21, 1982.

———. *The Falklands Campaign: A Digest of Debates in the House of Commons 2 April to 15 June 1982*. London: HMSO, 1982.

———. *The Falklands Campaign: The Lessons*. London: HMSO Cmnd. 8752, December 1982.

Historical Periodicals' Directory, vol. 4. Santa Barbara, 1985.

Hoffmann, Fritz L. and Olga Mingo Hoffmann. *Sovereignty in Dispute: The Falklands/Malvinas, 1493–1982*. Boulder, CO: Westview Press, 1984.

House of Commons. *The Falklands Campaign: A Digest of Debates in the House of Commons, 2 April to 15 June 1982*. London: HMSO, 1982.

———. *Handling of the Press*. Minutes, 20 October 1982. London: HMSO, 1982.

Howard, Michael Eliot. *The Causes of Wars and Other Essays*. Cambridge, MA: Harvard University Press, 1984.

———. *The Lessons of History*. New Haven, CT: Yale University Press, 1991.

Hughes-Wilson, Colonel John. *Military Intelligence Blunders*. London: Robinson, 1999.

Hunt, Rex. *My Falkland Days*. London: David and Charles, 1992.

Huntington, Samuel. *The Soldier and the State*. Cambridge, MA: Belknap Press of Harvard University Press, 1957.

Ingham, Bernard. *Kill the Messenger*. London: Fontana, 1991.

International Court of Justice. *Antarctica Cases (UK vs. Argentina)*. The Hague: International Court of Justice, 1956.

International Monetary Fund (IMF). *Blue Books 1981–1982.* Washington, DC: IMF, 1981–1982.

Jofre, Oscar Luis. *Malvinas: La defensa de Puerto Argentino.* Buenos Aires: Editorial Sudamérica, 1987.

Johnstone, Christian Isobel. *Lives and Voyages of Drake, Cavendish and Dampier.* New York: Harper Bros., 1840.

Jolly, Rick. *The Red and Green Life Machine: A Diary of the Falklands Field Hospital.* London: Century Publishing, 1983.

Keegan, John. *The Face of Battle.* Harmondsworth: Penguin, 1978.

———. *The Mask of Command.* New York: Viking, 1987.

Kemp, Peter, ed. *The Oxford Companion to Ships and the Sea.* London: Oxford University Press, 1976.

Koburger, Charles W. *Sea Power in the Falklands.* New York: Praeger, 1983.

Kon, Daniel. *Los chicos de la guerra: Hablan los soldados que estuvieron en Malvinas.* Buenos Aires: Galerna, 1983.

Langguth, A.J. *Hidden Terrors.* New York: Pantheon, 1978.

Latin American News Letter. "The Falklands War." London, 1983.

Le Bailly, Sir Louis. *From Fisher to the Falklands.* London: Institute of Marine Engineers, 1991.

Le Roy Ladurie, Emmanuel. *The Territory of the Historian.* University of Chicago Press, 1979.

Leed, Eric J. *No Man's Land: Combat and Identity in World War One.* Cambridge University Press, 1979.

Lloyd, Reginald, ed. *Twentieth Century Impressions of Argentina.* London: Lloyds Greater Britain Publishing Company Ltd., 1911.

Lloyds List. London, March–June 1982.

Love, Jim. "Coronation Point." In *Britain's Small Wars,* www.britainssmallwars.com.

———. "2 Para in Darwin Hill." In *Britain's Small Wars,* www.britainssmallwars.com.

Low, Charles R. *Maritime Discovery.* London: Newman, 1881, vol. 11.

Lundgren, David T. *Trust But Verify.* Annapolis: Naval Institute Press, 2000.

Mackinnon, Laughlin Bellingham. *Some Account of the Falkland Islands, 1838–1839.* London: A.H. Bailly, 1840.

Malvinas: Relatos de soldados. Buenos Aires: Círculo Militar, 1986.

Marcella, Gabriel. *The Malvinas/Falklands War of 1982.* Carlisle Barracks, PA: Strategic Studies Institute, U.S. Army War College, 1983.

Markham, Sir Albert Hastings. *Voyages and Works of John Davis, the Navigator.* London: Hakluyt Society, 1880.

Markham, Sir Clements. *Early Spanish Voyages to the Strait of Magellan.* London: Hakluyt Society, 1911.

McGowan, Robert and Jeremy Hands. *Don't Cry for Me Sergeant Major.* London: Warner Books, 1983.

McManners, Hugh. *Falklands Commando.* London: William Kimber, 1984.

Meléndez, Federico. *The Falklands: A Study in International Confrontation.* Carlsbad: Arcadia Publications, 1984.

Melvern, Linda. *The Ultimate Crime.* London: Allison & Busby, 1995.

Menéndez, Mario Benjamín. *Malvinas: Testimonio de su gobernador.* Buenos Aires: Editorial Sudamérica, 1983.

Middlebrook, Martin. *The Fight for the Malvinas: The Argentine Forces in the Falklands War.* New York: Viking, 1989.

———. *Operation Corporate: The Falklands War, 1982.* London: Viking, 1985.

———. *Task Force, The Falklands War, 1982.* Harmondsworth: Penguin, 1987.

Moineville, Hubert. *Naval Warfare Today and Tomorrow.* Oxford: Basil Blackwell, 1983.

Moore, Major-General Jeremy. Lecture by British Commanders on "The 1982 Falklands Campaign." National Defense University, Washington, DC, November 19, 1982.

Moran, Lord Charles. *Anatomy of Courage.* Boston: Houghton Mifflin, 1967.

———. *Dairies of Lord Moran.* Cambridge: Riverside Press, 1966.

Moreno, Juan Carlos. *La recuperación de las Malvinas.* Buenos Aires: Plus Ultra, 1973.

Morgan, Kenneth S. *Bristol and the Atlantic Trade in the 18th Century.* Cambridge University Press, 1993.

Morison, Samuel Eliot. *The European Discovery of America.* Oxford, UK: Oxford University Press, 1971.

———. *The Maritime History of Massachusetts, 1783–1860.* Boston: Houghton Mifflin Company, 1921.

Moro, Rubén. *The History of the South Atlantic Conflict.* New York: Praeger, 1989.

Mullen and Leuer. In *Close Combat: Light Infantry In Action*, Part 11, Newsletter No. 2–88.

Murguizur, Juan Carlos. "The South Atlantic Conflict: An Argentinian Point of View," *International Defense Review* 2 (1983): 135–140.

Namier, Sir Lewis Bernstein, and John Brooke. *House of Commons 1754–1790*. London: Oxford University Press, 1964.

National Maritime Museum, Greenwich. D8544.

———. D8539.

Neillands, Robin. *By Sea and By Land*. London: Orion, 1996.

Nott, John. *Here Today, Gone Tomorrow*. London: Politico's, 1992.

Nuttall, Zelia. *New Light on Drake: A Collection of Documents Relating to his Voyage of Circumnavigation, 1577–1580*. London: Hakluyt Society, 1914.

Orgill, Andrew. *The Falklands War: Background, Conflict, Aftermath— An Annotated Bibliography*. London and New York: Mansell, 1993.

Pack, S.W.C. *Admiral Lord Anson: The Story of Anson's Voyage and Naval Events of his Day*. London: Cassell, 1960.

Paret, Peter. *Clausewitz and the State: The Man, His Theories and His Times*. Princeton University Press, 1985.

———. *Makers of Modern Society: From Machiavelli to the Nuclear Age*. Princeton University Press, 1986.

Pendle, George. *Argentina*. Oxford University Press, 1963.

Penrose, Bernard. *Account of the Last Expedition to Port Egmont, 1772*. London: J. Johnson, 1770.

Perl, Raphael. *The Falkland Islands Dispute in International Law and Politics: A Documentary Sourcebook*. London and New York: Oceana Publications, 1983.

Pernety, Antoine-Joseph. *The History of a Voyage to the Malouines*. London: T. Jeffreys, 1771.

Perrett, Bryan. *Weapons of the Falklands' Conflict*. New York: Blandford Press, 1982.

Piaggi, Italo Angel. *Ganso Verde*. Buenos Aires: Sudamérica/Planeta, 1986.

Plaza, Juan. *Malvinas: Nuestra próxima recolonización de las islas*. Buenos Aires, 1970.

Pocock, Tom. *Nelson*. London: Pimlico, 1994.

Ponting, Clive. *The Right to Know: The Inside Story of the Belgrano Affair*. London: Sphere Books, 1985.

Potash, Robert A. *The Army and Politics in Argentina, 1945–1962*. Stanford University Press, 1969.

Pym, Francis. *The Politics of Consent*. London: H. Hamilton, 1984.

Quinn, David B. *The Last Voyage of Thomas Cavendish, 1591–1592.* University of Chicago Press for the Newberry Library, 1975.

Rand Corporation. *The South Atlantic Crisis of 1982.* Santa Monica, CA: Rand Corporation, 1989.

Ranelagh, John. *Thatcher's People.* London: Harper & Collins, 1991.

Rasor, Eugene L. *The Falklands/Malvinas Campaign: A Bibliography.* New York: Greenwood Press, 1992.

Reber, Vera. *British Mercantile Houses in Buenos Aires, 1810–1880.* Harvard University Press, 1979.

Ridley, Nicholas. *My Style of Government: The Thatcher Years.* London: H. Hutchinson, 1991.

Rock, David. *Argentina, 1516–1987: From Spanish Colonization to Alfonsín.* Berkeley: University of California Press, 1987.

Rodríguez Muñoz, Chacho, and Luis Garasino. *Malvinas: Album de la Campaña.* Buenos Aires: Fundación Soldados, 1999.

Rogers, George. Letter to Secretary of the Navy, 1832. Navy and Old Army Branch National Archives, Washington, DC. Courtesy of Rebecca Livingston.

Rogers, Woodes. *A Cruising Voyage Around the World.* London: Printed for A. Bell and B. Lintot, 1712.

Rommel, Erwin. *The Rommel Papers.* New York: Harcourt, Brace, 1953.

Roquie, Alain. *Poder military y sociedad política en la Argentina.* Buenos Aires: Emece, 1983.

Rowland, J.R. "Combat Readiness: Fifty Percent." In *Armour,* May–June 1982.

Saint-Exupéry, Antoine de. *Flight to Arras.* New York: Reynal & Hitchcocke, 1942.

Sancton, Thomas A. *Time Magazine,* May 31st, 1982, p. 37.

Sewall, Samuel. *Diaries,* Vol. 1. New York: Farrar, Strauss and Giroux, 1973.

Shakespeare, William. *12th Night.* Roslyn: Black's, 1937.

———. *King Lear.* New York: Penguin, 1972.

Shumway, Nicholas. *The Invention of Argentina.* Berkeley: University of California Press, 1991.

Sibley, John Langdon. *Biographical Sketches of Graduates of Harvard University,* Vol. 2. Cambridge: Cambridge University Press, 1881.

Simpson, John and Jana Bennett. *The Disappeared and the Mothers of the Plaza.* New York: St. Martin's Press, 1985.

Southby-Tailyour, Ewen. *Falkland Islands Shores.* London: Conway Maritime, 1985.

————. *Reasons In Writing: A Commando's View of the Falklands War.* London: Leo Cooper, 1993.

Spiro, Herbert J. "From Bureaucratic Politics to Philosophy of History: The Laws of Replication." Colloquium Paper, Woodrow Wilson International Center for Scholars, Washington, DC, 1979.

Starkey, Marion L. *The Devil in Massachusetts.* Garden City, NY: Anchor Books, 1969.

Strategic Balance, 1980–1985. London: Brasseys Ltd., 1980–1985.

Strauss, Barry S. and Josiah Ober. *The Anatomy of Error: Ancient Military Disasters and their Lessons for Modern Strategists.* New York: St. Martin's Press, 1982.

Sugden, John. *Sir Francis Drake.* New York: Holt, 1991.

Sunday Times of London, April, May, June 1982 and 22, 29 March 1987, for Argentina's plan of invasion: Plan Goa.

Sunday Times of London Insight Team. *The Falklands War.* London: Sphere Books, 1982.

————. *War in the Falklands: The Full Story.* New York: Harper and Rowe, 1982.

Thatcher, Margaret. *The Downing Street Years.* New York: Harper & Collins, 1993.

Thompson, Julian. *The Lifeblood Of War: Logistics in Armed Conflict.* London: Brassey's, 1991.

————. *No Picnic: 3 Commando Brigade in the South Atlantic, 1982.* London: Leo Cooper, 1985.

Thompson, Leroy. *British Paras in Action.* Carrollton, TX: Squadron Publications, 1989.

Timmerman, Jacobo. *Prisoner Without a Name, Cell Without a Number.* Translated by Tory Talbot. New York: Knopf, 1981.

Tinker, Hugh, ed. *A Message from the Falklands: The Life and Gallant Death of David Tinker, Lieut. R.N.* London: Junction Books, 1982.

Tustin, W. J. "Logistics of the Falklands War." In *The Army and Defense Quarterly* 114, no. 4 (October 1984).

Underwood, Geoffrey. *Our Falklands War.* Liskeard, Cornwall, UK: Maritime Books, 1982.

U.S. State Department Papers, Argentine Dispatches, September 26, 1832.

Vagts, Alfred. *A History of Militarism.* New York: Meridian Books, 1959.

Valcourt, Richard R. "Controlling U.S. Hired Hands." *International Journal of Intelligence and Counterintelligence* 2, no. 3.

Van Creveld, Martin L. *Command in War*. Cambridge, MA: Harvard University Press, 1985.

———. *Supplying War*. New York: Cambridge University Press, 1977.

Vaux, Nick. *Take That Hill: Royal Marines in the Falklands War*. Washington, DC: Brasseys, 1990.

Verbitsky, Horacio. *Confessions of an Argentine Dirty Warrior*. New York: New Press, 1996.

Villar, Captain Roger. *Merchant Ships at War*. London: Conway Maritime Press, 1984.

Villarino, Emilio. *Exocet*. Buenos Aires: Siete Días, 1983.

Visscher, Nicholas. *Chart D8537*. National Maritime Museum, Greenwich, England.

Ward, Nigel. *Sea Harrier Over the Falklands*. London: Cooper, 1992.

Waters, David W. *The Art of Navigation in England in Elizabethan and Early Stuart Times*. London: Hollis and Carter, 1958.

Washington Office on Latin America (WOLA). "Rattenbach Commission Report." Washington, DC: WOLA.

Weinberger, Caspar. *Fighting For Peace*. New York: Warner Books, 1991.

Weiss, Kenneth G. *The War for the Falklands: A Chronology*. Alexandria, VA: Center for Naval Analyses, 1982.

West, Nigel. *The Secret War for the Falklands: The SAS, MI6, & the War Whitehall Nearly Lost*. London: Little, Brown, 1997.

West, Dame Rebecca. *A Dictionary of Quotations*. New York: Barnes and Noble Books, 1995.

Williams, Judith. *British Commercial Policy and Trade Expansion, 1750–1850*. Oxford University Press, 1972.

Wilsey, John. *H. Jones VC: The Life and Death of an Unusual Hero*. London: Hutchinson, 2002.

Winton, John. *Signals from the Falklands*. London: Leo Cooper, 1987.

Wolff, Leon. *In Flanders' Fields*. New York: Time Inc., 1958.

Woodbury, Levi. Letter to Duncan dated June 10, 1831. U.S. National Archives, Washington, DC.

Woodward, Admiral Sandy, with Patrick Robinson. *One Hundred Days: Memoirs of the Falklands Battle Group Commander*. Annapolis: U.S. Naval Institute Press, 1992.

Woodward, John and Jeremy Moore. "The Falklands Experience." *Journal of the RUSI*, March 1983.

Woolf, Cecil and Jean Moorcroft Wilson. *Authors Take Sides on the Falklands*. London: C. Woolf Publishers, 1982.

List of Figures and Photographs

Index

Numbers in square brackets indicate photo plates.

Mather, Increase, 180
McManners, Hugh, 181
Menéndez, General, 83, 87, 117, 118, 177
Mercedes (Task Force). *See* Task Force Mercedes
Milans at Goose Green, 152–154, 168
Miller, Alan, 102n92, 127
mines
    amphibious attack and danger of, 82–83
    Goose Green's lack of, 132
Mission Orders for Goose Green, 120, 126–130, 150, 159, 243–248
Monroe Doctrine, 15–16
Montgomery, Bernard Law "Monty," Viscount, 107, 139n36, 143n83, 186n59, 191, 207n1
Moore, Jeremy, 67, 89–90, 96, 111, 114, 139n36, 177–178, 182
Morales, Lcdr C., 116
Moran, Lord, 113, 162, 195
Moynihan, Patrick, 39
Mt. Harriet, attack on, 152
Mt. Kent, need for full-scale attack on, 110–111, 112
myth, nature of, 147, 180–182, 191, 206, 214

N

Nairne, Sir Patrick, 198
Napoleon, 10
NATO. *See* North Atlantic Treaty Organization
Neame, Phil, 117, 134–136, 154, 166, 168–169, 184n27, 195
negotiations between Britain and Argentina
    assessment of Argentine junta, 211–221
    continued pre-landing hopes for, 67, 79
    defensive war, decision of Argentines to conduct, 95
    Goose Green, 168, 177, 178
    initial British reaction to invasion, 35–38
    prior to Falklands invasion (1970-1982), 25–28
    success of amphibious landing contracting Argentine options in, 87
    ultimate failure of, 49–61
    US intervention in, 46–49, 59–63
Nootka Sound Convention of 1790, 54–55n19
Norland, 77, 83, 92, 122, 123
Norman, Sgt. Barry, 147, 151, 152, 156, 157